Happy Birthday, Boy Ken

— and dew you keep a' smiling!

Keith Skipper

(Norfolk, 2005)

Keith Skipper's
NORFOLK DIARIES

HALSGROVE

First published in Great Britain in 2005

British Library Cataloguing-in-Publication Data.
A CIP record for this title is available from the British Library.

ISBN 1 84114 438 X

HALSGROVE

Halsgrove House
Lower Moor Way
Tiverton, Devon EX16 6SS
Tel: 01884 243242
Fax: 01884 243325
E-mail: sales@halsgrove.com
Website: www.halsgrove.com

Printed and bound in Great Britain by CPI Bath.

Contents

Introduction

Perhaps it was part of the settling-down process after so many years of footloose and fancy-free living in my native county. I had married just a few months before – not simply to avoid going into an old people's home, as suggested by a few of my closest friends – and prepared for domestic bliss with Diane at Blacksmith's Cottage in Hevingham, eight miles north of Norwich. My 40th birthday beckoned, the sort of milestone bound to concentrate the mind, if not completely cloud it, and I could find a bit more time after tea to prove the pen remained mightier than the sink.

Perhaps certain Orwellian visions began to haunt me with the dawn of 1984. Norfolk was changing far too radically for my liking as big developers were encouraged to see the area as ripe for missionary work, preaching a blunt gospel that big money talks louder than pastoral traditions. Prophets of boom in the property market pointed emphatically to supply and demand, with house prices pushing towards the ludicrous inflation ripping across other parts of the nation.

Perhaps I needed another outlet for my growing frustrations as new ventures and new jobs flew in the face of traditional images luring many people here in the first place. While the sprawl around Norwich was pronounced and predictable, an insidious middle-class spread was creeping up on most Norfolk towns and larger villages while smaller communities were being bullied into taking their share of newcomers seeking greener pastures. I had ready platforms from which to denounce such artificial expansion fired by short-term thinking and the fast-buck philosophy with regular columns in the *Eastern Daily Press* and *Norfolk Fair* magazine and a programme renowned for its parochial flavour on BBC Radio Norfolk five days a week. But a daily diary would allow me even more scope to be scurrilous about the end of much Norfolk civilisation as I knew and adored it.

Perhaps it was a combination of all these factors that enticed me into starting a routine destined to become an integral part of my life. I had filled hundreds of notebooks during 17 years as a journalist on the local news beat and continued to scribble prolifically around my roles as wireless presenter, after-dinner speaker, Village Hall entertainer and author in waiting. I had often flirted with January and even bits of February when it came to keeping a comprehensive daily record on my Norfolk rounds. Then all too soon good intentions were smothered by lack of basic disciplines.

When my wife bought me a 1984 diary pleading for constant attention I made the usual pledge to myself, albeit with a written declaration of intent at the front of the volume. It's worth recalling in full to show I meant business:

This is a personal record of Norfolk, 1984. It leans to some extent on reports and letters in the Eastern Daily Press *and also includes news and views from those who write or talk to me as host of BBC Radio Norfolk's* Dinnertime Show. *There's the occasional snippet from the national or international arenas, mainly to bring extra flavour to a local topic.*

But, for the most part, these are random reflections on the changing scene in Norfolk, my home county. My trips round the area, be they official or simply casual, can both uplift and depress. There are many pockets of rural resistance as the technological revolution dominates the latter part of the century. Is that resistance valid? Is it simply nostalgia rather than a genuine buffer against so-called progress? Can the dialect survive? Will the Village Hall prove stronger than the video? Do we have to accept the disappearance of so many pubs, schools, hedgerows and country traditions as inevitable? Will suburbia and dormitory villages continue to grow? How many people in the holiday trade really care about conservation or preservation? Is parochialism worth having? These, and other questions, are examined as Norfolk and I square up to 1984.

Well, over two decades later, I'm still testing Norfolk's temperature on a daily basis. A challenge that turned into a habit is now a proud obsession while I plough freelance furrows as writer, broadcaster and entertainer. 'Have you done your diary?' is no longer a question designed to make me feel guilty or lazy. I record, ruminate, rant and resolve as a matter of course. Some entries highlight my blatant prejudices, especially against the worship of cars, mobile phones in public places and experts who want Norfolk to be like everywhere else. I try to maintain a balance, however, by accepting I'm getting older, grumpier and less likely by the month to play cricket for England, win the Booker Prize for Cromer or pass my driving test before they put a dual carriageway across Holkham beach.

The following extracts from my diaries are chosen to give as varied a picture as possible at the end of one century and the beginning of the new millennium. Yes, there are recurring themes – all record-keepers should plead guilty to riding hobby-horses – but I hope there's plenty to amuse, surprise and reflect the truly endearing side of people and places in what remains a county where 'quality of life' is not a cheap cliché.

I do not shun controversial episodes in my career, such as differences of opinion with management at Radio Norfolk which led to my high-profile departure In 1995, or steer completely away from joyful times in my family life, like the arrivals of our two sons. They are part of an intriguing mixture of highs, lows, and in-betweens that make up the pattern of every existence. I also muster the temerity to comment now and again on holiday haunts strong enough to tempt me away from my beloved homeland.

Even so, this is primarily a chronicle starring good old Norfolk in all its cussed glory, determined to 'dew diffrunt' despite incessant pressures to toe the line, see the light, accept the inevitable and show proper respect for the rest of the world.

◆　◆　◆

January

January 1 – Strong winds, but weather mild along the North Norfolk coast as we take the New Year air. Cromer and Sheringham warm the hearts of winter visitors seeking reassurance that there are homely alternatives to unashamedly commercial Yarmouth. But, with economic pressures building up how much longer can they stay 'old fashioned'? Home to Hevingham via the back road to Aylsham, taking in a first visit to Silvergate, near Blickling. Perhaps expecting too much of a dreamy, rustic haven, we find simply a huddle or two of houses down a rough road and, of course, you have to meet horses and riders coming the other way! Strange how a name can conjure up all kinds of images until you go and have a look.

January 4 – With the New Year hardly out of its cradle, a stunning literary breakthrough to report. On the back page of today's *Eastern Daily Press* I spy the headline: 'Breckland to scrap honeycart.' Must be the first time such a description has been pinned on the old wagon in our local paper in a serious report.

January 6 – The Hon. Richard de Grey, son of the seventh Lord Walsingham, dies at Merton, near Watton, aged 83. I met him when he was scoring for Merton Cricket Club at home against my team, Caister. He wasn't slow to chide home players with some old-fashioned oaths if they were sloppy. He was presented with a shooting stick by the club in 1965 to mark his half-century with them.

Dick Condon – genial manager of Norwich Theatre Royal.

January 12 – Afternoon coffee and chat at Norwich Theatre Royal with manager Dick Condon, the genial Irishman who has married commerce to culture and sold it to Norfolk with remarkable success. Our conversations invariably come round to the business of communication, be it concerned with the media, the theatre or the simple matter of people talking to each other in the hope of finding better understanding. His impish sense of humour and ready chuckle make certain we don't get too deep. Comparisons between Ireland and Norfolk come easy, especially after my honeymoon in the Emerald Isle last August and a chat on the air with entertainer Val Doonican before Christmas. Dick agrees, but finds a marked difference in attitudes towards death. Norfolk people are much more reticent to talk about it. I suggest the Irish are more convinced they're destined for a better place!

January 18 – Pub with no beer is doing well at Diss! White Elephant has opened this week but the owner can only sell soft drinks until his licence application is granted. It's being opposed by previous owner, Norwich Brewery. Alcohol-free lager is the pub's best seller.

January 23 – After picture-postcard scenes left by the first snow of the year, we have the chilly reality culminating in tea-time chaos across Norfolk. Traffic snarls to a halt and hundreds of vehicles are abandoned. Virtually every social event is cancelled as the battle to get home stretches long into the evening. In conditions like these local radio really comes into its own. Several drivers jump out of their vehicles to ring in with information. Taxi firms call to say youngsters picked up from school two or three hours ago are perfectly safe in the cabs. Offers to put up stranded drivers for the night come in from all over the county.

February

February 2 – Walter Fuller gives up his barber's shop at Hemsby after 54 years. Walter retires and his timber shop will give way to new building development. 'The customers were dying off. The youngsters go elsewhere. I suppose the shop weren't posh enough for them,' says Walter. His last customer is Fred Armstead, who'd been going there for over 40 years. As he finishes, Walter shuts the door, pats the timber and tells it: 'You've been a good old shop...' It retains its 1930s' furniture and fittings right to the end.

February 7 – As the debate continues about Yarmouth's future as a holiday resort, with allegations that some businesses aren't pulling their weight and other interests are pulling different ways, I pop down for the afternoon. The place always evokes mixed feelings. Sunshine and donkey memories of over 30 years ago on Sunday school outings. Nearly three years on the local paper in the mid-

1960s when much of the old Yarmouth was being replaced by modern attractions. Perhaps I still yield to nostalgia and curse many developments along the Golden Mile, but I still like the resort at this time of the year. Bright and bracing on the front. Caravans huddled together trying to keep warm. Industries almost rubbing shoulders with the Pleasure Beach. Wellington Pier complex future shrouded in uncertainty. Giant Marina Centre a monument to the demands of modern holiday-makers. Posters from last year flap in the wind.

February 8 – Bright day ends with a truly golden sunset at 5 o'clock as we head home from a little shopping expedition in North Walsham. Glorious dusk with churches dipping in and out of the rays and one side of the sky mocking the other over a cluster of villages. I name them like the lines of an old Norfolk verse: Westwick, Scottow, Felmingham, Worstead, Sloley, Skeyton, Banningham, Colby, Tuttington, Oxnead, Brampton. Come to think of it, sounds more like a football team with Sloley at centre half. Was ever a Norfolk village more beautifully named!

February 14 – St Valentine's Day – and my heart is well and truly touched by a Dereham woman who sends me a Hamond's Grammar School* tie to transport me back to days at Swaffham when I was a lad. The old school is comprehensive now, but that tie of yellow and black stripes stares at me, defying the years and all the changes.
(*I attended Hamond's Grammar School from 1955 until

1962. Following the 250th anniversary of the school's foundation at a big reunion in 1986, the Old Hamondians' Association has grown and flourished with an annual dinner in Swaffham in May.)

February 24 – End of an era at Diss as the livestock market closes after 55 years. General decline in the number of pigs passing through is main reason. Last sale features two of auctioneer John Jennings' own pigs. Proceeds of £310 go to Guide Dogs for the Blind. When Henry Guy Apthorpe, founder of the market, held the first sale in September 1929, 65 fat cattle, cows and calves were penned, together with 400 pigs and a large entry of 275 lots of poultry.

February 25 – Grand local event as Hevingham Village Hall is officially opened. After my little warm-up chat, I hand over to Mrs Phyllis Benton. She does the honours and unveils a portrait of her late husband, Evan. He gave the land to the village on which to build the hall.

February 28 – It's 25 years ago today when the axe fell on one of the most enterprising and individualistic railways, the Midland & Great Northern, which threaded its eccentric way from Lincolnshire, through Norfolk to Norwich, Yarmouth and Lowestoft. 'The Muddle and Get Nowhere' line holds a special place still in the hearts of Norfolk people, and I think of it every time I go near Melton Constable, the headquarters.

Melton Constable station in its heyday.

1984

March

March 2 – Driving snow and high winds provide an ironic backcloth to that social institution, the cricket club dinner. Quite a hazardous journey to the coast for the annual celebration with my Caister colleagues – and we have some silverware, the Neave Plate, on display for the first time in the club's history. Main guest is Norfolk captain Fred Handley, the tall left-hander who opens for Ingham and the County. He falls just short of first-class championship level mainly because his dashing style always gives the bowlers a chance. Fred isn't the typical county skipper in that he doesn't have a clipped accent or the sort of social status that were traditional features for that role a few years ago.

March 5 – Ted Ellis, doyen of local naturalists, warns that industrial pollution and urban effluent are slowly killing the North Sea's marine life. 'The rivers of Europe are pouring filth into the North Sea and towns such as Yarmouth and Cromer are pumping pollution into it, and vast areas of the seabed are becoming sterile.' Ted points out that modern detergents are ruining the Broads. 'I did suggest this might be happening, but it was 15 years before anybody took the slightest notice. And they have spent millions since then trying to put it right.'

March 9 – All a bit embarrassing as Radio Norfolk's *Dinnertime Show* listeners creep into the studio to mark my 40th birthday in a couple of days with an impromptu celebration. And I have to react coherently on air. Old and new faces behind the regular names of prolific letter writers. On the accordion, John Hammond from Beccles, a former printer with a saucy line when it comes to writing limericks. This is our first meeting. Others include Ivy and Henry West from Corpusty; Dot Kent from Seething; June and Alf Pepper from Dersingham; Lil Landamore from Dereham; Tiger and Lily Tidman from Ketteringham; Connie Fox from Lingwood (on the move to Acle); Phyllis Tozer from Spixworth (a regular visitor with her home-made cakes) and Amy Elizabeth Chamberlain from Norwich. It's rather like a family reunion.

March 16 – Bodham's *A Night of Squit* in the Village Hall, with usual adjournment to the Red Hart pub next door after the show. Not sure who needs refreshment most – cast or long-suffering audience! Mixture of sketches with a local flavour, dancing and musical items, all very loosely held together by village enthusiasm on and off stage. Barry and Mik are the comperes trying to keep some semblance of order, but it all adds to the fun when things go wrong.

Fun and games at Bodham's A Night of Squit.

'Mastermind' was one of the highlights, with Ruddy Sparks collecting most of the honours for his version of a rustic Spike Milligan. Dressed as a parson, his verbal gymnastics and off-the-cuff antics make a delightful mockery of any rehearsals... despite the prompt cards he clutches in his hand all night.

(*Bodham – a village half way between Holt and Cromer. These sessions began in 1977 to mark the Queen's silver jubilee and villagers continued to entertain themselves and others until the 1990s.)

March 25 – Happy evening at Norwich Theatre Royal as Dick Condon spearheads a *This Is Your Life* to mark the retirement of theatre manager Stanley Fuller after 50 years of service. Old friends and colleagues spill out from behind the stage curtains to pay tribute as countless chapters unfold. Stanley and wife Hilda are all but submerged in a sea of memories and good wishes.

April

April 3 – Cromer for tea – and an invitation to chat from three Americans in the corner of the restaurant. They are enjoying their holiday in 'your wonderful country'. Yes, they really say it, and follow up with a host of questions including 'What do you really think of Prince Andrew?' and 'Whatever happened to Lord Snowdon?' They hail from New York and Philadelphia and their hunger for snippets of information about the royal family dominates the session. They are thrilled to learn that Sandringham isn't too far away.

April 12 – At last! A real whiff of spring with temperatures rising and sunshine paying more than a fleeting visit. All that after an overnight frost. So the weather turns kinder as Michael Montague, chairman of the English Tourist Board, continues his Norfolk tour. He urges us to step up the fight for better roads and praises the regeneration of Hunstanton's holiday trade. Over the past two seasons 'Sunny Hunny' has gone against the general tide in Britain and increased its tourist business.

KEITH SKIPPER'S NORFOLK DIARIES

April 13 – Survey work starts on £30 million Castle Mall development in Norwich. Sports Minister Neil Macfarlane opens the £620,000 King's Lynn sports complex. Controversial plans for a £4 million holiday centre with 70 chalets, a restaurant and leisure centre at Potter Heigham approved by the Broads Authority. And the first application to develop land at Drayton and Taverham officially earmarked for 2000 new homes is received by Broadland District Council. An average sort of day on the Norfolk development front and, no doubt, some of the changes will be for the better. But we seem to be moving at such a rate I wonder if there will be any room left by the end of the century. This is the second Friday 13 of the year – with another one to come in July.

(*The new homes at Drayton and Taverham were built to form the new community of Thorpe Marriott.)

April 18 – Stroll to work takes a different course in the sun. Past Norwich Castle and along Timberhill, an area soon to undergo drastic surgery in the name of development and progress. Easter Fair crammed onto the Cattle Market car park extending a rather lukewarm invitation. Fair magic seems to have faded in recent years and to many the tradi-

tional city noise, lights and packed arena are now no more than additional nuisances to all the traffic. I recall the tingle of excitement after the corn harvest two or three decades ago when after exertions in the field – and most was safely gathered in – a trip to the fair on Dereham market-place was a real pilgrimage of pleasure. Four threepenny bits would keep you going for an hour if you picked your rides and side stalls carefully. And there was the smell, the whirr, the half-discernible sound of music to keep you entranced if the money dried up. Most of all there was the sense of a local community brought together in a common search for enter-tainment at the end of long hours of harvesting. Brown arms and red faces from the villages. Self-indulgence on a Saturday night without a trace of guilt.

April 24 – North Norfolk crab fishermen out in force to bring in the first of this year's catches. The fishermen leave beaches between Trimingham and Cley daily at about 4a.m. at the start of the season, but in midsummer boats are hauled over the sand as early as 2a.m. Three miles out, they drop their baited pots and leave them for about eight hours. The crab season lasts from April to September. About 600–800 crabs are caught on each

Cromer crab fishermen bring home a tasty haul.

haul and sent to shops around the country. Cromer fisherman Richard Davies sends regular supplies to the food halls of London's top people's store, Harrods of Knightsbridge.

April 28 – Swaffham's best known landmark is given a new lease of life. The 200-year-old market cross has been saved from the ravages of lorries and cars and should be good now for another 500 years. Metal posts and a landscaping scheme set it on an island sanctuary in the centre of the market-place under a £16,500 improvement scheme. Much of the cash has come from the town trustees who put aside income from a farm on the edge of Swaffham.

April 29 – Stand by for aching limbs and annual regrets after the start of another personal battle to defy advancing years. A new cricket season for me opens with Caister at the charming St Andrew's Hospital ground at Thorpe, scene of our first cup triumph last summer when we beat Rollesby in the Neave Plate final. Imagine my surprise when captain Richard Hewitt tosses me the ball with an invitation to open the bowling! I haven't had a net, let alone a warm-up, so a couple of wides are greeted with less than hostility. Eight overs give away 21 runs and I fail to take a wicket, but it isn't a bad start in the circumstances. Caister win this friendly with one ball to spare.

April 30 – So the sun sets on one of the warmest and driest Aprils on record. But forecasters say rain is on the way. Farmers and gardeners glad to hear it, along with all the fire brigades doing overtime these last few days.

May

May 10 – As we plough the fields and scatter, new laws are to be introduced to control the use of pesticides. The moves follow strong pressure from conservation groups and trade unions who want greater statutory control over the chemicals. And what about this for progress down on the farm: 'Young cow seeks friendship with mature pedigree bull with a view to close relationship.' It's the start of Britain's first computer dating service for cows. At present the service is confined to Holstein beef cattle but it's hoped it can be extended to all other pedigree breeds. Think I know what they'll call the contact magazine when it comes: *The Farmer's Sutra.*

May 11 – Norfolk landowners are mounting an inquiry to discover whether the red squirrel is extinct in the county. William Bulwer-Long, chairman of the Norfolk branch of the County Landowners' Association, says: 'The red squirrel

has all but been driven out by the more aggressive grey squirrel, which is now doing enormous harm, particularly to the bark of young trees, which can easily be killed.' If the red squirrel proves to be extinct, the branch is to decide whether to press for the grey squirrel to be properly controlled. Thetford Forest is believed to be the last refuge of the red squirrel.

May 13 – My calendar motto put it perfectly: 'Think only of the past as its remembrance gives you pleasure.' An afternoon of unashamed nostalgia as I pay a visit to Winnie Chapman, celebrating her 73rd birthday at Sporle, near Swaffham. Winnie was one of the dinner ladies at Hamond's Grammar School while I was there. She retired 10 years ago but the mother-figure qualities are still burning bright as we roll back the years and exchange names of teachers and pupils with machine-gun rapidity. Winnie can match all my yarns as she recalls keeping watch for boys who dared to go out of the school gate without a cap, darning holes in the seat of their trousers, finding them a few coppers to spend at the tuck shop – and chasing one of the masters with a dishcloth before discovering his true identity! 'I thought he was one of the boys and he took it all in good part' she chuckles.

Winnie Chapman – cook of the old school.

KEITH SKIPPER'S NORFOLK DIARIES

May 17 – Warm welcome to the Norfolk dialect evening at the 37th Cromer and North Norfolk Festival of Music and Dance. I've been asked to adjudicate for the second successive May as competitors read a chosen piece written in dialect. Then they can do their own thing, tell yarns or present any items provided they stick to a maximum of five minutes. Familiar faces and voices along with organiser Jason Bell. There's 84-year-old Victor Dewing, determined to make the hazardous trek to centre stage with aid of his stick; ebullient baker Jack Gaskin, who punctuates his offerings with delightful mannerisms; art gallery owner John Hill; Bodham squit merchant Mik Godfrey; Holt housewife Christine Owen and Sheringham mawther Hilda Booty. Another delightful session – but no youngsters to join in the fun. Christine says teachers at school chastise the children for talking in dialect, and that's one of the main reasons they won't come out.

May 19 – Sir John Betjeman, the people's Poet Laureate, dies at his Cornish holiday home. He was a regular visitor to Norfolk and had a strong personal link with North Norfolk – a lifelong friendship with the Harrod family at Holt. The Broads held strong appeal while his celebrated passion for churches brought him this way as well.

May 20 – Heaviest rain for nine weeks in Norfolk and I'm charmed by the sight and sound on peering out of the bedroom window to confirm this is really happening. There are local youngsters over two months old who've never seen a shower.

May 27 – Rain lashes down to mock so many bank holiday schemes. I'm at Thornham, near Hunstanton, to open the village playing-field – but we have to make do with a hastily-rearranged session in the drill hall. With a neat sense of humour, locals bring a sod into the hall to give the 'opening' a tinge of authenticity, and then it's all the fun of the fête under cover.

May 28 – Comedian Eric Morecambe, one of my heroes, dies at 58 after another heart attack. He and partner Ernie Wise travelled over the bridge from music hall and vaudeville in the 1940s to make such a big impact on television. I was lucky enough to see them on stage in Yarmouth and at the Theatre Royal in Norwich.

June

June 5 – Evangelist Billy Graham on his way to preach in East Anglia as part of his *Mission England* venture, with Carrow Road in Norwich his starting point next week. Always a controversial figure because of his salesman approach to religion, he's being advised by many that he could be getting down to business and trying to make inroads into the 'heathen' of his own country. I recall his visit 30 years ago and how thousands were converted at his emotion-charged services. We went on a bus from our village to hear the message relayed in a church in Dereham. I remember being both impressed and frightened by the heady atmosphere created by this brand of evangelism.

June 7 – Long-service salute to Jack Stammers, who recently celebrated his 79th birthday. He has completed 60 years of continuous service as organist at Hempnall Methodist Church. He succeeded his aunt, Alice Stammers, and has played at every type of service or event.

June 10 – A pair of parrot crossbills, rare feathered visitors to these shores, successfully fledge three youngsters at Wells amid great secrecy. It's believed this is the first time they have ever bred in Britain.

June 15 – Return to familiar pastures. To Gressenhall Swan, near the village green, to judge a Boy George dressing-up competition for both sexes. Most of the evening spent meeting old friends, including *Dereham & Fakenham Times* photographer Brian Smith, with whom I covered many stories and presentation events two decades ago. Chummy Hammond, another Beeston old boy, is the pub landlord. I soon spot Gerald Burton in the corner. He and Reggie Purple formed one of the most lethal bowling partnerships in mid-Norfolk cricket when I was a lad scoring for Beeston and they were turning it on for Longham.

June 16 – More sunshine on the village scene as I open the popular two-day Buxton Fair. Organisers include Old Hamondian Don MacKenzie. I'd mentioned that I owed him a 'ding o' the lug' for chastisement at some stage of my grammar school career when he was a prefect – and he invites me to square the account on stage in front of hundreds of people!

June 17 – *A Night of Squit* at the Cromer Pier Pavilion Theatre is a big success. A full house and a lively programme featuring personalities who have become favourites on the local wireless: John Crisp, Bobby Benton, Mawther Maggie, Olly Day, Major Egbert Gladstone-Pyle and David 'Muck Carter' Lambert. Plus Chad, who's in full cry when the fuse goes at the end! I

1984

was confident such an event would be popular in this lovely end-of-the-pier setting when asked by Dick Condon to put the show together and to compere it.

(*This was the starting point for regular rounds on the local entertainment scene, with the Press Gang to the fore in more recent years. We have made occasional returns to Cromer Pier to give thanks for that chance in the summer of 1984.)

June 18 – After 40 years of silent slumber, the wheels of Letheringsett water-mill start to turn again. The Domesday Book recorded the existence of a mill there in the time of William the Conqueror. At Worstead, the foundation stone for the new Village Hall is laid a year after a referendum in the village decided where to build it. South Wootton and Massingham retain their titles in West Norfolk's inter-village sports. Winterton's new £2000 lifeboat dinghy is blessed by the rector of the village and Swaffham's Scout hut is prepared for a face-lift.

June 20 – Thunderbolts, lightning and torrential rain leave the county battered, dazed and mopping up for hours. Norfolk fire service deal with over 200 incidents. Shops and houses are flooded, roads awash and electricity supplies cut off all over the county. At Norwich Theatre Royal, flooding causes about £70,000 worth of damage to scenery, stage clothes and lighting equipment. The bucket-and-mop brigade come out at the Norfolk & Norwich Hospital as rainwater seeps through corridors and floods lift shafts. Murky water comes to within a foot or two of a theatre where an operation is in progress.

June 24 – In the small Flegg community of Mautby, they pay tribute to their most famous daughter. Five centuries ago, Margaret Paston – whose family letters are valued as an insight into life of the time – died at Mautby Hall. The anniversary prompts the village's 95 inhabitants to organise an impressive festival. Members of the Mautby clan are travelling from all over the world to the home of their ancestors. The village opts to hold the special weekend in the summer rather than wait until the exact date of the anniversary, November 4. Visitors are being asked to dip into their pockets to help towards a £10,000 repair bill faced by the church, mainly for the roof.

July

July 2 – While Wimbledon, the second test at Lord's between England and the formidable West Indies, and seaside shows are in full swing, Norwich Theatre Royal announces the line-up of this year's pantomime. It's

Goldilocks and the Three Bears, starring dynamic dancer Wayne Sleep. As if in deference to dark days to come, it's a wet, miserable Monday. Where to escape? There's a new exhibition on the Ice Age in East Anglia at Norwich Castle Museum. It opens with a surprise donation to the organisers – an old tooth. (And I went to the dentist today!) This mighty molar graced the jaw of a woolly mammoth 60,000 years ago and was found by a digger driver at a Lyng gravel pit last week.

July 4 – I see one of the new football clubs to join the Norwich and District Sunday League glories in the name of Road Traffic Act United. Yes, they're from Norwich Union. It must be their policy to come up with the most unglamorous title imaginable. Perhaps it started as a joke. Now they must be ruled offside.

July 5 – From the office to the river to launch a splendid exhibition on the Wherry *Olive* in early evening sunshine. The *Olive* was built in 1909 by Ernest Collins of Wroxham, and was in the hire fleet for parties of ten people with a skipper and steward until 1958. Then she was used as a houseboat for the next three years. Originally the sail was fitted with a boom, but this was dispensed with when a new Terylene sail was fitted in 1975. After extensive restoration work, she's now fulfilling her original role of taking parties of up to 12 people and crew. Photographs on display show trading wherries, pleasure wherries and an extensive look at the *Olive* herself from 1909 to the present day.

July 10 – To Aylsham Town Hall as Black Shuck comes out of hiding to star in *Marsh Fever*, presented by the Ipswich-based Eastern Angles Touring Theatre. Over 100 to greet the demon dog: 'He is a dark shadow in the marshes and minds of the area… if you want him, he exists' warns the programme. Supper afterwards at Marsham White Hart on the way home – and the other side of the canine world. Robbie, a 12-year-old black Labrador, big and friendly, struggles over as if to make a plea on behalf of his friends… 'Don't tar us all with the same brush!' He's got bad arthritis and his eyes are going. But I'm convinced he was given enough energy to come and put my mind at ease. Well, it was too much of a coincidence – wasn't it?

July 15 – Thunderstorms overnight and more downpours in the morning wash out Caister's all-day home cricket match with Reepham. The wife is just as disappointed as me as she spent most of yesterday preparing Sunday teas. We braved the rain to attend morning service at Hevingham church. Leak in the roof demands a plastic bowl to catch the drips. 'I thought it was a metronome!' quips the visiting vicar standing in for our local rector who is on holiday.

July 17 – An evening cricket match at Eaton Park in Norwich – and remarkable boundary banter to make it memorable as I play for Mann Egerton. A man, probably in his late 50s, and a woman, presumably his wife, are in heated debate throughout the game, totally oblivious to the sporting activities unfolding before them. He is a loud, pointing figure, accusing the woman of 'deceiving me for so many years and spending my money behind my back'. He accuses her of not being in when he called today, and of refusing to make any effort to straighten things out. Her voice, so quiet in contrast, does not carry but she looks sheepish and embarrassed. As the match ends, an easy victory for our side, the couple are still there with no sign of a truce. Strange little scene with more than a tinge of sadness. Chances are I'll never hear or see them again. But I can't help wondering what sort of world they're returning to after this open-air soul searching. Was it a chance meeting? Couldn't they have shown a little interest as I collected four cheap wickets?

July 25 – Another sad slant on our times. A Norwich inquest is held on an unknown tramp who died in Blickling Woods 'with no one to care a damn'. Coroner James Hipwell says this is the first time he's held an inquest on a person with no name.

July 27 – One of those delightful evening sessions that simply happen. Off-the-cuff decision to go to Sheringham for our evening meal despite threatening skies. Umbrellas and anoraks dominate the resort as carnival week reaches a climax, but there's an air of relaxation and friendship as we eat at The Two Lifeboats. We take the table nearest the window through which rain and waves catch the eye. Coloured lights rock and roll as the wind gets up. A couple from Rotherham in the bar tell us with broad smiles that wherever and whenever they go on holiday it just rains. I tell them some parts of the world would be delighted if they could do the trick for them. Strolling along the front, I break into an impromptu impression of Gene Kelly singing in the rain... totally unaware of an audience laughing above.

August

August 4 – Delightful afternoon on the Broads – African Queen style. We join Radio Norfolk colleagues David Line, Keith Roberts and Ian Hyams on David's replica Edwardian steam launch from Wroxham to Belaugh and then Coltishall

and back. I steer successfully on the way there and I'm surprised how quiet it is as soon as we pull away from a bustling Wroxham. Stop at Coltishall for a pint and an impromptu chat with Melissa and her great-grandfather who tells us he started driving steam trains before 1920. He's fascinated by the launch and breathes in the steam as if it's all part of his recipe for a healthy old age. Hundreds of holiday-makers take photographs as we pass by, sipping our wine and munching sausage rolls.

August 10 – Look out, Diss! They're out to turn you into a big slice of commuterland before the end of the decade! British Rail and the town's estate agents say Diss will become the boom town of East Anglia with rail electrification to London, house prices taking off and local businesses prospering.

August 12 – Eye-catching article in the *Sunday Times* by Godfrey Smith about all things English. His look at 'village' should spark a few lively debates in Norfolk: 'The contemporary English village is as much the nodal point of change, flux, tension and collision as the big city from which it is popularly suggested to be a portmanteau refuge.'

August 17 – Bold experiment by the Otter Trust at Earsham to release otters into the wild is proving a big success. There's every sign that the released animals are breeding happily. This experiment is the first time anywhere in the world that otters held in captivity have been sent out into the wild. Regular monitoring shows they've settled down and are behaving exactly like wild otters.

August 18 – Sunbathing holiday-makers at Gorleston run for cover as it rains straw. This unlikely 'cloudburst' lasts ten minutes and leaves police and visitors baffled. A large stretch of beach gets a light coating. One suggestion is that a mini-whirlwind has blown the straw from a field between Gorleston and Lowestoft and deposited it on the seafront.

August 21 – Remember when you paid a tanner or a bob for a haircut? Well, compared to the £18 handed over in London these days, I suppose £4.50 in Norwich has to be something of a snip. A local survey reveals that some men have given up going to the hairdresser's because it is too expensive. They get a friend or relative to cut it for them. It seems the barbershop days are gone; it's all stylists and salons now. All a far cry from when I was a lad in Beeston and used to visit Fred Neal for a trim at his house near the canning factory. Out in the garden in the summer months with a cloth round the neck – and he did very well considering he had fingers missing from one of his hands!

1984

August 25 – Start of the new Football League season – and what a rousing curtain-raiser at Carrow Road. Norwich force a 3–3 draw with champions Liverpool. Three penalties, one of them missed by City, an own goal by new home defender Steve Bruce after only two minutes, and an equaliser from the spot by Mike Channon with only a minute or so to go. Some fans miss the final drama through leaving early. They should have known better in a game like this.

August 28 – Farewell Norfolk for a few days as we head for the Cotswolds and West Country. First stop is Stow-on-the-Wold with its profusion of hotels, antique shops and art galleries. Youngsters on the street corner seem incongruous in such a setting, designed, it appears, simply for those seeking a traditional English refuge. A few stubble-burning scenarios on the way with smoke billowing over harvest fields scorched black and looking forlorn.

September

September 1 – I can't help noticing how folk in this part of the world talk like we Norfolk natives are generally portrayed on national television and radio… and they all mention Bernard Matthews when you say you come from Norfolk.

September 3 – The story of Tintagel is really the story of Cornwall; traditional industries of fishing, farming and mining have waned and tourism has turned into the golden goose. Although scholars may argue about King Arthur and his true location, businessmen have no qualms. Arthurian names abound. One local author tells me: 'We see nothing now but the common exploitation of these myths. It is the achievement of the twentieth century to turn a poem into a bazaar.' Clear warnings there for Norfolk with its Nelson connection, Black Shuck, Parson Woodforde and a few others.

September 6 – Home to Norfolk with reflections after 1,200 miles on English roads bound to be dominated by traffic. Car is king in city, town and village, and it is with no sense of pride that I wonder how many hours I've sat inside a piece of mobile metal during the last week or so.

September 8 – End of an era as doors close for the last time at Garlands, the Norwich store which has been a major attraction for customers of fashion over the last 122 years. I buy my mementoes – three shirts in the closing-down sale.

September 10 – Survey of wildlife casualties on a stretch of Norfolk road reveals the rabbit and hedgehog as most vulnerable creatures with the grey squirrel in third place. Another regular victim of heavy traffic is the coypu.

September 12 – Most emotional moment so far in my broadcasting career. The sporting years are rolled back as Errol Crossan, one of the heroes of Norwich City's epic FA Cup run of 1958–1959, flies back to Norfolk from his home in Canada. There was a grand Canary reunion last night, 25 years on, and Errol comes in to Radio Norfolk with a clutch of other former City players. He hasn't heard *The Ballad of Crossan and Bly*, composed and sung by my cousin Paul Wyett. When I play the record, Errol has to fight back the tears. I'm choked as well, but we recover in time to talk about those memorable ties that saw third division Norwich reach the FA Cup semi-finals, only to lose by the lone goal in a replay against Luton. After the programme I give him my copy of the record as a souvenir. He leaves, one of my boyhood heroes, the dashing little winger with a crew cut who helped write one of the proudest pages in Carrow Road history.

September 17 – Doyenne of Norfolk writers, Jane Hales of Holt, calls in for a *Dinnertime Show* chat. She's over 80 but still extremely sharp and cheerful and writing regularly for local papers and magazines. Her love of North Norfolk shines through much of her work, but she refuses to be labelled an eccentric just because she smokes a clay pipe! The late Dick Bagnall-Oakeley, schoolmaster, television personality and dialect expert, was a cousin, and Jane admits that his use of good old Broad Norfolk puts hers in the shade. She signs my copies of her books to add to a proud collection of local volumes with signatures in the front.

September 29 – Last cricket fling of the season as I play for the Chairman's XI against Hethersett on the village ground. Time for a quick chat and pint in the pub afterwards before heading to Garvestone to compete a hat trick of harvest suppers in the old Village Hall. One of my favourite occasions to reaffirm faith in some aspects of Norfolk rural life. Youngsters here to catch a flavour of what us veterans regard as so important, and let's hope they have the time and talent to maintain such traditions. A good day for warm reflections at the end of a Norfolk summer. The village cricket ground bathed in sunshine. The Village Hall resounding with laughter.

October

October 1 – Start of Arnold Wesker Week, events initiated by Radio Norfolk, thanks, in many respects, to the friendship between the internationally-acclaimed playwright and our news editor, Ian Hyams. Curtain up on *The Kitchen* at The Maddermarket Theatre in Norwich with the author and his wife, Dusty (from Starston) in the audience. The play has its roots in Wesker's experiences at the city's Bell Hotel and other restaurants in London and Paris. 'The world might have been a stage for Shakespeare, but to me it is a kitchen,' says Wesker.

October 2 – Wesker is my guest on the *Dinnertime Show*. High spot is a world première of something he wrote over 30 years ago while in Norfolk – and it was turned down by the *Eastern Daily Press*! *Sugar Beet* is a dialogue between two farm workers as they put their backs into it up and down the rows. The author does the scene setting while his nephew Keith and I take the starring roles. Time only for a couple of rehearsals – appropriately enough in the Radio Norfolk kitchen – and then we present it live.

Script conference – playwright Arnold Wesker runs through his lines with Keith Skipper.

October 5 – Wesker Week winds up with a grand lunch in his honour at The Maddermarket, and he reveals with a whimsical smile that there were suspicions he had been a spy for the Russians. On his departure from The Bell in Norwich 30 years ago, local detectives swooped to interview every member of staff about the kitchen porter and his girlfriend. They hinted darkly he'd been a spy in the pay of Russian intelligence. No one interviewed Wesker on the matter. As I say farewell the playwright grins when I suggest Radio Norfolk is now preparing for Ezra Pound Fortnight. It's been an interesting experience in the week commercial rivals Radio Broadland first went on air. Reckon we had the edge when it came to culture.

October 6 – Massive police operation in and outside the ground as Chelsea and their notorious followers come to Carrow Road. Sad indictment of the times that this kind of operation has to be staged just so a football match can be played. Climate hardly right for a free-flowing session, and a stuttering, niggling, unexciting 0–0 draw results. The sight of so many policemen, ambulance officers and stewards ringing the ground must feed cynical thoughts about the future of professional soccer.

October 12 – Go west, young man – to West Winch for the annual dinner of North Runcton Cricket Club. I share the stage with one of the game's biggest names, Jim Laker. Now a member of the BBC television commentary team, he's saddled for life with those remarkable test match figures of 19 wickets for 90 runs against the Australians at Old Trafford in 1956. I ask what he said to Surrey spin partner Tony Lock for mucking up his chances of a clean sweep. Jim simply smiles a forgiving smile.

October 13 – More travelling and talking, this time to Bradenham Harvest Horkey in the Village Hall. After supper and my mardle, out come the foxtrots and waltzes as Toby Rowe sets the pace with his 'geriatric disco'. Host of local characters to meet in the company of old friend, local auctioneer and cricketer John Dewing. There's Nelson pub landlord, John Larwood; Maurice Knights, proudly showing his photograph of potatoes that came up like cottage loaves; Milly Kerrison, leading light in the Brownies for many years and dubbed the Bradenham Skylark for her singing while riding a bike; then there's Jill, who plays the organ at Necton church; and Dulcie, who helps out at the Nelson on the green. She praises local youngsters who use the pub. Also time for a chat with dear old Hugh Parker, a pupil at Hamond's Grammar School in Swaffham from 1930 until 1936 before 40 years in the RAF.

October 21 – Pleasant job on a pleasant afternoon, opening the new Village Hall at Walsingham. I cut the pink ribbon as youngsters pitch into a football match just a few yards away. The hall is the result of 10 years of hard work spearheaded by local farmer Tom Moore in a village subjected to the sort of pressures few can understand. Religious fervour around the Walsingham shrines brings thousands of pilgrims every year, and that tends to take attention away from local activities. Plenty of characters to meet including Charlie Brown, who retired a couple of year ago as the Walsingham policeman with special responsibilities for visitors. He tells me of a colleague who claimed they were High Church where he went 'cors they burn that incest there'!

October 25 – We awake to learn Norwich City Football Club's main stand at Carrow Road has been ravaged by fire in the night. It will be closed for the rest of the season. Green and yellow plastic seats are melted and twisted in the blaze and flames tear through the roof. Underneath, the club boardroom is gutted and much of the club's history lost. An electrical fault is blamed for the disaster.

October 27 – Carrow Road show goes on. Norwich City take three points on a three-sided ground, beating Queen's Park Rangers 2–0 in splendid autumn sunshine. Main stand looks like a leftover from the Blitz. Rangers change in The Nest pub under the River End Stand. The Canaries use the police base as their dressing-room. Good jokes emerge as well: Will QPR be breathalysed before kick-off? Will home players be released for an identity parade after half-time? An RAF police dog demonstration team entertain before the match, jumping through burning hoops as part of their programme. What an ironic sight in view of the charred and twisted stand providing the backcloth. The muse settles easily on the shoulder: 'A perky Canary has emerged phoenix-like from the ashes of a traumatic week.'

October 29 – Good to hear some voices raised against the growing campaign to dual the A11 road in the name of progress. It's being pointed out that such a project would bring more accidents, more pollution, more noise and more stress to the roads and the people of Norfolk.

November

November 1 – Fakenham publisher Jim Baldwin calls with first copies of Old Barney's broadcasts on Radio Norfolk. *Dew Yew Keep A'Troshin'!* is my first venture into the book business and we're having the official launch at Fakenham before moving on to the Great Ryburgh Boar pub for a spot of socialising. Chad, a regular entertainer on my *Dinnertime Show* and a former art teacher, has illustrated the scripts with Dick Condon, manager of Norwich Theatre Royal, writing the foreword. A second volume is already sorted out. Keeping this diary has instilled a new brand of discipline into my jottings. Let's hope I can carry it on and maintain the energy and enthusiasm to make a little mark on the local book scene.
(*I wrote and recorded Old Barney's weekly reports on Radio Norfolk for over seven years, and three volumes of his rural correspondence were published in all and a cassette produced of some of his earliest broadcasts. Old Barney joined the ranks as soon as the radio station opened in September, 1980 – and I was amazed that many listeners thought he was a real person who biked into the studio every Saturday morning!)

November 3 – Weather turns colder with blustery winds and showers. Hardly ideal conditions for those celebrating bonfire delights this Saturday evening. As I write, a few rockets light up the sky and I'm reminded of that Guy Fawkes session I missed over 30 years ago after helping chum Tubby Rye to prepare the bonfire. I was wearing a brand new pair of rubber boots. Such was my enthusiasm to add to the pile that a tine of the pitchfork ripped through one of them. The gaping hole was immediately noticed when I got home for tea. Punishment was being forced to stay indoors while celebrations were unleashed into the Beeston sky. How I cried at the sheer injustice of it all. It could so easily have made me bitter and twisted for the rest of my days.

November 9 – Norfolk motorists will soon be confronted by signs warning of toads crossing the road. Special signs are going up after a successful pilot project designed to save thousands of toads which would otherwise be squashed by vehicles during the migration period between March and May.

November 13 – Tell us something new! The Norwich Society warns that as two pubs close every month, a vital part of the city's heritage is disappearing. It is estimated that there'll be only 100 left in five years' time. Back in 1870 there were 780 pubs in Norwich. Now, despite extension of the city's boundaries, there are only 205. Road widening is partly to blame for knocking down many pub buildings. Although breweries claim closures have been on financial grounds, a large number closed by the big breweries are now thriving under new ownership.

November 17 – Chimney sweep comes early to prepare us for winter. A grey, damp and uninviting day, but we take a trip to North Walsham for a spot of shopping. Herring for tea. While Norwich is clearly already seriously afflicted by festive shopping mania, it's a more leisurely pace in the towns.

November 18 – Delightful Sunday afternoon at Worthing Mill, near North Elmham, where I'm asked to open an exhibition, *Rural Bygones*, by local artist Bill Cooper. Evocative scenes from a fast-fading Norfolk canvas – but plenty of old faces to come back and haunt me. Margaret Watson and Janice Mitchell, fellow pupils at Beeston village school, and John Dawson, son of Harry, our grand old Sunday school teacher, lead the parade. I shared a harvest or two with John at Primrose Farm, and paintings on the wall remind us it used to be a bit quieter. A threshing scene draws plenty of attention, but several viewers stress what a mucky and messy old job that was even if it has a romantic hue up there. Grand mixture of country people nodding and chatting their way round and helping to keep it all in perspective.

November 19 – The Spinners, going strong on stage and records since 1958, drop in for a chat on the *Dinnertime Show* after last night's performance at Norwich Theatre Royal. Easy to see why they remain so popular; natural and amiable manner make it sheer fun to chat and they break into song around one microphone at the drop of an eyelid. Calls come in while they are on air to say thanks from fans for last night's show. There's genuine warmth in their reciprocal greetings.

November 26 – King's Lynn lands a starring role in *Revolution*, a film about the American War of Independence. Creation of sets and filming over a period of five months starting next February will bring extra work to the town with all it's spin-off benefits. Lynn waterfront, particularly around the Purfleet, will be made to look like New York in the eighteenth century. Buildings will have to be painted and local contractors used to restore them to their original state afterwards. Dozens of locals will be taken on as film extras and American tourists are expected to flock west to Lynn. The film-makers visited dozens of towns all over Britain before selecting Lynn.

(*Despite a star-studded cast, headed by Al Pacino, *Revolution* was panned by the critics and slid unceremoniously into cinema history as an expensive flop.)

December

December 2 – One of those days spent waiting for winter… cool enough for a fire but not yet time for huddling or ignoring the world outside. Last leaves are floating down in a wind without spite, and you can still hear the birds singing proper tunes. It's been a lingering autumn and that certainly helps the dark period of the year hurry by. New family in the village at church in the morning to almost double the average congregation.

December 3 – Intrigued to note the *Eastern Evening News* will be going tabloid in the New Year. This switch to a smaller format is in response to a survey of what readers want. It means that on January 28 the paper will revert to the size it was 15 years ago.

December 7 – Receivers called in at Dereham's Jentique and Metamec factories, with over 500 jobs at stake. Attempts being made to find buyers for the furniture and clock-making works. Dealing in the company's shares on the stock exchange is suspended. The continuing reces-

sion is blamed for the troubles. Dereham Mayor Michael Fanthorpe says the factories represent 'the employment pulse of the town. It that pulse stops not only will the firms need intensive care – Dereham will too.' The company opened in 1923 with a 12-strong workforce making model boats. Furniture production started in the 1930s and Metamec clocks first chimed in 1944.

December 8 – One of my brightest ideas of 1984 comes to fruition on a clear but chilly night in the tiny parish of Ovington, near Watton. I launch Norfolk's first village twinning project between Ovington and Bodham, near Holt. Over 20 enthusiasts from Bodham, forty miles away, arrive by bus for a 'getting-to-know-you' social event. The hosts turn on the style with splendid home-made entertainment. A good sing-song soon breaks the ice, although it's nippy going for performers changing in a tent at the back of the tiny Village Hall! Cultural exchanges are taking shape with Ovington set for a return visit in March. It's always seemed strange to me that many places are twinned with locations in Europe or even further afield – and yet they have no idea about many other places in their own county. This sort of 'missionary work' can be fun as well as worthwhile.

December 11 – Tears at Dereham as about a quarter of Jentique and Metamec workers are made redundant. A total of 129 are given their cards late in the afternoon, and there are no guarantees of long-term survival for the other workers. Ian Hare has to leave after ten years: 'I'm shattered. I'm 51 years old, so there's not a lot of chance of getting another job. In a few years it will be strange to see someone going to work…'

December 13 – Ever wondered what sort of language today's children will talk and write tomorrow? Some people are trying to make plain speaking more fashionable, but it's a tough job when you get a chunk like this from the Social Security (General Benefits) Regulations for 1984: 'Benefits paid to one person in respect of another as being a child in respect of whom the payee is entitled to child benefit, or as being the wife or husband, or an adult dependent of the first mentioned person shall, unless it is required to be repaid, be treated as having been properly paid for any period for which it is not in fact payable in cases where under a subsequent decision either.' What a lot of ole squit!

December 21 – Memory-jerker of a session as we head for The Stag pub at Westacre to break a charity bottle and savour a seasonal mardle. Beaming across the room is the face of 77-year-old local Joe Bly, one of the preachers who made regular calls at Beeston chapel when I was a lad. I recognise him immediately and there's the same rich voice that lit up many a Sunday sermon. Old names flow as Joe tells me he's made a remarkable recovery from illness. He certainly looks well, but there's a tinge of sadness as he recalls last week's closing of the old Methodist chapel in Westacre.

December 22 – Best seasonal yarn so far. Comedian Roy Randall has the stuffing knocked out of him by his pet turkey Samson. He swoops from a garden fence and sends Roy crashing to the ground at Topcroft. He's knocked out and taken to hospital but discharges himself after three hours. Roy goes to Newmarket – accompanied by a nurse – where he's topping the bill at a review at a cabaret club.

December 27 – Sandringham House under tight security as members of the royal family start arriving for their traditional New Year holiday. Big freeze continues and a power cut at Attleborough leaves 300 homes without electricity on the coldest day for a year. Gritting lorries are out and fog is an additional hazard. Frozen points delay Norwich to London trains by up to an hour.

December 28 – North Norfolk district councillors give the go-ahead for a new piggery at... Baconsthorpe!

December 31 – Made it! It is with pride that I make these jottings on the last day of 1984. My daily diary is complete, the first time I've managed such a marathon. Another cause for celebration is Diane's birthday and we stage our second 'at home' for friends and neighbours at Blacksmith's Cottage. Local vicar Christopher Basil Morgan is one of our guests and he greets 1985 with a short prayer after Old Lang Syne. More logs ready for the fire we're bound to need tomorrow. Greetings and fond hopes ring out on a clear, crisp night. A full diary. Sleep comes easy. I'm sort of organised after all!

End-of-year lights at Blakeney captured by artist Andrew Dibben.

January

January 6 – Bleak weather continues – but superstars have to brave the elements to earn an honest crust. Actress Meryl Streep has been on location at Castle Rising filming for her latest picture, *Out of Africa*. She dashes away to catch a plane to Kenya where much of the production will be shot. Filming at Castle Rising was scheduled to finish yesterday, but was extended after snow. Earlier scenes had been shot with lime sprayed on the set to create a wintry effect, but then the film-makers decided to repeat them with the real thing. Secrecy at the Norfolk location has been very tight. Miss Streep stayed at the Duke's Head Hotel in King's Lynn, but was at the Castle Rising set by 7a.m. each day and didn't leave until after 5.30p.m.

January 13 – *Poppyland* unfurls on BBC television, and perhaps the North Norfolk coast will become an even bigger target for holiday-makers as a result. Clement Scott, journalist and theatre critic, fell in love with that stretch of coast leading to Sidestrand and Overstrand from Cromer and his flowery writings inspired poets, authors and artists to follow his tracks. Local accents for this television production are predictably bad – same old Mummerzet tones – and I resent some other aspects of this intrusion as well. Clem watches the locals hard at work in the mill and sighs how envious he is of their way of life. Couple of weeks with his jacket off would have changed his poetic tune! I fear many modern visitors still nurse the same sort of romantic illusions and those responsible for selling holidays are delighted to perpetuate them.

January 15 – Henry the heron continues to dine in style at Heacham. Sue Torrey has a long-standing arrangement with her feathered friend – a tasty meal of half a dozen sprats a day. They met up 12 years ago after Henry had been hit by a car. He arrived at Sue's home in a cardboard box one January night. After a few days in a cage, Henry was let out. He stayed around until March, but he was back in October and remains a regular visitor. He knows a good thing when he tastes it.

January 16 – Andrew Clarke of Burgh St Peter drives ten miles by tractor to get to Langley School so he won't miss his Biology O level exam. Andrew, a sixth former, was hoping to get behind the wheel of a car but the family home was snowed in. The tractor drive took 45 minutes.

January 27 – A century of rugby football in Norwich is celebrated with a service of thanksgiving thought to be unique in the sport's history. The centenary service is conducted by former Norwich Rugby Club President, the Right Revd Aubrey Aitken, Bishop of Lynn, at the club's Beeston Hyrne headquarters.

January 29 – Pantomime treat at the Theatre Royal in Norwich, a splendid show with sumptuous costumes, colourful action and telling effects. Wayne Sleep is the star but his dancing skills never become too obtrusive. Box-office records are being broken. One sour note is a front page story in the *Eastern Evening News* (which reverted to its tabloid size yesterday) in which Wayne Sleep attacks Norwich people as 'rude' and 'thick'. This refers to an incident in a local restaurant and the dancer is angry that one comment in a lengthy interview has been hauled out for the big headline treatment. At the end of this evening's panto performance he says this should not be taken as a general criticism. Well, he shouldn't have said it in the first place. Oh, no, he shouldn't!

January 31 – Serious danger of North Norfolk becoming a cult spot for tourists next summer. After the *Poppyland* drama a couple of weeks ago, the show at the end of Cromer Pier gets national exposure on BBC 2's *Forty Minutes* programme, highlighting how it's all run on a showbiz shoestring. It's one of the few remaining shows of its kind and the curtain will go up again in a few months. This brand of family entertainment with a nostalgic flavour has a brave survival spirit but some sense it's only a matter of time before it disappears. A valuable 'cradle' for young artists who have to muck in and become all-rounders, but many still see it as no more than a harmless anachronism in an age of instant and expensive entertainment.
(*Happily, fears of a final fling for Cromer's end-of-the-pier show proved unfounded. It continues to flourish and that spotlight in 1985 sparked renewed interest.)

February

February 1 – I'm reading *Sharpen the Sickle*, a history of rural trade unionism by Reg Groves. There were almost 30,000 full-time farm workers in Norfolk in the late 1950s and early 1960s. That's shrunk to only 7,000, although some will argue that the rate of productivity continues to increase. The agricultural revolution of the past two decades means numbers will carry on falling. When I was

Hard labour – harvesting the sugar beet crop.

a lad in the village of Beeston it seemed natural for so many to work on the farms with others joining in at harvest and threshing time. Perhaps the sugar beet crop demanded the hardest labour, interminable rows of chopping out and then knocking and topping in snow, frost and mud. My modest attempts at farm labouring made it abundantly clear I could stay well away from all that romanticising in years to come.

February 7 – Singer Matt Monro dies of cancer at 54. One of my favourite performers, I recall meeting him at the Brundall Vauxhall cricket ground when he opened some smart new facilities. He was appearing at the Windmill Theatre on Yarmouth's Golden Mile, a fine singer admired by Frank Sinatra.

February 12 – Strange sight at Acle on another frosty morning – early risers see three suns! A spokesman for the Institute of Astronomy in Cambridge says it's caused by atmospheric conditions. On very cold mornings the sun's rays are sometimes refracted by ice particles in the upper atmosphere and strange optical illusions can result.

February 17 – Sunday outing for lunch in a Beccles pub. We go via Loddon where ducks waddle up from the frozen river in the hope of titbits. Through Haddiscoe and St Olaves into the ugly sprawl of Bradwell. There's no distinctive gap between this chunk of Yarmouth's suburbia and the town itself. Industrial bits and pieces in Southtown are getting out of hand. Southtown Common is a small oasis in this sea of roads and haphazard development where many homes are up for sale. No surprise there. The sounds must be frightening while the sights can hardly be justified whatever 'benefits' this industrial mayhem brings to the resort. A relief to get out along the Acle Straight. So much sky above the marshes. Thank goodness they can't build here! Windmills dotted on the gentle canvas each side of a road that should be boring, but it holds recuperative powers for me after Yarmouth's cramming and claustrophobic environment.

February 21 – Opening day at Griston, near Watton, as the new Wayland Prison welcomes its first residents. Twenty of them, including one 'lifer', arrive at the £17 million complex. Each week another score will pass through the giant steel door until the prison is full with 494. The prison, on an old RAF missile site west of the village, isn't yet complete. Some cell blocks are still being fitted out. Some local councillors call it a 'holiday camp', but deputy governor Alfred Jennings hits back: 'It's far from a holiday camp. It is a modern prison, providing facilities long overdue in the prison service.'

February 22 – We're told thousands of new homes need to be built in the Norwich area to keep pace with demand and to prevent house prices rocketing. And a big search will be mounted to identify building land in the city, its suburbs and satellite villages. County Council estimates put the need for new homes in this area at over 1,500 a year for the next five years. Whitehall figures, inevitably backed by local builders, put the need even higher at about 2,000 a year. Special studies will be carried out in villages like Mulbarton, Cringleford, Poringland and Stoke Holy Cross. One member of the county planning committee, Tory John Birkbeck, says he's horrified at the prospect of Norfolk ceasing to be a rural county and becoming just like the rest of England. However, his views seem to be drowned out by 'needs for new industry and influx of people to attract investment into its outdated roads system and Norwich Airport'.

February 26 – The long-neglected country skill of hedge-laying enjoys a little revival in Norfolk. An agricultural training group is asked to arrange a basic course in the arts of hedgelaying. A total of seven farm staff showed interest and a suitable stretch of hedge at Swardeston received much-needed repair work.

March

March 3 – The miner's strike is over after exactly a year – and the battle for the peace begins. NUM delegates go against Arthur Scargill and other union leaders and call off the bitter strike without a settlement. Some still claim the miners had every right to battle to save their pits and communities. Clearly an energy revolution is on the way. We experienced an agricultural revolution in this area after the last war, and that's why so many jobs on the land had to go. No doubt, there were painful times as life on Norfolk farms underwent drastic surgery in the name of progress. Families and communities had to move or adapt to new ways of making a living. Those who remain working on our farms under a completely different sort of regime are protesting loud and long about poor wages. One of the responses will be that more money for the workers must mean even more cuts in jobs. Yesterday, over 100 farm workers marched through the middle of Norwich to complain at low pay.

March 4 – Sad to hear of the death of Ethel Battelley at Dereham. She was 77 and the mother of one of Norfolk's most talented sporting families. Ethel was the cleaning lady at the *Dereham and Fakenham Times* press office when I worked there in the early 1960s. We always enjoyed a good Monday morning mardle with Ethel bringing me up to date with all the weekend news fit to print.

March 5 – An increase of 8.5 per cent in farm workers' pay  after two days of tough bargaining by the Agricultural Wages Board. Farmers don't like an increase higher than the rate of inflation and warn they'll be forced to shed labour to absorb this increase. Farm workers' leader Jack Boddy says: 'If they dispose of workers it will be pure vindictiveness… this increase represents a small shuffle by employers, but it's a big step forward for farm workers.'

Jack Boddy – farm workers' leader.

March 6 – So Norwich City are off to Wembley for the first time in a decade after beating Ipswich 2–0 at Carrow Road in the return leg of their Milk Cup semi-final. City win 2–1 on aggregate thanks to an 87th-minute goal from Steve Bruce. The Canaries meet Sunderland in the final, and the natural hope is that they'll do themselves – and their supporters – a better turn than they managed on previous Wembley visits in 1973 and 1975.

March 12 – More people are moving into Norfolk – about 5,000 every year – and there's no sign of a let-up. Chief planning officer Martin Shaw tells county councillors that the number of people coming to live here exceeds official census office estimates. About half of those moving in are over 50.

March 16 – Extra time for winter! Snow and sleet as I head for Swaffham to help launch a book called *Cap and Apron to Cap and Gown* for Jean Rennie. This vigorously determined Scots lady went to the University of East Anglia in her 70s and completed a BA degree in History. She had the qualifications to go to Glasgow University in 1923, but with her father unemployed she had to take what work she could get. The story of her time among 18-year-olds underlines her victory in the fight to make up for lost years and opportunity.

March 24 – A truly memorable Sunday. The Canaries win 1–0 to earn their first Wembley triumph in the Milk Cup

Wembley glory at last – Canary captain Dave Watson holds the Milk Cup aloft.

Final against Sunderland – and it's a triumph for the fans as well. Their impeccable behaviour draws praise from the police and is dubbed 'The Friendly Final'. Asa Hartford's shot is deflected home by a Sunderland defender early in the second half. The Wearsiders miss a penalty but there's no denying City's extra pace and skill deserve to carry the day. I'm a member of the Radio Norfolk commentary team, sharing summarising duties with former manager John Bond. I watch Wembley gradually come alive from 8.30 in the morning as the first fans mill around outside. It's like a giant rosette unfolding after midday, green and yellow, red and white, and the stage is set for a clash of the unfashionables. At the end, Sunderland supporters, fighting back tears, exchange hats, scarves and banners with City followers. And they exchange smiles and handshakes. It's so old-fashioned and refreshing. It brings a 1959-size lump to the throat.

April

April 6 – Sporting pilgrimage to Walsingham for Fakenham Town Football Club's centenary dinner. It's a night made for memories and I dip into my cuttings for reports of local derbies between the Ghosts and Dereham in the 1963/64 season, my first full campaign as a reporter on the local touchlines. Fakenham goalkeeper Sid Negus is one of the colourful characters on parade, smiling at amiable jibes from all quarters. I join in with this extract from one of my reports: 'Negus had an amazing piece of good fortune in a scrimmage. He lost sight of the ball, twirled round in ballet fashion to see whether it was nestling in the back of the net or had gone over the top. He must have been surprised when it dropped into his arms!' It's the way I told 'em.

April 9 – Raw material of Norfolk life surfaces on a trip to the Two Lifeboats at Sheringham for a meal and a yarn. Peter, a local musician who fills in during the days by digging gardens in the area, points to local fisherman 'Plug' Emery as a fount of good old Norfolk sayings. For example, if it's raining he suggests: 'Dew yew come in on out onnit!' Another little gem for bonfire night as 'Plug' tries to ensure safety after the fireworks have been lit: 'Stand well clear o'yerself!' I jot down these little sayings and here they are for posterity.

April 12 – Unusual home for sale in the King's Lynn area – a two-bedroom windmill complete with bathroom, living room and kitchen plus French ovens and much of the original machinery. The West Winch windmill was saved from demolition and converted into a house by Wally Price. He died last year and now his widow Elsie reluctantly decides to part with it. The cost is £125,000 with two cottages, or £95,000 without.

April 22 – Costessey pigeon fancier Bernard Lince welcomes home a special bird. He's had to wait longer than usual for it to return… seven years, in fact. The bird went missing in 1978 when it was six weeks old. Last week it was rescued at Margate during a gale and, thanks to the identity ring on its leg, it's back with Bernard.

April 24 – Sir Harry Secombe in Norwich to record *Highway*, his Sunday evening religious programme. He forgets his braces as he goes to appear before the television cameras. In a timely supporting role, local press photographer John Folkes whips off his own blue braces and passes them to the star presenter.

Sir Harry Secombe forgot his braces.

April 26 – The small South Norfolk village of Shelfanger is digging into its past with an exhibition of bygones. It could have been a booming spa and attracted royalty if a scheme by a local doctor had taken off a century ago. Dr Anthony Farrington discovered the water in his well was rich in minerals. He launched the Norfolk Spa to sell his 'constitutional waters' in bottles. He tried to enlist the backing of the Prince of Wales and the Great Eastern Railway agreed to run a branch line to Shelfanger if business was good enough. Bottles were sent all over England, and even to France, and hundreds flocked to bathe in the waters. But the novelty wore off and the spa failed. What sort of place would Shelfanger be today if that initial boom had continued?

April 27 – Snow stops first-class cricket at Derby, and sends a wintry shudder through Norfolk. However, there's plenty to warm the soul at Hemsby as Ada Feakes, aged 103 and still going strong, officially opens the new £130,000 Village Hall. Ada was there when the old hall was opened in 1920. She now presents a clock to go over the plaque she has unveiled. 'It's got large numbers so the older people can see the time' she chuckles.

May

May 1 – Traditional May Day celebrations see Morris dancers in action in Swaffham town centre at 6a.m. They dance on the bandstand and there are a few mystified looks from folk collecting their morning newspapers. The group dispense with the ivory horn normally blown lustily to herald their arrival.

Morris dancers greet the May Day dawn.

May 2 – Off to Southwold for fresh air and to buy a few books. It remains my favourite coastal haunt, unashamedly tied to the past. There's natural politeness in the shops and restaurants, an unhurried feel to the place, a real pride in being different to other more brash members of the seaside family. Big old houses looking out to sea are so quiet, sentries from another age. Cannons, relics of the Napoleonic wars, stand guard with no apologies for being so far behind the times.

May 3 – Now Norwich reels from redundancy blows. The Laurence Scott & Electromotors workforce is to be cut by 236. Another 65 jobs are being shed by Jarrold Printing works while the Corona drinks factory is to close with 68 redundancies.

May 8 – My VE celebration day with a difference is to join Hickling Women's Institute for their 67th birthday party. A chat about dialect with a few examples along the way goes down well with the sherry, sandwiches and cakes. They do sing 'Jerusalem' at the start, but the general WI tone is changing, not least as a result of so many newcomers in our villages. A real mixture of accents and classes here.

May 16 – Motorway mania in the area reaches a peak as Transport Minister Lynda Chalker opens the new Attleborough by-pass. She tells flag-waving pupils from Attleborough High School that by the time they reach half her age they will have 'the A11 that Norfolk really deserves'.

May 20 – Local milkman rises to occasion as his float sinks. Roger Warne jumps clear after a burst water main causes major subsidence. This all happens at 5.30a.m. in Gorleston. The float sinks to the depth of the milk platform. East Anglian Water Company workmen are first on the scene and use a hydraulic lift to extract the float from the hole.

May 24 – A bit like 'The Prodigal Son Goes Home'. An evening full of yesterdays at Litcham Methodist Chapel for a chat about my work and interests. My last call here was to read the lesson for dear old Harry Dawson about 25 years ago when he was on his preaching rounds. Plenty of familiar faces and voices, including Joe Bly, Gordon Bailey, Norman Wagg and Cyril Jolly. Cyril's gentle examples of dialect and humour are a sheer delight. Pint and mardle afterwards with Derek Knock at The Bull. I like Litcham more now than I did as a lad when local rivalries produced a kind of tribalism.

May 25 – Discovery day for the wife and I as we go back to nature. Stroll round the village before tea in warm sunshine, and a voyage to the unexplored down Bingles Turn, following the footpath to the woods. New houses disappear as Forestry Commission trees beckon. Carpets of bluebells. Birds and bracken. Sadly, no sign of deer that live in the woods. We feel rather ashamed that we haven't ventured that way before in over two years of living in Hevingham. I'm wearing slippers, testament to the surprise turn our stroll is destined to take.

May 26 – Coventry win their final match 4–1 against champions Everton – and so Norwich City are relegated to the Second Division just 63 days after lifting the Milk Cup at Wembley. Talk about a sweet-and-sour season! My first cricket outing of the summer is a cup match against Electricity at Angel Road in Norwich. They bat first and struggle to make 95. Caister are on a dodgy 22 for 4 when thunder, lightning and rain force the tie to be abandoned. I'm umpiring at the time and pleased to get off.

May 30 – Home Secretary Leon Brittan in Norfolk to open Wayland Prison – and he pledges the Tories will speed up anti-hooligan measures after last night's European Cup Final tragedy. Fans ran riot before the match between Liverpool and Juventus in Brussels. Nearly 40 die and hundreds are injured in this ugly war on the terraces. Some fans suffocate and are trampled to death as a wall collapses.

May 31 – Norwich City's passport to Europe as Milk Cup winners is snatched cruelly out of their hands as the FA bans all English clubs from next season's European competitions. A devastating blow after relegation misery last week.

June

June 1 – One of Norfolk's best-loved characters, Aubrey Aitken, Bishop of Lynn, dies at 73. A keen all-round sportsman, he played cricket and rugby in his younger days, but it was his love of Norwich City Football Club that enhanced his sporting reputation. Aubrey was made an honorary life vice-president of the club in 1979, first time they had gone outside Carrow Road to make such an appointment. I bumped into him regularly as a reporter for home matches and we shared many a chuckle in the boardroom

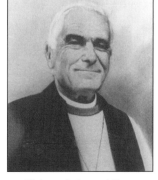

Bishop Aubrey Aitken.

where his pithy comments were kept tactfully from the ears of directors! His last sermon three weeks ago was in the Hempnall group of parishes. The congregation gave him three cheers. 'Here was a good man who believed it was better to light a candle than to curse the darkness' says the *Eastern Daily Press* in its leader column.

June 5 – Countryside writer Rosemary Tilbrook is back on the warpath. She writes in the *Eastern Daily Press*: 'Far too much of the foaming roadside verge in this part of South Norfolk has been minced to smithereens. The sun comes out, warms the verge with life – and along come the dreaded cutters.' She's sick and tired of the insidious erosion and overall mismanagement of roadside verges which ought to play an important role where matters of conservation are concerned.

June 8 – The government's *Civil Defence and the Farmer* guide is published with up-to-date advice from Whitehall to keep farming going after a nuclear attack. Polythene sheets, a bucket of dirt and an ample supply of straw bales make up the survival kit. But Norfolk farmer David Barnes of Forncett St Peter thinks it's all a waste of time. 'If we spent a month putting all they say we need together, we still wouldn't have enough time.'

June 12 – As first copies of my latest epic, *A Load of Old Squit* comes through from the publishers, I'm interested to note that Eastern Arts are launching a scheme in which parties of schoolchildren and teachers have the chance to visit regional writers whose work demonstrates a direct relationship with their environment. Author of novels for older children, my former *Eastern Daily Press* colleague Jack Gordon is main spur behind this idea after his walking tours amid settings that have influenced his work. He says his perambulations by the Wash often inspired discussions on the nature of the Fenland experience.

Jack Gordon

June 22 – Plenty of heavy clouds as we drive into South Norfolk, but a fine afternoon to bless Kenninghall Fair. Hearty lunch at the Red Lion with the Holman family and amiable stroll on the recreation ground interspersed with chats. There's Peggy Hogg, who has biked from North Lopham to give me a kiss; Ma Sutton, who bets me I daren't tell a saucy joke on the wireless; and Olive and Tom Knox, who inform me they used to live next door to my family at Holmdene Cottages at Beeston. Olive 'knew' me before I was born! She remembers Mum pregnant with me, and Tom recalls how Vic, my dad, helped him carry baths of water up the yard for washing purposes.

June 27 – Royal Norfolk Show organisers face a £50,000 bill after two days of rain. But despite the lowest attendance since 1976, officials still hope to go ahead with a major expansion plan at the Costessey site. For all the problems surrounding this mud-and-thunder show, loyalty of Norfolk people deserves a big salute. After battling our way home and cleaning up, we head for Gorleston and a production of Arnold Wesker's *Roots* at the Shrublands Youth and Adult Centre. The Norfolk accents are happily authentic – I would have walked out in disgust had they not been – and we enjoy this treatment of a play that still provokes 26 years after it first put the county on a national stage.

July

July 3 – To mark the close for good at end of term of Sea Palling Village School, teachers and pupils organise an open day. It features an exhibition tracing the building's 106-year history. Margaret Bale, headmistress since 1976, says the event is organised 'because we want to go out with a flourish and not a whimper'.

July 4 – A day wallowing in cups of tea and nostalgia. Morning session at Chambers shop under the town sign at Dereham signing books and renewing acquaintance with old friends. Then we take our refreshments to Beeston lily pits and a spot of shade before moving on to see my old village schoolmistress Marjorie Tann and her husband Frank. They retired to a bungalow in The Street. Tea and a symphony of names and memories. It's a pity to break up but we have one more Beeston call to see Aunt Margaret and Uncle Cyril down Herne Lane. Perhaps there's just too much to think and talk about in one afternoon, and my mind is brimming over as we head home past the dog roses and fields of turning corn.

July 7 – On the cricket trail at Hindringham. I smack my first boundary of the season – but we're all out for 87. The home side ease to victory by eight wickets as the Wimbledon men's singles final comes to the boil. Boris Becker, only 17 and unseeded, is champion. I'm 41 and trying to defy the years.

July 12 – Words to ponder left behind by the Archbishop of Canterbury, Dr Robert Runcie, in his talk to Norfolk clergymen. 'To use a Norfolkism, you've got a proper job on here' he exclaimed. The cosy rural stereotype no longer fitted the facts. 'High-tech' and 'agri-business' had long replaced the loom and the plough. Such changes were two-edged in their effects. On one hand they fashioned a future filled with financial security and material wellbeing, while on the other quickened the disintegration of deep-seated patterns of rural life. 'Indeed, in this diocese as elsewhere, I suspect there's a growing separation of 'rural' and 'agricultural'. Actual use of the land now requires much less labour and the life of the village can become a kind of optional extra to those who manage and live on the farm.' Intriguing that outsiders high and low can often see our changing patterns much more clearly than we can see them ourselves.

July 25 – The day some people in Norfolk thought the world was about to end. A nuclear attack warning siren wails out – but it's all caused by human error. British Telecom engineers are working on the air-raid early-warning system. They are updating equipment. Something triggers off the sirens for about 30 minutes. Places most affected are Norwich, Harleston, Bungay, East Harling, Wymondham and Attleborough. One worried resident says it's all very well being told that it's a mistake this time, but what does he do next time?

July 28 – Heavy rain appears to make our Sunday visit to Brisley nothing more than a formality, a little pilgrimage of habit rather than with any realistic hopes of action on the cricket field. But both sides are determined to fill the time usefully before The Bell opens over the green. We field first in intermittent rain. Brisley get sharper showers when it's Caister's turn to bat, but return after one brief visit to the pavilion. Female spectators shake their heads in amusement and amazement, and there are moments when even we hardy lads wonder what on earth we are doing on a day like this! We win, but the real pleasure is in our visit to The Bell for a pint and reunion with mine hosts, Ada and Henry. Ada was born here in 1900. She's a pillar of the local church. Henry's a little bit younger. They run one of the most delightfully old-fashioned public houses you'll ever find. It's like going round to see auntie and uncle for an evening chat. The front room is for the more retiring customers. We enjoy the living room atmosphere – armchairs, table, piano, photographs on the sideboard. Of course, it will all slide into local folklore when this charming old couple have to call it a day and the pub is transformed to meet the 'needs' of a modern age. Ada and Henry go with the setting.

July 29 – A right royal week coming up in the area, and the Queen Mother, 85 in a few days, sets the big ball rolling at Worstead as she opens the new £100,000 Village Hall. She says this is 'a shining example of what can be achieved when people have the will to help themselves'. The Queen Mother will be at Sandringham Flower Show on the last day of the month accompanied by Prince Charles on his first visit to the event. The Queen and Duke of Edinburgh head for Yarmouth, Lowestoft and Oulton Broad next week.

August

August 3 – The Siege of Stoke Ferry has been lifted! Traffic which has clogged the West Norfolk village's narrow winding streets switches to the new by-pass. Within minutes of MP Sir Paul Hawkins cutting a ribbon across the £2.6 million road, heavy lorries have been spirited away.

August 9 – Richard and Eliza Moore celebrate 70 years of marriage at their Yarmouth home. Mr Moore is 91 and in excellent health. 'I've been smoking since I was 14 and perhaps working in a brewery for 40 years has helped as well!' So much for the traditional recipe for good health and old age. Mrs Moore is 88 and looking well.

August 11 – Grumpy skies but willing spirits at Bodham for the first village twinning cricket match with Ovington. Social in the Village Hall for all ages rounds off another grand little chapter in this saga. As rain blows across the scene before the start of the match, farmers in fields nearby are forced to withdraw their combines and so lose a few more precious harvesting hours. Meanwhile, 13 people are taken to hospital as gales lash the Sheringham to Cromer raft race.

August 18 – They are celebrating a sporting coup at picturesque Castle Rising – a cricket match against Italy! The contest is arranged following a village visit to Italy last month, the first English club to tour there. That trip included matches in Milan, Florence, Rome and Naples. The Italians are on their second visit to this country. Their squad of 20 includes ten 'pure' Italians; the rest are British and Sri Lankan who live there, but all are qualified to play for Italy under International Cricket Conference rules. Meanwhile, Lowestoft carry off the Bob Carter Cup at Lakenham in Norfolk's main showpiece final. They dismiss Swardeston for 112 and get home with six wickets to spare. It's Lowestoft's second win in three years and earns them the first £500 cash prize put up by the sponsors. I don't like this idea at all. It must encourage pot-hunting instincts and provoke more unsporting behaviour. It also means certain players with less successful clubs will have their loyalties seriously tested.

KEITH SKIPPER'S NORFOLK DIARIES

August 31 – We fly out of Norwich for the Channel Islands. Brief stop at Jersey and then on to Guernsey for a week. We are staying a few doors from Hauteville House, where writer Victor Hugo lived and worked in exile for 15 years. The main town of St Peter Port is built on cliffs surrounding the bay. Our first trek into town underlines that local reputation for friendliness. As we take lunch at a restaurant a twinkling lad from outside town engages in chat at the adjoining table. He was 83 last Wednesday, he celebrates his diamond wedding next year – and spent 60 years in greenhouses. I tell him he ought to be bigger. Then the rain starts and we take waif-like refuge in a doorway. A woman comes across to offer a lift in her car back to the hotel. Not bad adverts for the place.

September

September 12 – After uplifting holidays in Guernsey and in the Cotswolds, I prepare to go back to work. Neighbour Brian lends us a pint of milk and brings round some plums to mark our homecoming. The rector rings to see if we are going to church on Sunday morning. I know what he's after and so volunteer to read one of the lessons. He'll be round soon to collect sponsorship money for his round-the-churches cycle ride. The gasmen are busy digging up the road outside our cottage. Home, sweet home!

September 17 – Eckling Grange at Dereham celebrates 25 years as a Christian home for retired people. It was founded by the late David Potter, originally to provide homes for retired missionaries and Christian workers. Now it's a retirement haven for Christians of all denominations with 44 residents in the Grange and 72 others living in bungalows on the complex.

September 24 – My favourite weather! Misty morning and then the sun fingers through branches to bring that lovely restful feel of early autumn. Celebrations to go with it at Horsham St Faith, on the outskirts of Norwich. They've won their big fight against developers who planned a massive housing estate there, putting up 260 houses and so more than doubling the size of the village. Environment Secretary Kenneth Baker rejects an appeal by the developers, so ending a battle which first united residents at the end of 1983. The plan was opposed by the parish, district and county councils, and Mr Baker agrees that such development would substantially alter the character of the place and lead to loss of agricultural land. What a marvel – Whitehall goes along with the wishes of local people!

September 27 – Rackheath church provides a delightful story in the Norfolk countryside. Five years ago it was a vandalised shell. Now it's a beautiful little place. Restoration is complete with the fabric renewed and the interior redecorated. A monthly service is held there and many more visit this building in its serene setting surrounded by fields.

September 28 – After last night's trip to Wreningham Village Hall to pull the first pint in their smart new bar, it's back to a regular haunt for a harvest supper. Garvestone Village Hall – and what a pleasure to see inhibitions pushed aside in the name of fun and laughter. Folk of all ages and sizes join in dressing up, passing the parcel, singing songs and generally cavorting in the old fashioned country spirit.

October

October 1 – A day to pluck off the calendar and store away. Glorious sunshine all the way, the peak of a spell that has confounded all those who suggested a soggy summer was best gone… let autumn and winter do their worst! Trouble with the drains at home, so the man comes round with his long stick, amiable advice and a bill for £28 (inclusive of VAT). As he leaves, we head into the Norfolk countryside to claim some of summer's overspill.

October 7 – Howard Rotavators giant Harleston factory closes with the loss of 200 jobs. And the local job centre manager warns that some might not find work for six months.

October 12 – Nurse Edith Cavell's rocking chair, which she took to Belgium from Swardeston vicarage, is brought home. The surprise gift from Belgian guests is presented at the village sign unveiling. The return of the chair is highlight of another successful Cavell Festival. Meanwhile, more than 200 gather by a railway bridge in a sun-drenched corner of North Norfolk to pay tribute to an outstanding man: David Pinkerton, a British Railways bridge engineer and volunteer worker on the North Norfolk Railway, died when he lost his footing and fell from the bridge he was constructing on the Sheringham to Weybourne line. He was 28. A stone is set in the bridge wall dedicated to his memory.

October 16 – Memorable event at Cinema City in Norwich. I host a Norfolk Night as the radio station's contribution to the Triennial Festival Fringe. It draws acclaim from public and press alike. Our audience includes Sir Timothy Colman, Lord Lieutenant of Norfolk, and there are many requests for more evenings like this to salute local characters and writers.

October 18 – To Old Buckenham for the local Women's Institute's 17th birthday party. A true country flavour and mardling reaches a climax after the cake has been cut and passed round with the sherry. We sit opposite the couple who run the local Post Office and stores, so they're in a prime position to catch the flavour of the community. The local vicar is a few seats along on the top table and he's formed an unofficial 'Men's Institute' for the hard-working, long-suffering chaps who like a pint and a chat while the girls are busy at their meetings. I'm rather surprised to hear there's no love lost between Old Buckenham and New Buckenham. Evidently, arguments have flared over boundaries, with 'them' making claims to items such as the cattle. Shades of civil war! I suggest it could be a good idea to have an annual set of fixtures between the two to get rid of high feelings. Surely a cricket match and inter-village quiz could do the trick…

October 25 – Renewing old acquaintances and finding new friends at Bradfield Cricket Club's centenary dinner. I reckon 1885 was a vintage year – Dereham and Fakenham Football Clubs were formed, Gladstone was Prime Minister and 37-year-old W.G. Grace scored 1,600 runs and took 118 wickets. Early years at Bradfield saw men and boys come in from the farms to play cricket, with crop rotation dictating on which ground they could play. Coincidentally, one of Norfolk's last surviving wherrymen, Jack Gedge of Swafield, celebrates his 100th birthday. He was already at work on wherries when Queen Victoria celebrated her diamond jubilee. His father and grandfather were wherrymen as well.

November

November 1 – As the weather strikes a much colder note I find this cheering description of a 'lady-in-waiting' at the start of a month with a notoriously small fan club: 'November is a faithful handmaiden of Mother Nature, making leafy patchwork quilts for the garden beds, shooing southward loitering birds, carrying fruits of the harvest to men in her generous arms, bustling about till her work is finished. Then, complacently, Autumn sits in a corner, with a shawl drawn over her tired shoulders, waiting till her sister Winter tiptoes in, snowflaked and sparkling, ready to take over in the seasons' cycle.' With these words to warm us, we head for Cromer and some late-afternoon shopping with a cup of tea to follow. There's still life left in the sun as it paints glorious colours and shapes as it bids a defiant good evening. That mixture of skies and landscapes dotted with churches has a haunting quality at this time of year.

November 5 – Reunion after more than 20 years with Keith Hodson. I trod the boards with him in Thetford Festival Players' production of *Rape of the Belt* as a young reporter in town in the early 1960s. He was a towering Heracles to my diminutive Theseus, a comic contrast that helped us get a few laughs. We chat on air about those dramatic old days and he gives an impromptu example of his current work as a children's entertainer. He is Kernel Marvo. He lives at Wolferton on the royal estate.

November 8 – Jim Hanley, at the heart of the Norwich shoe industry for over half a century, dies at 80. He joined the board of directors at Norwich City Football Club in 1947 and became chairman soon after. He was later appointed club president – and continued to play tennis well into his 70s.

November 22 – A fleeting television appearance in the annual *Children in Need* marathon. I represent Radio Norfolk in the local studios, but I can't call it either an entertaining or edifying experience. This whole frantic drive for money, desperately needed though it be, is turning into a massive excuse to provide free advertising for firms and business interests who see it as the ideal vehicle for such a purpose.

November 26 – Former colleague John Kitson, now chief reporter for the local paper at Thetford, paints a sad picture of the town in a hard-hitting article. 'A trail of broken shop windows in the pedestrian precinct, fights in the market-place and an atmosphere of the big city rather than the rural town has become the rule rather than the exception… it is the most heavily-industrialised town for its size in Norfolk, and is increasingly and aggressively urban. At certain stages of the clock, and especially at weekends, it is also an unpleasant place in which to be should you stray into a number of areas. One experienced police officer described it as a powder keg at weekends. For some Thetfordians, the 1960s vision of the expanding town has gone more than a little sour.' Overspill changed Thetford. It brought new opportunities – but destroyed old values.

December

December 2 – I enjoyed my first chat with Fakenham rector Hugh Buckingham on Saturday after switching on the town's festive lights. I note he's just had his first book published, *How to be a Christian in Trying Circumstances*. This was rejected by 12 publishers with Anglican Church connections before being accepted by Epworth Press – publishers for the Methodist Church.

KEITH SKIPPER'S NORFOLK DIARIES

December 7 – Canaries in the afternoon at Carrow Road – and the annual turkey supper at Beetley Village Hall in the evening. A splendid parish do with the seasonal fare piped in and carved by one member of each table wearing a chef's hat. I enjoy a mardle with Joe Freestone, who used to drive buses for Carters of Litcham when I was a lad. He now runs buses of his own in Beetley and we cover many miles down memory lane.

December 9 – Warmest night of the year! I make my debut as Father Christmas, handing out presents to mentally and physically disabled youngsters at the Vauxhall Centre in Norwich. I'm soon sweltering in that heavy costume while eager children bring their own hazards. I threaten to take one lad back to Greenland to help work in the present-making shop as he tugs my coat and tries to remove my whiskers. He returns five minutes later – to tell me his mum says he can go with me! Get out of that one, Santa!

December 15 – Carols and lessons in the village church, and an exceptional turnout on a wild Sunday afternoon. Cynical thought – but I do wonder if the blacking-out of a snooker final on television has anything to do with that. Diane reads the first lesson. I read the last. We both have obvious colds, but survival spirit is fed by that community feeling easing along the pews. Darkness is falling as we leave, and Diane says she loves to see a church with lights on.

December 21 – Shortest day of the year. Brightest display for a long time from Norwich City at Carrow Road as they trounce Millwall 6–1 to show how much they like life at the top of the Second Division.

December 22 – the brand new Bishop of Norwich attends Morning Service at a country church. The Right Revd Peter Nott is preacher and celebrant at St Mary's in Old Hunstanton. The quiet coastal setting is far removed from the pomp and ceremony of this enthronement on Friday in Norwich cathedral. 'I belong here in parishes like this just as much as I do in the cathedral,' he says.

December 27 – A woman who lived a solitary life and took a vow of silence more than 40 years ago dies at the Anglican Shrine at Walsingham. Sister Mary Phillida, formerly Lady Phillida Shirley, was 69. She was the daughter of the 11th Earl Ferrers, and before devoting her life to prayer, reading and contemplation, was a talented pianist. She worked at the Foreign and Commonwealth Office for a number of years, making use of her fluent French. She took her vows in 1943 and lived a life of almost total seclusion in her own small hut at the Walsingham shrine.

December 29 – Blanket of snow over Norfolk, although not so thick as we head for Cromer and Sunday lunch before a bracing stroll along the front. Biting winds as I christen my new binoculars, moving in on gulls wheeling over the sands. If only I'd had such support along the lanes of mid-Norfolk when I was a young naturalist-cum-detective.

December 30 – As I congratulate myself on completing two whole years as a diary-keeper, I salute John Boggis of West Raynham. He's nearly home for the 39th time! He has been filling a page of desk diary every day since 1947. He started during the rough weather of that year as a reminder of what it was like. I'll take him as a perfect example.

1986

January

January 1 – Just ribbons of snow left along the Norfolk headlands and beet still waiting for a lift to the factory.

January 2 – Certain constant themes running through the past two or three years look like staying with us: closure of village schools; changing face of local landscape; insidious spread of suburbia; the endless campaign to 'give' Norfolk facilities that could prove so damaging in the long run; dilution of the local dialect. Add these all up and there's the prospect of a frightening picture to hang up on the end of the century. I feel a verse coming on to sum up my feelings…

Now she saves her warmest smiles for strangers
Who jilt so easily when they find another.
But we must stay true, not just to memory,
In case she needs our love tomorrow.

January 3 – Yarmouth saddened by the death of comedian Dustin Gee, who was due to appear at the ABC Theatre in the summer. The 43-year-old impressionist dies in hospital after a heart attack during a pantomime at Southport. He appeared at the Britannia Pier with his partner Les Dennis in the summer of 1984. Last time a summer show star died before the Yarmouth season was in 1976 when Sid James died two months before he was due to take to the stage of the Windmill Theatre.

January 15 – The two Weasenhams are split by an unholy row. Weasenham St Peter votes for the parishes to be joined, but at Weasenham All Saints the parish council has already decided against. That leaves the two parish council chairmen smoothing over a row that dates back to 1978 when the two parishes went their separate ways after years of joint consultation.

January 16 – A Mulbarton couple's long wait for a family ends with the arrival of quads! David and Julie Ames married nine years ago, and have been trying for children for more than six years. Julie was given fertility drugs – and they did the trick four times over. Gemma, Kate, Clare and Benjamin arrive within five minutes of each other at the Norfolk & Norwich Hospital.

January 21 – Interesting session with the team behind The Mardler, North Norfolk's talking newspaper for the blind at their Aylsham headquarters. I enjoy making a contribution to their latest hour-long cassette and it's clear they have the enthusiasm and know-how to make the project a lasting success. The idea is booming right across the area with little armies of volunteers using their various talents to provide weekly magazines.

January 23 – Downham Market conservationists celebrate as the town's southern by-pass is open after 14 years of campaigning. They believe the road will make the town a healthier, cleaner and safer place to live in. The by-pass, finished four months early, skirts the southern edge of Downham. Joy also for Mattishall widow Marjorie Baker. She can now build the home she and her late husband planned together. Planning applications were twice turned down by Breckland District Council but now the refusal is overturned by a government inspector. After 30 years working in the two village schools Marjorie considered the appeal site perfect – directly opposite Mattishall Middle School. 'It will be lovely to sit outside and see the children coming out. It will give me so much happiness.'

January 25 – Darts match with a difference at Hemsby… both teams are at home. While regulars at the Lacons Arms step up to the board and sip their pints, their opponents are more than 5,000 miles away in sunny California. Scoring is done by phone and Hemsby win narrowly. The idea grew out of Fred Carr's trip to California last September where his daughter and son-in-law run an English-style pub. Meanwhile Burns' Night celebrations include a happy little session at the Stonemason's Arms in Aylsham. Landlord Jock Cairncross parades a dish of haggis round the pub, while his father celebrates his 87th birthday by singing traditional Scottish songs.

January 27 – Postmistress Elsie Gillingwater calls it a day after 58 years behind the counter at Langley's only village shop. At the age of 83 she's swapping regular opening hours for her picturesque garden overlooking the Yare Valley a few miles from Loddon.

January 28 – Big celebration at Stiffkey as the local football team score in the last minute to win their first game in over two years. Regular anchormen of the North West Norfolk Sunday League Second Division, they last tasted success in October, 1983. This 2–1 victory over Colkirk Reserves breaks the sequence. Club chairman Stanley Sutton says: 'It's remarkable. We lose all these games, but still get 14 players turning up because they love to play.'

KEITH SKIPPER'S NORFOLK DIARIES

February

February 1 – Norfolk continues to shed its distinctively parochial colours, and I'm convinced that the number of outsiders now holding key positions in local government will hasten the process. Planners who have seen something take off in another area automatically assume it will work here.

February 12 – Former Prime Minister Lord Wilson – Harold of the pipe – makes his acting debut at Gorleston. He's shooting a scene for Anglia Television's drama series *Inside Story*. It's about the battle for a Fleet Street newspaper. Lord Wilson plays himself, presenting journalistic awards. 'It's been nice to come and see the area from which my wife comes' he says. Mary Wilson hails from Diss.

February 14 – A typically forthright article in the *Eastern Daily Press* by Doreen Wallace, doyenne of local writers, underlining some of the reasons why our village life is changing so drastically. 'Now the real villagers come under the threat of losing their schools and their post-offices-cum-shops. Will the newcomers care? They have cars. If they have school-age children, their schools are elsewhere, and they seldom, if ever, shop in the village… the most useless 'foreigners' are those whose country retreat is only meant for weekends and summer holidays. They don't even arrive unless the weather invites. They can never become part of country life.'

February 19 – The battle to keep our village schools safe continues. Banner-waving children pack Norfolk County Council chamber to hear the future of their schools debated. Only one certain to be closed as a result of this meeting of the southern schools advisory committee. Tiny Tibenham School will be shut and its ten pupils offered places at neighbouring Aslacton. Education Secretary of State Sir Keith Joseph dips into his own pocket to help boost the library at Methwold Primary School. This follows an appeal by headmaster David Tinsley to leading politicians, local firms and dignitaries. Sir Keith's £5 buys a book called *Going To School*.

February 25 – British Rail confirm reports that a naked couple made love on an Eastern Region train while a member of the royal family travelled in the next compartment. The incident happened last September on the London to King's Lynn service.

February 27 – A Norfolk vicar says the vast majority of incoming retired people would be far better off staying

Swaffham – a moving plea from the vicar.

where they have always lived rather than trying to settle in an entirely new area. The Revd Kenneth Reeves, vicar of Swaffham, remarks: 'People should not move when they retire. They should adapt to retirement where they have always been rather than leap off to the 'idyllic' Norfolk countryside.' Retirement-led migration from other parts of the country increases Norfolk's population by about 5,000 a year. Most are retired or nearing retirement. The Swaffham vicar adds 'They come in expectation of a much gentler way of life. This is a figment of the imagination. They think there is a sense of belonging in rural areas – but they do not find it.'

March

March 4 – A team of youngsters start battling through the undergrowth on a major Ormesby conservation project. Batches of logs are to be delivered to the elderly as a squad of Youth Training Scheme students work on a clean-up and conservation project on a strip of land next to the village playing-field. The eight-strong team are all doing a YTS Farmstart course to learn about agriculture and horticulture.

March 6 – Fakenham could die as a town – a stark warning from the president of the local chamber of trade. He hits out at apathy among the traders after news that the trades fair has been cancelled through lack of support. It would have been the first fair of its kind in Fakenham for over 20 years.

March 13 – Farm workers' leader Jack Boddy urges a fresh look at rural problems as Common Market food mountains and EEC budgetary troubles increase pressures for change in the countryside. 'If we are going to maintain a rural community then agriculture is the most important industry in the world. We have got to spend money on ensuring the rural environment is worth living in… I don't want to see again what happened in the 1930s when farms were completely desolate. Heaven help us from ever returning to that kind of society.'

March 14 – The 60th anniversary of the founding of the Norfolk Naturalists' Trust is marked with a special lunch at the Cley hotel where it all began. Timothy Colman, Lord Lieutenant of Norfolk and grandson of the trust's founder president, Russell Colman, unveils a plaque at the George and Dragon Hotel to commemorate the jubilee and to launch a year of celebrations.

March 16 – Pleasant Sunday lunch at the refreshingly old-fashioned Tudor House restaurant opposite Cromer Parish Church. Real strength in the sun and a promising flavour to a Sunday that reinforces the feeling we must not allow this day to slide into 'just another shopping session' category. By putting the day under such threat, we've been forced to look at some of the reasons, and to be affected by some of the feelings, that make it so special. I suspect commercial instincts will win, but a quiet stroll round the likes of Cromer on a day like this, coupled with a gentle ride home, fills me with a powerful sadness.

March 19 – A wrong done to Hoveton around a century ago is to be put right. When the Great Eastern Railway reached the Norfolk Broads in about 1890 it named the station near Wroxham Broad, Wroxham Station – even though the new railway halt was established in the parish of Hoveton. Now there are plans for British Rail, North Norfolk District Council and the Broads Authority to get together to clean up and improve the station area. British Rail will put up new name boards on the platform announcing 'Hoveton and Wroxham.'

March 28 – Village coalman Maurice Pryer calls it a day at Feltwell. 'I started to get chilblains for the first time this winter, so I've decided I've had enough' says 63-year-old Maurice. He's been a coalman for 46 years. His grandfather started the family business at the turn of the century, digging peat out of the fens and then selling it to householders as fuel.

April

April 2 – Lady Harrod raises her influential voice against too much new housing in Norfolk. She claims many villages are being spoilt with old houses and cottages being replaced by unsympathetic buildings. 'Control seems to be lacking in conservation areas. For instance, in the middle of Stiffkey there's an intrusion of quite unsuitable houses which have a very bad effect on what was once a pretty street. Planners have a hard job and pressures are on them now as never before, not only because of increasing population but even more because of a huge demand for holiday homes, particularly in our coastal villages. But statutory powers to deal with conservation areas were designed for just this sort of situation. I hope planners will stand firm before all the character is lost.'

April 4 – Norfolk lifeboatmen can look forward to a warm homecoming after cold sea voyages. Every year John Young, who lives in San Francisco, sends 200 bottles of whiskey to England to be shared out between lifeboat stations around the country. This year's beneficiaries are Hunstanton, Wells, Sheringham, Cromer and Yarmouth. It all started when Mr Young visited Norfolk and got to know the Cromer crew.

April 8 – Arthur Rudd, one of the areas best known football administrators, dies at 82. He was president and patron of the Building Scene Eastern League which he helped form as the Eastern Counties League in 1935. He was league secretary for nearly 40 years and lived at Gunton Cliff, Lowestoft, where his high house with large turrets became a local landmark.

April 24 – Bill Edrich, one of Norfolk's most famous sporting sons, dies at 70. 'A farmer's boy came to Lord's to reap such a rich harvest' – that's how he summed himself up in the last sentence of one of his books, *Cricket Heritage*. Back in 1947, a team made up solely of the Edrich family, and skippered by Bill's father, challenged and beat Norfolk's county side. It was on the international stage that Bill became a cricketing legend, despite

Bill Edrich.

having his career cut by the second world war during which his bravery as a bomber pilot won him the DFC. He returned to captain his home county in 1959 and led them until 1968. I relished many a vintage Edrich display at Lakenham where the qualities that made him such an outstanding performer for Middlesex and England still shone through.

April 30 – Three men are rewarded for helping to preserve Norfolk's character with outstanding conservation and restoration work. They collect awards from the Norfolk Society. Cabinet maker Simon Simpson is praised for his restoration of a group of old farm buildings at Panxworth, near South Walsham. John Carrick of Swanton Morley transformed three cottages, condemned 20 years earlier, into smart homes. Kenneth Jelly collects an award on behalf of Saham Toney Parish Council, who have created a nature reserve by landscaping an overgrown area of the village.

May

May 1 – Norfolk naturalists fear a famous colony of wild otters has been wiped out. They say a dying female otter found at Cley Nature Reserve could well be the last from North Norfolk's once well-known haven. Two other dying otters were found in this area last year and post-mortem examinations revealed high levels of farm chemicals in both creatures.

May 6 – Aircraft noise from RAF Coltishall prompts cries for mass sound-proofing, a petition and for villagers to refuse to pay their rates. One resident tells the Coltishall parish meeting that noise has become 'an excruciating and nerve-racking screeching din.'

May 7 – Swaffham auction market owner Tyrone Roberts stops auctioning pet animals at his weekly market following complaints from the RSPCA about conditions. He has been selling pets such as mice, gerbils and cage-birds. He'll continue to auction 'food animals' such as hens, ducks and geese.

May 9 – Sad little story from Thetford. A dance to raise funds for the town's twinning activities is given the elbow by local people – and organiser Judy Spiller is left to dance alone. The knees-up at the Carnegie Room fails to attract a single soul, with only Mrs Spiller and two helpers there to listen to the Mildenhall band which plays on gamely without an audience.

May 13 – Another little chapter of local history slides into the notebook. North Lopham butcher Dick Frost is shutting the shop which has reputedly been trading in the village for 200 years. Dick, now 70, started work when he was 15. Father Robert had taken over the shop in 1912. Dick recalls making deliveries with a pony and cart to the surrounding villages of Bressingham, Fersfield, Garboldisham, Kenninghall and South Lopham.

May 30 – Old friend Jack Murton, the paper boy who delivered his first copies on the day war broke out in 1914, decides to take a well-deserved rest. That's a round going on for 72 years. He's guest of honour today at a special ceremony at Longham to mark his retirement. Jack, 81, lives at Tittleshall with his wife Frances. He prides himself on never having missed a single round. 'Even when the villages were snowed in the papers had to get through – even if we needed to use a tractor' says Jack. At the end of last year he gave up two stops on his 45-mile round trip which took him to Beeston, Litcham, Great Dunham, the Lexhams, Mileham, Tittleshall, Wellingham and Longham. Now his family will take over the driving while Jack supervises operations from home. Jack has never tired of the job: 'I used to deliver medicine, get the milk in and also make one old fellow's bed every day.'
(*Jack's wonderful round was to end less than four months later. He died in September.)

June

June 7 – Start of my fête-opening season with a pleasant afternoon at Wacton, near Long Stratton, for their annual event to raise money for the chapel, church and Village Hall. On the green for the first time, and the tradition of good weather holds good: 'Only three wash-outs in 40 years' says one of the organisers. I win second prize of £3 in the bowls competition. No luck on the teddy bear stall. Refreshments in the barn. The growing world of Long Stratton seems to be pushing hard towards little Wacton, but the independent spirit shines on in this community of about 250.

June 10 – North Elmham's civil defence organiser urges villagers to stock up with dried milk and tinned food in case of a nuclear emergency. 'It is being prudent and being prepared' says Squadron Leader Eric Harrison. 'One never knows when these emergencies are going to arrive.'

June 12 – On the road for another Women's Institute diamond jubilee celebrations, this time at Shipdham. I sing for my supper and there are plenty of memories to share. Ethel Riches, at 90 the oldest gal in the village, regales me with yarns about her days looking after Shipdham pubs. She sings and twinkles the evening away.

June 21 – Norfolk Night at the Princess Theatre in Hunstanton as part of the local festival. I organise and compere the event, a mixture of local writings, characters and humour. A simple formula but there's plenty of scope for variety. One idea is to give the Norfolk dialect treatment to scenes from Shakespeare and other classics. Colin Riches has blessed Bible stories with the dialect treatment, so there's no reason to think it won't work in other areas. Bound to be many more invitations to take this sort of show on the road.

June 28 – Nostalgia all the way! To Litcham Primary School in the afternoon to open the fête and then enjoy a mardle with old friends. Then it's on to Swaffham for the 250th anniversary of Hamond's school. Nearly 100 guests for a dinner at the George Hotel and the perfect excuse to recall classroom days as far back as 1912. Ten old boys present attended the 200th anniversary celebrations in 1936. I'm asked to provide a yarn or two, and so there's the inevitable memory of spending a day in the toilet at Fransham railway station rather than face a geometry test and the possible wrath of teacher Mickey Moore. At the dinner, I sit next to Don Urry, a cheerful colleague on the *Dereham and Fakenham Times* 20 years ago.

June 29 – Gentle stroll around Swaffham after last night's reunion. I peep through the windows and gates at Hamond's to catch a few glimpses of my grammar school past. It seems only natural to move on and take in Beeston and Fransham before returning to the present. The railway line has gone at Fransham. They are trying to close the school at Beeston. Protest banners are pinned on the door. I'm angry. This is where it all started. I vow to help fight the battles ahead.

July

July 3 – If bells could say good-bye, Aylsham Parish Church clock would be chiming its own fond farewell to Ron Lansdown. He has cared for it for nearly half a century. Ron, 71, climbs the steps, all 69 of them, to the church tower for the last time to keep the clock ticking over perfectly.

Aylsham church dominates the town skyline.

KEITH SKIPPER'S NORFOLK DIARIES

July 5 – A Weybourne pig farmer is seeing spots before the eyes. He had mated a black sow and black boar... but could hardly believe the results. Robin Woodhouse went to his Upper Sheringham pig pen to find three of the ten piglets born were spotted. Some of the others were black and white saddlebacks and the rest were black. In more than 35 years connected with pigs, Robin's never seen anything like it. 'There is a genetic throwback.'

July 9 – Minor Counties cricketers meeting New Zealanders in a three-day game at Lakenham. Wymondham College handicrafts teacher Andy Seeley marks his retirement by watching the start of the contest. He's lived and worked at the college since its official opening in 1951, and he has another special reason for being at Lakenham. He's made the electronic scoreboard at this ground in the middle of Norwich and plans to make more and sell them during his retirement.

July 12 – To Crimplesham, a couple of miles from Downham Market, to open the village fête. It should be held on the playing-field, but persistent rain forces the event indoors. Only a few signs of panic as stalls go up in the Village Hall – and the evening barbecue is on as well. No school, pub or Post Office in this village, but there's an obvious community spirit. Norfolk cricketer Robin Huggins, captain of North Runcton, drops in when his match falls foul of the weather. He wins top prize of £50 in the draw.

July 18 – Proud residents of Hapton, a small community five miles south-east of Wymondham, unveil their village sign. Four years ago when the fund-raising started for the £650 sign, villagers were irritated because Hapton didn't have a single indication to let motorists know they were passing through.

July 22 – Ted Ellis, much-loved Norfolk naturalist, dies at 77. Tributes pour in to the man who explained the intricacies of flora and fauna to anyone who shared his enthusiasms. Dr Tony Irwin, Keeper of Natural History at Norwich Castle Museum, says: 'I don't think there's going to be his like again. His breadth of knowledge has never been equalled and our knowledge of the natural history of Norfolk is down to Ted.' Malcolm Freeguard, Director of the Audio-Visual Centre at the UEA, was instrumental in the university's decision to award Ted an honorary doctor of science degree in 1970. 'He was probably the last of the great self-taught naturalists, but he was also important to academic life.' Ted was a pioneer in the field of conservation long before it became fashionable. He became a

Ted Ellis – 'probably the last of the great self-taught naturalists'.

celebrity through his prolific writing and broadcasting but remained a modest man with the joy of nature constantly shining in his eyes.

August

August 2 – A beautiful evening beckons as we take the long way to Cromer and back. Sun-kissed diversions include a peep at the small village of Thurgarton, which reinforces my view that 'old-fashioned' rural settings are still there if you find time to look for them. Coming back as the light fades, I'm amazed again how quickly one leaves the town and finds the country on the road to Felbrigg and Roughton. Harvest fields glow in the evening calm and I get my first feeling that autumn can't be far away.

August 3 – Sunday forecast proves only too accurate as we head for Wells in a downpour. My uplifting task is to crown the carnival queen and salute her attendants. They shiver with cold rather than fright at the ordeal. Rain refuses to relent but organisers take it all in their good-natured stride. They're used to it: this is the third successive year of rain on the big day. Thunder, rain and lightning disturbs the normally tranquil Abbey of St Benet's as the Bishop of Norwich holds the annual service.

1986

August 7 – On stage for *Keith Skipper and Friends* at the second Mundesley Festival. A full house enjoys this parade of local talent including a traditional Norfolk fisherman's clog dance by Richard Davies, coxswain of Cromer lifeboat. He is accompanied on the melodeon by Tony Hall, well-known on the local folk music scene as well as regular cartoonist for the *Eastern Daily Press*.

August 18 – The world bread-and-butter making record comes home to Norfolk, thanks to a farmer's wife and a flour technologist, with a little help from Daffodil the cow and a combine harvester. John Stubbing of Norwich millers Read Woodrow & Sons, slices over 11 minutes off the world bread making record by clocking up a field-to-loaf time of 29 minutes 37.94 seconds. In the same Cambridgeshire field, Greta Allen of Manor Farm, Barnham Broom, sets the first ever udder-to-butter record at 17 minutes 23.5 seconds.

August 22 – A 14-stone St Bernard dog is recovering after being stranded in a dyke for two days. Patch went missing from his Hickling home. Plaintive barks were heard coming from a deep ditch near Hickling Broad. The loveable hound has wandered off before. This latest adventure ought to ensure he thinks a bit more before setting out again.

August 25 – Stirring example of the old family spirit at Methwold's village carnival and fête. Fifteen members of the Willis family are in the decorated float parade, having come from London, Leiston, Portsmouth, Stoke-on-Trent and other points on the compass. They take second prize – but earn top marks for loyalty.

September

September 2 – Sun out as I unveil the Best Kept Village award sign at East Harling. They can't make it a hat trick here after successive victories as no village can win three times in a row. Meanwhile, campaigners overshadow the award ceremony at Boughton, in the west of the county. Parents and pupils stage a silent protest in their fight against a county council decision to close the village school.

September 3 – Another popular Norfolk nature expert dies. Billy Bishop, 73, was warden on the Norfolk Naturalists' Trust Cley Marshes nature reserve for 42 years. He took over in 1937 from his grandfather Robert, who was the first warden there. Friends often recalled how he clinched the job as warden after a local hotelier had written a reference describing Billy as 'a wonderful poacher.' He fulfilled his main ambitions by attracting bitterns, bearded tits and avocets back to breed at Cley.

Bernard Bishop took over from his father in 1979.

September 13 – Brightest news for some time! My old village school at Beeston is among those given a reprieve in the Litcham area. I drop a line of congratulations.

September 21 – Our big day as Danny Richard Skipper arrives at 3.37p.m., weighing in at 7lb 3oz. I defy my own fears and misgivings by being present at the birth at the Norfolk & Norwich Hospital. The nurses are wonderful. They find me little jobs, like tying up their aprons, to make me feel part of the miracle. Danny arrives with a yell. He's in my arms within seconds. I tell him Norwich City are second in the First Division after winning 4–1 at Aston Villa yesterday. He seems pleased.

September 28 – A peal of bells is heard for the first time in nearly 250 years at Barton Turf Parish Church. At a packed service a ring of six bells is dedicated to the memory of Lady Delia Peel, a former lady-in-waiting to the Queen Mother. The bells last rang out in 1739 before falling into disrepair. The trust set up to honour Lady Delia paid to have the surviving bell and machinery restored and five new companions added.

October

October 1 – Blackberry picking start to the month as the afternoon warms up. What a good way to say hello to some of our neighbours. Mum with a pram is a traditional icebreaker. Dad with a basket for the hedgerow raid offers another opportunity to exchange banter. Only a matter of yards from home we find a hedge packed with fruit, and I'm amazed no one has seen fit to take advantage. Congregation outside the shop for baby inspection, and a woman offers a bag of apples to go with the blackberries. Perhaps the rosy glow has largely gone from many communities, but now and again a little session like this puts fresh heart into an old cynic.

October 2 – Drive in the sunshine to one of Norfolk's rural havens, the picturesque village of Heydon. Not a bad choice for Danny's first outing into the heart of the countryside. Seemingly frozen in time, the village is used regularly by film-makers who want the genuine bygone flavour.

October 28 – Robbers of our ancient history are busy in Norfolk. One expert reckons the monetary value of heritage being spirited away runs into tens of thousands of pounds a year.

October 31 – I can't get there, but about 800 friends and

colleagues, and those who knew him simply for his enthusiasm, charm and gentle wit, gather in Norwich Cathedral to celebrate the life and work of naturalist Ted Ellis. The clergy wear their scarlet and widow Phyllis also chooses not to wear the black normally associated with sombre, formal occasions. Hymns, readings and prayers are all in harmony with the theme of thanksgiving. A trust has been set up to create the Ted Ellis Nature Reserve at Wheatfen Broad in Surlingham. It aims to acquire the 100 acres of marshes and tidal channels where Ted lived and worked for more than 50 years and preserve it in his memory.

November

November 5 – Difficult now for Norfolk people to close their eyes to aggravation. Violent gang warfare is fought almost nightly on Norwich streets. Mobs of young thugs roam the council estates, fighting each other and terrorising passersby. Police have trebled their strength to deal with the explosion of gang violence in the city centre. Yesterday, 19 youths from rival gangs were dealt with by a court after squaring up for 'the fight to end all fights' at the city's Sloughbottom Park.

November 18 – Jeanette Cox, a former air hostess, wants to 'put North Norfolk on the map'. Why do they all say that as if it's not already there? She's the district council's new tourism and leisure officer, and one of her main aims is to extend the four-month holiday season. One can forgive natural enthusiasm for a new job, but she ought to take care not to rattle the natives too much. For some of us, North Norfolk has moved into the best part of the year. Yes, it is a bit selfish, but it's only through this sort of attitude it will survive in a meaningful way into the next century. Sharp lessons at Yarmouth and on the Broads have not been taken to heart. Their problems are obvious, even if rewards have been financially considerable for a few. Looking beyond the county, we can see what has happened to parts of the West Country when tourism took over. There's no way back.

November 22 – My first visit to a sailing club dinner. Singing for my supper at the Yare Sailing Club function held at the Norfolk and Suffolk Yacht Club in Lowestoft. BBC television colleague over the road Mark Wells, the club's commodore, extends the invitation, and I'm agreeably surprised at the way things are changing. Not long ago, cut-glass accents and cash would have been prerequisites in many such clubs, but there's a healthy cross-section here who do it mainly for fun and laugh loudly at each other's foibles and failings.

November 24 – Italian soccer giants AC Milan make another swoop on the British transfer market – for Norfolk's Sallie Jackson. The club sign up the 20-year-old from Mattishall. Her lucrative two-year contract includes a healthy salary and use of a luxury apartment. According to her dad Trevor it is Sallie's power in the air that has attracted the Italians: 'Really good centre halves aren't too common in women's football.'

November 30 – Former waitresses at the Norwood Rooms shed a nostalgic tear or two at their first and last reunion in the Norwich dancehall and banqueting suite. They are waited on themselves as they hold their own special 'hennight' before the Norwood turns into a bingo club in the new year.

December

December 2 – A stricken RAF jet screams low over a village school near Diss before exploding in a field just a few hundred yards away. The two crew escape death by a split second as they eject safely. Wortham School head Judith Thomas says: 'But for the grace of God and a few hundred metres, the plane would have landed on the school. We are really lucky.'

December 4 – Sprightly pensioner Charlie Blackburn solves a spooky mystery that has haunted many a Norfolk villager for nearly half a century. He confesses 'I was the Dunstan Ghost'. The tiny village near Norwich was sent into a frenzy in the winter of 1937 when a driver reported seeing a white spectre looming in his headlights on a late-night country drive. His sighting made newspaper headlines and explanations flooded in about how the 'ghost' could have been mist or even a white cow. Now Charlie reveals his best-kept secret… on his diamond wedding anniversary. 'The ghost was me. I was out poaching wearing a sheet.'

December 5 – To Aylsham to switch on Christmas lights. I try my hand at conducting the local band. They make a good job of 'Silent Night' despite my efforts. Over two hours strolling round the shops to pass on seasonal greetings. Red Lion Street is closed to traffic and the amiable atmosphere must suggest to the strolling player that this is the way ahead. With Danny behaving perfectly, we wind up at a bookshop. An ideal finale.

December 14 – Danny christening at Hevingham Parish Church – where Diane and I tied the knot in August, 1983. It's a double booking today as next-door-neighbour Christopher Robert Collins, now nine months old, also has

1986

Christening day for Danny Richard Skipper as proud parents look on.

a close-up of the font. A busy time in church this morning as well with the annual carol service and village school pupils showing their expertise with handbells.

December 19 – I join the celebrations at Frettenham Rose and Crown, a village pub totally transformed by four months of hard work. I pull a pint to present to Titch Baker, a regular here for more than 40 years. It's an endearing atmosphere. You can almost see the caps and hear the rustic tones. There's no juke box. There is an open log fire. There must be hope.

December 23 – Norfolk loses yet another leading naturalist with the death at 78 of Robin Harrison. A former warden on the Breydon Water Nature Reserve, he wrote and illustrated a weekly column under the name of Robin in the *Eastern Evening News* for 50 years.

December 31 – A memorable year, with Danny bringing so many new dimensions to our lives. He's thriving, but I can't help wondering what sort of Norfolk he'll grow up in. We can't return to the past but we ought to learn from it. Those lines I wrote at the start of 1986 seem just as relevant:

Now she saves her warmer smiles for strangers,
Who jilt so easily when they find another.
But we must stay true, not just to memory,
In case she needs our love tomorrow.

◆ ◆ ◆

January

January 1 – Skies scowl and weep but the rain cannot wash away a familiar theme. Improving Norwich links with the outside world could rebound on the commercial life of the city, warns Tom Carr, senior partner with estate agents Percy Howes & Co. The irony of improved communications is that they could push up labour costs and increase house prices. 'Not everything will be marvellous even if you bring the M11 to Cringleford,' says Mr Carr.

January 11 – Heaviest snow of the winter so far, a big white blanket covering the village by dinner time. Jamie, the lad next door, volunteers to clear our path to the road. He's hardly finished before another sharp flurry covers his tracks. Youngsters are out with their sledges and bobble hats and a couple of them use our garage door for target practice with snowballs. There's an appealingly old-fashioned flavour around the parish. You can't hurry either in a car or on foot. Trouble is the chaos it's likely to bring when we try to get to work tomorrow.

January 13 – Another tough battle to get into the city – but the show must go on. A Rover Rescue land rover ploughs through the snow to pick me up and get to the studios just in time for my programme. Hundreds of cancelled events and all the latest information make up the bulk of three hours on air. I can't help wondering how many people have found their local wireless station for the first time!

January 14 – All schools in the county closed as drifting blocks many roads. We're reminded of the important things in life – bread, milk, heat, friendship – as Norfolk squares up to the challenge. Rest of the country is keeping us company now. Norfolk villages some way from main roads are the worst hit.

January 15 – Many villages still cut off. Stories of more mercy dashes and airlifts to save the ill and infirm. Most minor roads impassable and train and bus services drastically curtailed. Sixty marooned sugar factory staff at Cantley tuck into bacon and eggs as food is dropped by helicopter. Norwich Theatre Royal is flooded as a fractured pipe sends hundreds of gallons of water cascading through four floors to the basement.

January 16 – Dozens of funerals postponed in Norfolk because of treacherous roads rather than frozen ground.

In winter's grip – but one family step out with purpose.

The Gorleston to Yarmouth ferry is late for the first time in 36 years. A 27-hour battle to take vital heating oil to Mundesley Hospital. Sheringham police use sledges to reach cut-off Sustead with bread, milk and eggs, while snowploughs end four days of isolation in Ringstead, near Hunstanton.

January 23 – Most of the snow is gone after a week of trying to get back to normal at home, work and school. Plenty of bouquets for Radio Norfolk's part in keeping the area fully informed and cheerful throughout the emergency. Proud to say I got in every day.

January 28 – The Queen and Queen Mother enjoy a good old Norfolk mardle with members of Sandringham Women's Institute. Housewives Jean Simmons and Betty Woodhouse, who live on the royal estate, entertain the two royal visitors with Norfolk impressions and stories in West Newton Parish Hall.

February

February 1 – Sherry the Shetland pony makes a spectacular appearance at the pantomime service in St Peter Mancroft Church in Norwich. According to the programme, Sherry is down to make a 'contribution' while Michelle Summers reads a farmyard fable. Perhaps Sherry misunderstood 'contribution' because with back to audience she answers a call of nature which causes the vicar, Canon David Sharp, to call for bucket and shovel.

February 13 – After 50 years in footwear, Dick Ward leaves his job at the Norwich CWS shoe factory. He's the last man to retire voluntarily before it shuts down and all 133 of his workmates lose their jobs.

February 14 – Royal flavour at Carrow Road as the Duchess of Kent officially opens the new £1.7 million stand and releases 2,000 yellow and green balloons from the pitch before kick-off.

February 16 – Joe Bly, a local preacher of the old school, dies at 79. He loved the Norfolk land along with the pulpit, and always gave his sermons with a smile. Glad I met him again in recent years, on his home ground at West Acre and at a Litcham School fête last summer.

February 18 – A six-year pest control campaign to get rid of the coypu from Norfolk and Suffolk waterways is almost over. Ministry of Agriculture scientists at Norwich say the rodents are all but extinct after the scheme to kill the 3,000 left in East Anglia. They have been the scourge of farmers since breeding pairs escaped from fur farms in the 1930s. In 1960, the coypu population in Britain reached its peak of 200,000.

February 19 – County planners decide that the welfare of Dersingham people must take priority over the needs of the micromoth which inhabits a nearby bog and give permission for a by-pass to be built across the land. The move infuriates conservationists who regard the bog as a vitally important ecological site.

February 24 – Ethel Rogers celebrates her 100th birthday at Scole Lodge nursing home. 'I don't feel ill. I don't feel 100. In fact, I feel all right. But I seem to be a curiosity.' She's worried about her weight.

February 26 – Dereham Festival is laid to rest. The annual meeting of the festival committee holds an inquest into the poorly-supported 1986 programme, but there are no efforts to keep it going. A festival has been held in Dereham every two years since 1976. 'There is nothing else but to kill it off. Dereham never misses anything until it's gone,' says Terry Davy.

March

March 11 – My 43rd birthday and books feature large in the celebration. Diane and Danny furnish me with both volumes of Forby's *Vocabulary of East Anglia*, first published in 1830 and precious additions to my shelves of local books. I feel they will fuel ambitions to produce a Norfolk dictionary before too long.

March 15 – Round Tablers from around Britain are in Norfolk to start their diamond jubilee year – and they give a standing ovation to their two remaining founder members. Tom Tillett, aged 84, and Frank Winter, 86, are applauded as they enter the massive marquee on the Norfolk Showground at Costessey. Tom and Frank were part of the group of young men who used to meet with the organisation's founder Louis Marchesi back in the 1920s.

March 27 – A policeman dies and at least eight people are taken to hospital in Norfolk as gale-force winds bring havoc. Sergeant David Bowles from Necton is crushed to death by a falling branch as he clears a debris-strewn road at Shipdham. In Norwich, six people are treated in hospital after being blown over by strong gusts and a woman is injured by a collapsing bus shelter.

KEITH SKIPPER'S NORFOLK DIARIES

March 28 – Annual trek to Bodham for the village's notorious *A Night of Squit*. Signs of better organisation and a smattering of rehearsals, plus real musical accompaniment, won't do the Bodham reputation much good! Rustic off-the-cuff antics are the true trademarks that must not be lost in any indecent haste to ape the professional. Bodham's lack of shame upon the stage, and old-fashioned delight in the audience, are rare commodities. A friend with me suggests it's like going back over 40 years when village events and Village Hall support was like this much of the time.

March 29 – Rolling back the years at Dereham with 34 old colleagues from the former Mitford and Launditch Rural District Council gathering to renew friendships going back to the days before the council was disbanded in 1974. Former clerk and chief executive Maurice Turnbull says: 'We're one of very few councils who keep in touch like this.'

April

April 1 – A future where young Norfolk people may find themselves priced out of the county's housing market is indicated in a report, *Village Homes for Village People*. The Norfolk Rural Community Council criticises the government's 'lion's share' funding for housing in urban areas to the detriment of rural villages. The national report says the shortage of affordable housing for local people in villages is reaching crisis proportions. It says the extra purchasing power of outsiders above those earning income from rural industries, like agriculture, is pushing house prices beyond the means of local people. We're going to hear a lot more about this one.

April 9 – The first electric train into Norfolk arrives at Thorpe Station on time after its history-making run from London. At the controls is Stan Bunton, who began as a train driver in the age of steam. Rail travellers have to wait until May for the official opening of the new high-speed service.

April 17 – Out into the Norfolk countryside for a spot of spiritual replenishment after a Good Friday stint at the office. Long way from the predictable snarl-ups, you can smell nature pushing through the hedgerows as we saunter through Swannington, Cawston and beyond. I'm in the back of the car with Danny as we sample the sunshine. He drops off, lulled perhaps by the peace and beauty of the local scene on the warmest Good Friday for years.

April 25 – A letter in the *Eastern Daily Press* from Jonathan Dunning of Sprowston makes my day. Norfolk must not be spoilt to appease tourism, he says. 'What need have we for modernisation and development? Norfolk should be run primarily for its inhabitants. It is pleasant to see tourists visiting us; no doubt their money is very welcome. But we must not prostitute ourselves to their desire for easy access to us and for lots of facilities to enjoy once they are here. Seeing tourism as our salvation is very short-sighted. It may bring a brief financial reprieve but will probably destroy our inherent characteristics.' I'm glad to have some company when it comes to criticisms of the tourism bandwagon.

April 29 – Norwich City defender Ian Butterworth goes down as the man to score the most expensive own goal in history. His mistake on Saturday against Coventry at Carrow Road gave a woman her eighth draw – and made her Britain's biggest ever pools winner with a total of £1,032,088.40. She's a Bexley housewife. Perhaps she'll send him a few bob!

May

May 2 – Caught in sudden showers at Aylsham and an estate agent provides one stop for shelter. The girl at the desk talks freely and imparts the news that one house-seller in North Norfolk is insisting that it goes to someone who has lived in this county for at least two years. A comforting stand as the rain beats down.

May 3 – Perhaps many of the runners in the Norfolk marathon are glad of all this wind and rain. Our annual ritual, watching the good, the bad and the struggling pass by on their way into the city. Out of respect, we eat a salad this year instead of the traditional Sunday spread.

May 5 – A refreshing journey into the Norfolk backwoods as the sun goes down. I join artist friend Ken Walton on a natural pilgrimage a few miles up the road, down the tracks after ambling through Ingworth. Here the black sheep are grazing all round, including the churchyard. But the treat of the evening is a wood awash with bluebells – yes, you can paddle in them – just past a couple of remote cottages. An elderly gardener looks up from the row he's digging. He's hardly moved when we return over half an hour later. Time and pace mean little out here.

May 16 – Thousands of birdwatchers converge on Cley, bringing the village to a standstill. But they're disappointed when the star attractions fail to turn up. The excitement drawing enthusiasts from all over the country was the sighting of a pair of slender-billed gulls on the Cley marshes, the first recorded visit to this country. Police are called in to sort out the traffic tangle.

A flutter of birdwatchers.

May 20 – Blakeney Village Hall is held up before the nation as a model for the shared use of leisure facilities for sports and arts events. The building, opened in 1982, is one of nine leisure facilities studied for a joint report by the Sports Council and Arts Council.

May 22 – Belton is the ugliest village in Norfolk, claims Norfolk councillor Cora Batley. Discussing a plan to landscape an area in the village, she tells the borough council's development control sub-committee: 'Belton is the ugliest village in Norfolk. I think it needs more trees and more grass in that area. I would have thought people would be only too pleased to have an open space with grass, seeds and trees.' Bill Dougal interjects: 'I think Hemsby is the ugliest village.' The committee approves the improvement scheme.

June

June 1 – A Broadland nature reserve, saved from the 'ravages of mankind', is put on the conservation map. Ludham Marshes, 180 acres of prime grazing marshland, has been acquired piecemeal by the Nature Conservancy Council over the last five years. It is now declared a national nature reserve. Lord Buxton, chairman of Anglia

TV, and an ardent conservation campaigner, opens the reserve and recalls boyhood days when he came bird watching in Broadland. 'It never entered anyone's head then that it needed protection to safeguard it against the ravages of mankind. It was just there. It's rather incredible that within a generation or two it's under such threat.'

June 10 – A priceless piece of heritage is destroyed by developers at Thetford – to make way for a housing estate. English Heritage discovered a 25-square metre hole amid the ancient ruins of the Canons of St Sepulchre when it thought a deal was about to be struck to save it for the nation. Regional director Jeffrey West says there's nothing they can do. 'The site is completely destroyed and there's now no point in preserving it.' The housing estate, naturally, will be called Priory Gardens.

June 18 – Diane takes Danny for his first dip at St Augustine's swimming pool in Norwich. Evidently, he laps it up after initial caution. I envy the lad his chance to learn something many of us didn't. Not too many opportunities in the middle of Norfolk when I was a boy. Yet one hears so many youngsters complain at being bored today in city, town and village. I've tried to discuss the matter with

Hevingham youngsters who congregate in the bus shelter on the main road. They are noisy, occasionally destructive and often rude when you request a little more thought for families living nearby. It's best to chat to them individually because you make little headway with a gang, all of them bidding to outdo the other. I don't want a return to the ultra-strict ways of yesterday, but there's bound to be a backlash before long.

June 20 – One of our favourite days of the summer. Weather improves as we head for the Waveney Valley and a garden fête at Denton Lodge. Sir Jeffrey and Lady Dorell are our hosts in this beautiful setting. We meet at the farmhouse home of Hilda and Tim Thomas before and after the fête. The Archbishop Sancroft High School band provide the music and views across the valley simply add to the pleasure.

July

July 5 – *Songs of Praise* at Foxley Parish Church. I read a prayer for Norfolk and there are two instalments from Colin Riches' Bible stories given the dialect treatment by Brian Winterbone. I enjoy a mardle with John Parfitt, brother of former England and Middlesex cricketer Peter Parfitt. John was a regular in the Dereham side during my reporting days in the town. He passes on a delightful yarn about his father's funeral at this church. They didn't think many would want to carry on to the crematorium – but all the old cricketing mates from the villages decided they'd like to go. They all piled in and one of them realised the parson was missing. He'd called to John: 'There's suffin' here your old dad wouldn't like.' John was perplexed: 'What's that?' Back came the reply: 'Well – he'd never go to a match without an umpire!'

July 10 – Dick Condon, whose flair, showmanship and sheer hard work brought such success to the Theatre Royal in Norwich, receives an honorary Master of Arts degree at the University of East Anglia. His 89-year-old mother Kate flies over from Ireland for the ceremony. The public citation reads that Dick 'brought the style of the travelling circus to Norwich and showed its relevance to filling a theatre, to making it not only profitable but something of which everyone is proud.'

July 11 – The saviour of Bittering church, next door to my home patch of Beeston, returns to dedicate a plaque to his old comrades in the fight to restore it. The twelfth-century church fell derelict in 1954, but the Revd Robert Dodson, Rector of Gressenhall, supported by the Squire of Bittering, William Napier, launched a campaign to have it reinstated as a Parish Church. Their efforts were rewarded in 1961. Canon Dodson, now 83, comes out of retirement in Scotland to take a memorial service for Bittering's patron, who died in Madrid last year.

July 17 – To the Phoenix Hotel in Dereham to talk to a group of visitors to Norfolk. My brief is to give them an armchair guide to the county – no easy task with two Germans in the audience! It comes home to me just how difficult it is to summarise the characteristics and qualities of the place.

Sea Palling before the 1953 floods.

1987

Some have Norfolk connections and they respond enthusiastically, especially when it's time for a bit of squit. Obviously, I stress the dangers and pressures facing us, with the tourist industry asked to take its share of criticism. One visitor asks if there's such a thing as a Norfolk dictionary or glossary. That convinces me this must be a publishing priority on my list.

July 21 – Pleasant little diversion in the shape of an afternoon call at Sea Palling. It is a strange little creature; scruffy close to the beach, but reasonably tidy among the caravans. Locals continue to work in their gardens as holiday-makers stroll by. A genuine Norfolk hybrid living several lives at once. I suspect winter is the favourite.

July 23 – Memory-packed evening at Beeston School, the little seat of learning I left in 1955. A fête to raise money for the school takes us back as a family to my educational roots. I feel proud to carry Danny through the playground into the classrooms where I had my first lessons.

August

August 1 – The glorious heyday of the Norfolk wherry is fleetingly recaptured as five of the majestic vessels unfurl their mighty sails and cruise on Wroxham Broad. It's thought to be the first time for over 40 years that five wherry-type crafts have sailed together. They're united today to mark the 75th anniversary and renaming of one

of their own kind, the *Lady Edith*. As the sun sets over the *Broad*, the *Olive*, the *Lady Edith* – now renamed the *Norada* – the *Hathor*, the *Solace* and the *Albion* take to the water.

August 3 – Sheep grazing in a Norfolk churchyard are earning their keep and providing the raw material for a thriving cottage industry. While the Norfolk Horn sheep graze between the gravestones in the churchyard at Worstead, members of a craft guild spin and weave their fleeces to enhance the church fabric. Kneelers, hassocks, an altar cloth and other items have been spun and woven by local people.

August 9 – Two years of silent Sundays in a Norfolk village come to an end as church bells ring out again. During those two years the Little Walsingham church bells, the heaviest ring of five in the county, have been painstakingly refurbished by the Whitechapel Foundry in London where two of them were cast in 1691. The two oldest were cast in Norwich in 1569.

August 11 – On the road as one of the judges in the first competition to find Norfolk's best-run Village Hall. Sutton, near Stalham, is our first call, and then we head for the more palatial building at Blakeney. Last stop today is Brancaster Staithe, where the hall was built in 1946. Happy reception committee includes founder-member Olga Mitchell. She recalls the first event, a dance on the

Norwich feels the force of the 1912 floods.

concrete floor with 'black stuff on it that covered us all as we moved round!'

August 12 – Day two of our grand Norfolk tour. We start at Old Catton where the building went up in the late-eighteenth century. On to the splendid 1983 hall at East Tuddenham, where the balcony is a dominant and pleasing feature. Yaxham next on the list – and what contrasts here! We inspect the church room built in the late 1890s for the use of the Sunday school. Just over the way a splendid new Village Hall is taking shape. The local community policeman is among those waiting to receive us. 'We knew you were coming – so I'm here for crowd control!' To the final contender at Hempnall where caretaker Ernie Downing makes me chuckle with his yarns. We tot up the marks and Hempnall is a clear winner with East Tuddenham second and Sutton third. A most worthwhile exercise and so much dedication and hard work to admire.

August 13 – Leonard Rudram, known as 'Mr Winfarthing', dies at 92. Apart from military service in the first world war, he spent all his life in the village. He left the village school at 13 to work in his father's carpentry, wheelwright and funeral business which he eventually took over. He held the position of Parish Church warden or sidesman for 48 years.

August 21 – Back to Norwich Prison with the *Dinnertime Show* four years after our first visit. This is the prison's centenary year and our visit coincides with a renewed debate about overcrowding. Lack of proper resources is a recurring theme as we talk to acting governor Ken Lay, several of his officers and some of the inmates.

August 25 – What a day! Worst summer deluge for years and Norfolk suffers blocked roads, burst sewers, swamped houses and drenched crops. The downpour, with over three inches of rain recorded in 18 hours in some parts of the county, comes on the eve of the 75th anniversary of Norfolk's worst ever floods on August 26th, 1912. Over six inches of rain then fell on Norwich in just 12 hours.

September

September 1 – Start of my favourite months has misty promise. Strange goings-on at Yarmouth. A large shark gives holiday-makers a scare as they take a trip round Scroby Sands. The 15ft fish is a harmless basking shark, but they're rarely sighted so close to shore. Meanwhile, waves of money spiders drive trippers from the beaches… and they just love the candyfloss.

September 12 – Last of the summer wine. And what a pleasant brew as we head for the church fête at Hindolveston. It's held in the old village school. The local silver band plays throughout and that old fashioned community spirit shines through. The pub and school have gone but the village has kept its shape.

September 13 – Nearly 3,000 Catholics walk the Holy Mile from Walsingham to the Shrine of Our Lady at the annual national pilgrimage. Black Africans and white South Africans, toddlers and disabled people stand under blue skies at the Slipper Chapel for a mass conducted by Cardinal Basil Hume, leader of the Roman Catholic Church in Britain.

September 18 – Stargazers claim lights from Norwich's proposed new hospital could ruin 15 years of hard work and make their telescopes useless. They say the sky at night will be too bright to spot faraway planets from their observatory off Colney Lane.

September 23 – Sheringham reflects following the death of Jimmy 'Paris' West, fisherman and lifeboatman whose legendary exploits at sea earn him a special place in the town's heart. He dies at 91 and was a member of one of Sheringham's oldest established fishing families. He was the last surviving member of the crew of the old rowing and sailing lifeboat, the *J.C. Madge*, which accomplished the most famous sea rescue in Sheringham's history 71 years ago. He inherited the nickname 'Paris' from his father, who died when Jimmy was two, from a strained heart suffered at sea.

Jimmy 'Paris' West, Sheringham's legendary fisherman and lifeboatman.

September 30 – Village blacksmith Robert Thrower of Long Stratton dies at 78, the last in a long line stretching back to the nineteenth century. His great-grandfather walked to London in 1851 carrying a horseshoe which won him a prize in the Great Exhibition. His grandfather, George Thrower, set up a blacksmith's shop in Saxlingham Thorpe in 1895. One of 12 children, Robert followed his father into the profession at the age of 13.

October

October 2 – Ada Fakes dies in hospital just three days after her 106th birthday. Born at Winterton, she moved to Hemsby when she was 16 and lived there for the rest of her life. Active and independent all the way. And tributes pour in following the death of Swaffham's Merle Boddy. Councils, trades union, politics, the mentally handicapped, the arts, youth centre and town twinning matters are just some of the issues she was involved with.

October 3 – Whissonsett youngsters answer back! In a week when older residents have unleashed a barrage of criticism against local youngsters, a group of young pub regulars help balance the books by presenting £500 to two causes. The dozen from The Swan public house give £300 to the vicar towards the cost of repairing a vandalised stained-glass window and £200 to cancer research. They've raised the money through sponsored events, and they describe as 'nonsense' claims by older villagers that they've had to put up with constant screaming, bad language, stone throwing and abuse from youngsters on their way to the pub.

October 13 – A vet who started Norfolk's first mobile service a few days ago is inundated with calls from pet owners wanting him to take his caravan surgery to their village. Alan Slater of Harpley, near Fakenham, is the vet with the busy rounds.

October 15 – Hundreds of Norfolk homes could disappear under flood water unless millions of pounds are found to strengthen crumbling embankments. Flood threat facing homes from Happisburgh to Beccles and as far inland as Norwich is spelled out by city engineer David Hawkes. Rising sea levels combined with crumbling embankments pose a real risk of a tidal surge flooding hundreds of acres bordering main rivers. The areas most at risk are low-lying parts of Yarmouth and the environmentally-sensitive Broadland area.

October16 – The Big Blow roars in during the early hours to create a trail of havoc and destruction. Trees topple like dominoes and it's a tricky and dangerous business just getting to work. Thousands of homes are without electricity and it could be days before some have power restored. At Bradwell, three-year-old Matthew Nuttall escapes with only cuts and bruises when a chimney collapses, burying him in slates and rubble in his bed. Forty rig workers have to be airlifted from a gas rig off Cromer. Lorry driver John Nunn, from Scole Common, near Diss, jumps clear of his lorry as a toppling tree brings power lines down onto his vehicle. A falling chimney crashes through the roof into the kitchen of a Yarmouth guest house seconds after owner Pat Shepherd has walked out. Thirteen people die as the gales leave a trail of destruction across southern England.

October 17 – Lull after the storm. We drive into Aylsham for shopping, with signs of damage all around. So sad to see so many lovely old trees flat out like fallen soldiers across the fields.

October 19 – Sentimental journey to Swaffham Assembly Rooms for a chat to the Wissey Group Women's Institute members. A full house from Swaffham Afternoon, Swaffham Evening, Stoke Ferry, Northwold, Goodestone, Castle Acre and Great Cressingham. I used to eat school dinners in this fine old building while I was at Hamond's over the road – and Suzie Besley, widow of our headmaster Major Besley, greets me at the door. She is my hostess for the evening.

October 20 – A memorable evening at Hales Chequered Flag pub, chatting to locals about their community past and present. Hales is the first name out of the Radio Norfolk *Dinnertime Show* village bran-tub. I paint a little picture of what life used to be like by dipping into Kelly's *Directory* for 1900, then it's up to listeners to provide memories and information. The idea could be a winner.
(*This potted local history exercise embraced nearly 300 villages in seven years. It attracted hundreds of guests representing their village on a Friday; some of them gleefully admitting it was their first trip to Norwich in years. Old school chums were reunited, retired teachers met pupils they hadn't seen since before the war and members of the same village cricket team savoured an innings together for the first time in decades. I sifted through over 5,000 letters to compile *Village Post*, published in 1996.)

November

November 9 – Ken Brown's seven year reign as Norwich City manager ends this morning. He's sacked, but goes with dignity and tears in his eyes. I recall the day I first met

KEITH SKIPPER'S NORFOLK DIARIES

Ken Brown – sacked after seven years as Canary manager.

him in 1973 just before he and John Bond left Bournemouth to continue their partnership at Carrow Road. As Bond's assistant, he helped him through the dark spells with a ready smile and keen sense of humour. Brown never changed when Bond left and there were always questions about a nice chap surviving in this jungle. He deserved his successes, especially in the Milk Cup final at Wembley, and leaves behind far more good will and friends than most of his predecessors.

November 13 – All sorts of campaigns to 'plant a tree' after the devastation caused by last month's gales. To be applauded – but so much goes on to destroy or dilute Norfolk's rural flavour without anyone batting an eyelid. Campaigns for road and rail improvements, spearheaded by the *Eastern Daily Press*, usually refuse to make any allowances for the changes such 'progressive' moves must bring. The latest nasty to creep out of the woodwork is radioactive waste and it appears to produce a penchant for looking for quiet little bits of Norfolk in which to dump it.

November 14 – History lessons at Methwold High School take on a whole new meaning after the discovery of Roman ruins close to the school playing-fields. Lessons are no longer restricted to the classroom for second year pupils. They are spent trudging through a neighbouring cornfield in the hope of uncovering some Roman treasure. The site was a Roman villa or farm and youngsters have found tiles, several in excellent condition, used in floors as well as roofs.

November 21 – Closed 54 years ago, the old Ovington School building stages a day full of memories as 26 former pupils and another 20 guests hold a reunion. Built in 1855, it was used as a private school until 1870 and then became a Church of England primary until closure in 1933. It's now the Ovington Village Hall.

November 30 – A thousand years of Norwich's past are about to be examined in detail. Some of the results will probably finish up as exhibits in the Castle Museum. Today sees the start of a £500,000 archaeological dig, a curtain raiser to the building of the city's projected multi-million Castle Mall shopping complex.

December

December 3 – A slice of Norfolk history refuses to stand still. A rare 120-year-old hollow post windpump, derelict on Ranworth Marshes for more than 80 years, is on the move to How Hill. With Broads Authority backing of £28,000, the restoration project should be completed next May. It was impossible to restore it on site, and How Hill, the Broads Authority's environmental centre, is an obvious relocation point.

December 5 – Poultry merchant Stanislaw Zak retires from his Norwich market stall after 35 years – and calls for the market to be flattened and rebuilt. He came here as a Polish pilot during the war. He says stalls like his are threatened by the modern trend for out-of-town shopping. 'It wants a clever architect to redesign the market, bulldoze the whole lot and level it up. Then the food stalls should be kept separate from all the others,' says Stanislaw. But he predicts shoppers will eventually tire of using supermarkets.

December 12 – A dozen fund-raisers celebrate a silver jubilee. The Blakeney Twelve, villagers who have raised £60,000 for the elderly and needy, mark their 25th anniversary by serving a special Christmas banquet to 150 pensioners.

December 17 – Plans unveiled for a £100m-plus London Dockland-style transformation along the banks of the Wensum in Norwich. The scheme is aimed at making Norwich a tourist and leisure magnet for the next century. Dubbed the Riverside, the 30-acre development should be completed by the mid-1990s. Estate agents warn that homes built as part of the plan could become a 'yuppie paradise' doing nothing to meet local housing needs.

December 19 – It has taken ten years for Blo'Norton to get

Gillian Shephard – unveiled Blo'Norton village sign.

its village sign. So nobody minds waiting an extra five minutes today as the unveiling flag refuses to budge. South-West Norfolk MP Gillian Shephard heaves on the rope but the Union Flag stays firmly in place until parish councillor John Dickson comes to the rescue with a long pole. A colourful rural scene in cast aluminium depicts a farm worker, sheep and Blo'Norton church.

December 21 – Norfolk turkeys have good reason to keep a low profile this time of the year – but noisy ducks at Hethersett are driving villagers quackers. The birds are causing sleepless nights and South Norfolk District Council pledges positive action. Local tenants are being asked not to feed the culprits in a bid to make them seek sustenance elsewhere.

December 25 – Christmas Day at Blacksmith's Cottage, probably our last after months of searching for a new home. I can't help smiling after lunch and all the present opening when Danny makes for empty jam jars near the door instead of putting in overtime with his new toys. 'Twas ever thus!

December 30 – Norwich City stalwart Dave Stringer is appointed team manager at Carrow Road after seven weeks as caretaker boss. The 43-year-old former Canary defender gets the job after successive victories against Derby and Chelsea.

◆ ◆ ◆

January

January 2 – Guardians of rural England urge Norfolk people to make this the year to speak out for the countryside. The Council for the Protection of Rural England points to major conservation issues at stake in this county – house building, the possible abolition of structure plans which monitor long-term development and the future of farming.

January 9 – One of Britain's smallest cinemas has been completed in a Norfolk back garden, and with seating for only 12 the house is almost always full. For the past 20 years retired motor fitter Johnny Briggs has lavished every spare minute building the tiny Toftwood Playhouse. He got the seats from the Regal in Wells when it closed down while the windows came from an old Nissen hut. Attention to detail has even gone as far as a miniature Wurlitzer rising from the stage.

January 11 – George Ewart Evans, father of the oral history movement in East Anglia, dies at Brooke aged 77. His books on the old ways of farming and rural conditions of the region are now an integral part of history libraries throughout this country and abroad. Born and educated among the miners of South Wales, he moved to Suffolk with his family in 1948. George came to realise that the older villagers were the last remnants of a rural culture destroyed by mechanisation. He set about recording details of their lives and their language. I bought three more of his books a couple of weeks ago.

January 16 – A new Village Hall which didn't cost a penny is officially opened. The old hall at Postwick, four miles east of Norwich, was sold – and a brand new one built with the proceeds.

January 18 – Uncle Harry's funeral at Thornham chapel just over the road from the butcher's shop he ran for several years. The service is relayed to many people on a damp, grey afternoon lit up by many little reunions and cheerful tales of Harry on his rounds and singing and preaching in local chapels. 'A personality – and never lost for words' is the main tribute at the funeral service.

January 23 – I join Brooke Women's Institute for their birthday supper in the Village Hall. I enjoy a chat with

Ploughing match at Guestwick – the sort of scene George Ewart Evans relished in his oral history work.

John Cossey, the blacksmith at Brooke who tells me of his part in the book *Horse Power and Magic* by George Ewart Evans. I look it up – and there's John at the start of a chapter on women and the heavy horse. He first drew George's attention to the success of women in handling these animals.

February

February 3 – Vintage motorcycle enthusiast Tom North recovers a rare machine – unearthed near New York more than 20 years after it was stolen from him. Mr North, of Rougham Hall, left the Brough Superior, renowned as the Rolls Royce of motorcycles, in a London motorcycle park in April, 1967. As a young barrister he used to ride it to Lincoln's Inn from his Soho home. It disappeared and he gave up hope of ever seeing it again. Then a British motorcycle dealer bought the bike offered for sale by 'an ex-motorcycle enthusiast, ex-Hell's Angel'.

February 4 – Helpful Norwich landlord Albert Brighton is hopping mad after helping a motorist out of a tight spot in his pub's car park. After directing the man out from the Coach and Horses, the driver ran over his foot – and then escaped in the landlord's car!

February 12 – Seaside landladies are set to go back to the classroom at Yarmouth to learn new tips of the trade. In a bid to shake off the old image, which has made them the butt of countless jokes, landladies and other hotel owners are being given the chance to brush up their skills. 'The days of the smaller guesthouse are numbered,' says borough publicity officer Tony King. He says the course will help landladies manage their business better.

February 16 – Shopkeeper Michael Whitmarsh is in the money – after stumbling on a pile of cash during building work at the village store at Redgrave near Diss. Stepson Mark, 17, unearthed a hoard of coins, some more than 350 years old, when a dividing wall was taken out. There's been a shop on the site since 1679 and it is thought a man called Thomas Brough hid the coins in Victorian times. What on earth for?

February 19 – Broads Authority planners decide a wooden kiosk put up 'temporarily' at Hoveton 20 years back, must go. It was originally used as a ticket office for boat tours, but an application had been made to use it for the sale of ice-cream and trinkets. Now it must go when planning approval runs out next month.

Keith Skipper opens Bodham's new Village Hall. He's pictured with parish stalwarts Barry Toyn and Austin Fisher.

February 20 – I'm invited to Bodham to officially open the new Village Hall. I've grown very fond of the locals in recent years with regular visits to their notorious *A Night of Squit* in the atmospheric old Village Hall. Now the £35,000 model is here and we all wonder if the old-fashioned spirit will survive. It's flattering to be asked to usher the village into a new era.

February 29 – February goes out with an icy growl, making that extra day in leap year memorable as we huddle to keep warm. Meanwhile, Winifred Scales celebrates her 21st birthday – with her 59-year-old daughter! Winifred, of Norwich, a leap-year baby, has waited for 84 years for her coming of age. She celebrated her diamond wedding a month ago.

March

March 2 – Sprightly 90-year-old Richard Cogman wins a vote of appreciation from the Lord Mayor of Norwich as the man who has been a city council tenant longer than anyone else. Mr Cogman and his wife Olive have lived in council houses for 65 years, the past 59 in a house on Henderson Road.

March 3 – Passengers escape from a double decker bus minutes before it slips into a 26ft hole on Earlham Road in Norwich. Families are forced to flee from nearby flats and houses as gas escapes from a ruptured main. The bus turns into a bucking bronco as the front rises high into the air. Old chalk workings in the area are blamed. Only a handful are charted, including those under the Catholic St John's Cathedral nearby. Last month a 60ft hole opened up in Kett's Hill, wrecking one home and forcing the evacuation of five others.

KEITH SKIPPER'S NORFOLK DIARIES

March 13 – Evensong at West Somerton church is a double celebration for the Jones family of Ormesby. Baby Emma Jones is christened on the day a new lych-gate made by her father Daniel is formally dedicated. St Mary's is a special church for Mr Jones and his wife Julie. They were married there and their three-year-old daughter Danielle was also christened there.

March 14 – Trams could be the solution to Norwich traffic chaos, according to a former city planner. Alfie Wood, the first Norwich City planning officer, says they should take a lead from Europe and America and reintroduce a tramway system. His suggestion comes as planners weigh up the idea of a park-and-ride system to ease streets congested by commuters.

March 17 – A living memorial to the work of former warden Billy Bishop is opened on Cley Marshes. Billy's Wash is a 30 acre expanse of water specially created to attract different types of birds throughout the year and dedicated to the memory of Billy, warden for 42 years.

March 20 – Coastguards at Cromer fire their breeches buoy rockets for the last time. The spectacular display of setting up the bosun's chair equipment, used for 180 years to rescue crews from stricken vessels, has been a regular training exercise for the volunteers. Now the equipment is being withdrawn from service and the busy Coastguard section will now concentrate on co-ordinating rescue services and honing its cliff and beach rescue skills.

March 22 – Axe heads more than 2,500 years old are among finds in a major Bronze-Age hoard dug up by amateur archaeologists in north-east Norfolk. The exact location, and identity of the finders, is being kept secret to protect the site from robbers armed with metal detectors.

March 25 – A Norfolk farmer who has been charging people 25p to look at a six-legged cow at car boot sales is condemned by the RSPCA. But despite branding the display as 'sick' the RSPCA say they can take no action because the animal is healthy and well looked after. The deformed cow has extra 'legs' growing out of its shoulders.

April

April 1 – Good weather sparks the inevitable charge on to the Good Friday roads with caravans leading the way. North Norfolk's newest tourist attraction opens. Hundreds take the plunge at the £2.5 million Sheringham leisure pool. Years of controversy over the most expensive leisure project in the district council's history are waved aside as swimmers hail The Splash as a tropical paradise. Council chief executive Terry Nolan enthuses: 'We have brought the Riviera to Norfolk.'

April 9 – Sharp reminder that summer is not here yet. Sudden snow showers early in the morning. I peer out of the window and see a top-level conference over the seed potatoes with Fella, Les and Tom. They poke and prod the soil as if to rouse it from winter slumbers. Contrast that with the sad little sight we note on the way up Grapes Hill into Norwich. Two youths are running through a sea of daffodils, kicking, trampling and generally mocking the flowers.

April 12 – A boyhood dream turns to reality, thanks to the contents of an old milk churn. Diss businessman Peter Gillings started putting small change in the churn 25 years ago in a long-term bid to own a new Harley-Davidson motor bike. He takes delivery today of a £8,000 machine after emptying the contents of the churn on the sales floor of a local motor company. A bank manager is on hand to take delivery of the savings. The bike would have cost £430 had he bought it 25 years ago.

April 19 – Farewell gathering at Blacksmith's Cottage for friends and neighbours before the packing begins. Local vicar Christopher Morgan drops in as well. Hardly a wake, but nor is it a celebration. More of a reflective session as we prepare for the big move.

April 21 – At last! On the move to 25 St Mary's Road in Cromer, a turn-of-the-century house with plenty of space and character. I plan to travel by train to and from the radio station in Norwich. We've always liked Cromer, especially on Sunday afternoon outings, and it still seems relatively sane at the peak of the holiday season.

April 26 – What an embarrassing start to our seaside saga! I am laid low by a bad back caused by nothing more strenuous than putting up a calendar on the study wall. A doctor diagnoses a strain and tells me to keep it warm and to rest for a couple of days. Perfect excuse to avoid heavy-duty work.

May

May 7 – We decide to have a picnic in Bluebell Wood, down that make-it-up-as-you-go-along track beyond Ingworth. We discovered this delightful spot last year. A shock awaits us in the shape of scenes of devastation left behind by the October lashings. Twisted trunks and branches. Painful gaps even though bluebells are pushing through and pretending it is just the same. Barbed wire blocks the entrance.

May 9 – The new D'Oyly Carte opera company, brought back from the dead by Dick Condon, makes a triumphant return to the Theatre Royal in Norwich. Charles Roberts waxes lyrical in the *Eastern Daily Press*: 'We were promised, and expected, a fresh approach. But this is more than fresh. It is rethought, reimagined, recreated at every step of its sparkling way. All deserve medals.'

May 12 – Norwich students, cracking up under the strain of university life, are flooding counsellors with pleas for help. They now face a two-week waiting list to see psychiatrists at the University of East Anglia's Samaritan-style help service.

May 17 – Desperate job hunters are trekking from Scotland and the North to East Anglia – only to have their visions of easy employment and housing vacancies shattered. Reports of this region's booming fortunes are giving a false impression and many jobless and homeless people hoping to find a land of opportunity end up at Citizen's Advice Bureaux instead.

May 18 – A few days after failing my fifth driving test, I note that some do make a real go of it. Twins Mike and Dave Butler have a double cause for celebration as they pass their tests on the same day. The Fakenham teenagers drive to success with the same examiner.

May 29 – The ancient well at Bawburgh is the setting for a special ceremony to commemorate the village's patron saint. Parishioners gather for the blessing of the well dedicated to St Walstan, who was born here in AD970. Waters from the well were reputed to possess miraculous powers and it was a centre for pilgrims for centuries. However, since the 1950s it has been covered after the water was ruled unfit for human consumption by the then Forehoe and Henstead Rural District Council.

May 31 – A new twist from the top. Norfolk landowners are urged to help villagers who are being priced out of their birthplaces. 'I believe it is very important that people like us, with a stake in the countryside, do what we can to make certain that villages don't stay pickled in aspic,' says Viscount Coke of Holkham Hall. 'Unless villages evolve and we allow rural workshops in, they will die and they will become commuter dormitories,' warns the chairman of the Norfolk branch of the Country Landowners' Association.

June

June 1 – Early journey 'over the border' to Sheringham to open a marvellous exhibition of family mementoes. The Old Sheringham Families Day forms part of celebrations marking 150 years of lifeboats in the town. Photographs, heirlooms, clothes, paintings, newspaper cuttings and traditional fishing equipment are among the exhibits.

June 7 – Norwich is voted the most courteous community in Britain. The Polite Society visited pubs, shops, hotels and public services across the country and dubbed Norwich 'the city with a smile'. Lord Mayor David Bradford, ready to receive a commemorative silver salver, says: 'We ought to try and live up to our reputation. This has come as a shock to me because normally Norfolk people are fairly reserved.'

June 15 – Crime is rising faster in the Diss area than anywhere else in Norfolk. The town's police chief, Inspector Steve Halstead, tells local councillors that the Diss section showed an overall 24 per cent increase in crime compared with the same time last year, and a 33 per cent rise in the number of burglaries. He hopes to raise the number of foot patrols in town. 'The police cannot do everything. We need the people of Diss to work with us.'

June 18 – Family reunion and homecoming rolled into one as the sun shines down on Beeston. Youngest brother

St Mary's Church, Beeston.

KEITH SKIPPER'S NORFOLK DIARIES

Michael marries Maxine at St Mary's Church. The old homestead looks warm and inviting as we drive through, memories stirring, affections rising. The church peers down on the parish as it has done since the fourteenth century. A memorial to boxing hero Jem Mace demands a visit, and we smile as we notice a horizontal gravestone for 'Henry Cooper' just opposite.

June 19 – Off to Walsingham on Carnival Day. We meet for refreshments at Abbey Farm, home of Tom Moore, a farmer with his heart firmly in the village. Tractors and floats wait for the off after judging and the colourful cavalcade with the Norwich Pipe Band up front snakes through the streets. Tom likes to walk at the head of the parade and I accept his invitation to join him. We are the local pilgrims today, smiling at the irony as priests and nuns pop out to watch.

June 23 – Norfolk's soaring property prices hit new heights with a garage in a coastal village being sold for £26,000. And the North Walsham woman who buys the garage at Blakeney believes she has a bargain. Ann Farrow was prepared to bid up to £30,000. 'I own the property adjoining the garage. I sat there and was determined to have it,' she says.

July

July 3 – Romantic memories of the traditional Sunday school treat are tinged with realism as rain falls on Brisley Green. Ferried by farm trailer from all over the Brisley and Elmham Deanery, children gather for a picnic and open air service on the village green. The event goes ahead in the semi-shelter of the cricket pavilion.

July 9 – Long trek to Ingoldisthorpe to open the school fête. It's a Church of England voluntary aided village school with a wonderful warm regard for its history. They are celebrating their 130th birthday. Classroom exhibitions are matched by Victorian dress for pupils, teachers and friends on the playing-field outside. We go to Dersingham for tea with old friends Geoffrey and Doris Rye. It is over 30 years since I last visited their home with my mate Michael Rye and his parents for Sunday afternoon tea and cakes.

July 14 – Funny who you bump into on the train journey between Norwich and Cromer. My companion for the return trip this afternoon is an Australian doing the grand tour on retirement. He used to be a full-time table tennis coach. He has seen his country rise to 25th place in the world, although, as he points out, the Aussies much prefer outside sport given their climate. A spot of industrial trouble means a delay at North Walsham as the rain beats down.

Our Aussie friend, complete with sou'wester, is looking forward to a couple of days on the North Norfolk coast.

July 16 – After opening the village fête at Billingford, we strolled across to St Peter's Church for the impressive flower festival. Danny sits to listen to the organ music. The church is in a lovely setting, with fields of rippling corn dotted with poppy red acting as a backcloth.

July 26 – Major new housing developments are producing box home 'ghettos' according to a leading Norfolk architect. Chris Lambert accuses developers of riding roughshod over planning guidelines. He blames cash-hungry developers for building the type of homes worth the most money and the territorial Englishman for aspiring to his 'castle'. He says the best developments often date back to the 1950s when people were content to build and buy solid terraced houses or semis. 'I think there has been an enormous rush of very second-rate and rather boring sterile stuff.'

August

August 7 – We know it's another scorcher inland – but the mist blots out the sun for much of the time along the seafront. Our Sunday afternoon stroll takes on a rather eerie flavour as we peer down on the beach but can't see the sea! The annual Sheringham to Cromer raft race is cancelled as Coastguards decide visibility is too poor.

August 8 – Horning scores a hat trick of awards in the Norfolk Best Kept Village Competition, carrying off the prize for villages with more than 500 people, the award for the best kept village green and Community Improvement Project award for the bowling green clubhouse. Caston are first time winners, taking the prize for best kept village with a population of less than 500.

August 15 – Business student Bernard Wooldridge, who is 38, reckons firms are dismissing his job applications because they think he is too old. He's fed up after giving up a secure job to go to college to try to better himself. He's unemployed despite having applied for about 30 jobs in Norfolk. Although he has a Higher National Diploma in Business and Financial Studies, and a background in engineering, he has been turned down without an interview. 'They cannot say so, but I'm sure it is because I am too old.' However, major city employers say they do not consider 38 is necessarily over the hill. They claim they still recruit on qualifications rather than age.

August 19 – Questions are being asked why the county

emergency services were not told nuclear waste was being transported through the centre of Norwich. And Labour shadow energy spokesman John Garrett says he's ready to tackle the government to stop imported nuclear fuels travelling through the city.

August 20 – Day out in Ditchingham to open the impressive new play area. A rubbish dump has been transformed into a marvellous local facility with part of the scheme dedicated to conservation. We are close to the Suffolk border in Rider Haggard country, with houses on the march across the meadows. This little lung is sorely needed.

August 22 – Early to rise in time for a live link-up with Radio 2's Derek Jameson show. It isn't easy to weigh up Norfolk in a few minutes, but I'm asked to give a few impressions to a national audience of the way our county is changing. Development, the Broads and the need to preserve some of our characteristics are the main topics.

September

September 6 – The sun is warm as the mists lift. Freshly-harvested fields look a treat. This remains my favourite time of the year and I intend to savour the lovely mornings with a stroll to the railway station and a gentle journey into Norwich. I find something fresh and stimulating in every trip, and I have soon got to know several fellow passengers.

September 11 – Champion cook Les Stothard strikes a blow for male equality as he leaves the women standing in the cookery classes at Swanton Morley's Horticultural Society Show. He stuns the village cake and jam making champions into silence with five firsts, a second, a third and three highly commendeds to win the trophy in the domestic section, covering cakes, preserves and wine.

September 15 – Strong onshore winds bring a tide of death to North Norfolk beaches with rotting seal carcasses washed up along the coastline. National Trust warden Joe Reed says there are now about 100 seals left of the original 700-strong colony at Blakeney Point.

September 21 – Danny is two today with Norwich City top of the First Division, the Olympics in Korea in full swing and Cromer slowing down fast after the summer season. We enjoy tea at the Tudor House restaurant opposite the church. The lad can't manage too many fish fingers and chips.

September 23 – A poetry festival gets off to its traditional start with a stiff drink on a station platform. The eight poets taking part in the King's Lynn Festival are served with a potent cocktail of Armagne and champagne at the beginning of their weekend of readings and meetings.

September 30 – I'm invited to take part in a debate about the countryside on Anglia Live in the Norwich television studios. A good idea – but the demands of 'entertainment' offer few chances to pursue important strands of many arguments. For instance, a farmer says pulling up the hedgerows affords much better views!

October

October 8 – I head for Wicklewood and one of the most delightful engagements of my career. I'm invited to unveil a plaque at Oak Tree Cottage, birthplace of The Grand Old Mardler, Fred Wigby, a big favourite in the Radio Norfolk *Dinnertime Show*. Cottage has been renovated and looks a picture as family and friends salute Fred. The inscription reads: 'Birthplace of Frederick Wigby, 23 October, 1912. Noted Norfolk author and storyteller.' Fred remarks with a smile 'I never thought this would happen when I was running about here with the backside out of my trousers!'

*Unveiling a plaque at the birthplace
of Fred Wigby in Wicklewood.*

October 15 – Blakeney for tea and then on to the Village Hall for the Great Pumpkin Spectacular! Organised by the Blakeney Twelve for charity the event swells into a grand community affair as pumpkins of all shapes and sizes arrive for judging. I have that task, with the sections including Best Decorated and Most Like Its Owner. Good village fun with a purpose.

October 18 – Village spirit wins through for Arminghall church as the parish three miles from Norwich raises more than £11,000 to restore its crumbling tower. The parish council appealed for state aid to repair the church a decade ago, but were told they were not high enough up the priority list. Two years back they called on the 100-strong parish to rally round and help raise the money needed to return the thirteenth-century tower to its former glory.

October 25 – The name Hooker Close suggested by a Norfolk clergyman for a new housing development near his church is thrown out following objections from people considering buying the properties. Councillors in West Norfolk approve Cuthbert Close as a suitable alternative. The name change is approved after it is suggested that it carries 'rather unfortunate connotations'. The Rural Dean of Lynn, Canon Maurice Green, says when he submitted the name he was ignorant of its associations with women of ill repute. He explains that Richard Hooker was a sixteenth-century notable at the time of the Reformation and a great Christian theologian.

October 29 – Grand day at Roydon, near Diss, where I'm asked to open the new community centre. The villagers stress how they want to retain their own identity. 'We don't want to be like Costessey is to Norwich' is a common comment as they celebrate.

November

November 2 – The growing Norwich parking crisis prompts department store Bonds to open their new multi-storey car park with fewer than half the spaces ready. Bonds say the decision to open spaces for around 250 cars in the planned 700-capacity car park is because of the desperate situation in Norwich. Meanwhile, businesses where profits have plummeted because of road closures strongly back a chamber of commerce probe into ways of paying compensation.

November 6 – A plaque commemorating the 300th anniversary of the Great Fire of Bungay is unveiled in the market-place. One person died, 300 families were made homeless and 400 buildings were damaged or destroyed by the blaze.

November 12 – A book-signing session at Chambers shop under the town sign at Dereham entices me into a few reflections on the town where I worked in the early 1960s. It is busy, full of traffic and forced to come to terms with a growing yobbish element. This is all too familiar in some of our villages as well as towns and cities.

November 20 – Winter in the air with a sharp mixture of

sunny bursts, scudding clouds and showers of sleet and rain. Danny and I brave the winds along Cromer front for a cobweb-moving stroll. He refuses to put on his gloves. We take a walk along the pier where he's fascinated by glimpses of an angry sea frothing below. 'This is what we came to Cromer for!' I call as we turn for home.

November 24 – Death at 75 of veteran Norfolk socialist Bryan Barnard. He was always ready with a quiet but sincere welcome whenever we went to Beetley. As a full-time Labour agent he helped mastermind Sidney Dye's famous victory in the South-West Norfolk constituency in 1955 – the only one in the country to win a seat from the Conservatives. He also spent a period as agent to controversial publisher Robert Maxwell.

November 27 – Chauffer-driven trip to Dereham to turn on the town's festive lights in a packed market-place. A blue Rolls picks us up and brings us home again – a treat Diane really appreciates after so many miles of driving on my behalf.

December

December 2 – Firemen answering an emergency call are forced to lift cars onto pavements to allow their vehicles through congested Cromer town centre. One more sad reflection on these car-crazy times.

December 8 – Earth tremors which shake the region are most probably the result of a sonic boom, and not an earthquake as first imagined. Mystery surrounds the cause of the tremors and rumbling noises making windows rattle and lights flicker in areas as far apart as Cromer and Cambridgeshire.

December 10 – Time to take our shopping more seriously as December breaks into double figures. We invest £5 in a real tree, and it's not that easy to carry it home down The Loke. Beware low-hanging branches! Bernard Matthews scoffs at a Norwich City Council warning which could turn thousands of families vegetarian this Christmas. He's amazed at a council suggestion that people might like to give turkey the bird and have a non-meat nut roast with their trimmings. 'I'm surprised the council have the temerity to suggest such a thing when they are in the county with Europe's biggest turkey producer employing 2,500 people. I don't think it's patriotic,' says the turkey boss.

December 12 – Nancy's Café at Cley serves up its last cuppa. Birdwatchers show their gratitude by presenting a colour television set to the gloriously named owner – Nancy Gull.

December 23 – Travel agents report booming business as record numbers of people head for a Christmas away fixture. Norwich travel firms say there's been a late rush of bookings with skiing holidays and the Canary Islands top of the pops with fun seekers.

December 28 – A teacher's seven-year promise to his class is not forgotten by his former pupils. Just before he left Diss Junior School in 1981, Peter Everall told his fourth-year class: 'I will buy you all a drink when you are 18.' Well, 15 of that class duly turned up at the Saracen's Head in Diss to take up his offer. Making up the numbers are 10 ex-pupils from other classes, and even one dad. The drinks bill, sir? 'It wasn't too bad because most of them had soft drinks.'

December 29 – A picturesque Norfolk village turns to East European reeds to rethatch its fourteenth-century church because Norfolk reeds 'do not last'. But their decision to use Rumanian reeds angers Norfolk thatchers who leap to the defence of home-grown products. Parishioners at Woodbastwick face a £10,000 bill for work on the listed St Fabian and St Sebastian Church, built in 1311.

December 31 – How I resent the pace at which so many precious parts of the Norfolk scene are being altered. A few signs of honest protest during the past year, but the snowball is getting bigger as it rolls unchecked down the hill. It is impossible to be too optimistic about the future as so many influential voices point to development and change as the only sensible partners to take. We diehards have a platform or two, but we're too often patronised or ignored.

1989

January

January 1 – Disturbing news of how Dereham market-place erupted into a battlefield early this morning when over 150 youths went on the rampage. Seven policemen are hurt as they come under attack from a barrage of bricks and stones hurled by crowds of drunken youngsters. Police struggle for nearly an hour to control the turmoil which evidently broke out shortly after 1a.m. when one youth was arrested as he grabbed light bulbs from the town's Christmas tree and flung them at passers-by. Welcome 1989!

January 7 – A Norfolk railway line is coming back to life more than two decades after it was closed by British Rail. Enthusiasts have spent almost a year clearing a site between Dereham and Fakenham for the first phase of a new tourist attraction. The relaying of the first section of track is a dream come true for members of Fakenham and Dereham Railway Society. The initial half-mile of track starts to go down at County School, between North Elmham and Guist. Passenger trains on the old Wells-Dereham line stopped in 1964 and the track was scrapped in 1986.

January 11 – After eight years of intensive trapping the campaign to wipe out the coypu is declared an official success. The 24-strong team of trappers will each receive a termination bonus for getting rid of the South American rodents, introduced into East Anglia in about 1929. The original population of 3,000 expanded rapidly to an estimated 200,000 by the 1950s.

January 29 – Fred Steadman retires after working for 51 years on the same farms in his home village. Fred of Hindringham has worked at Church and Waterloo Farms since he left school at 14. He has seen farm work from the era of the horse to that of the machine. He particularly enjoyed the community spirit which working in gangs generated in the old days. Fred is currently involved in the local pantomime.

February

February 6 – Thieves who stole a huge digger from a building site could already have smuggled it abroad. The £24,000 digger disappeared from a site near Caister beach. It was being used to lay drains.

February 14 – Twins George and Ernie Harbour are honoured for more than 30 years' service to the Royal Observer Corps. The pair from Dereham are presented with certificates by the Lord Lieutenant of Norfolk, Timothy Colman. George, chief observer at the Honingham post, and Ernie, chief observer at Gressenhall, both enrolled in 1957.

February 15 – Pedestrianisation of Yarmouth market-place is given enthusiastic response by traders and shoppers. Borough planning officer Mike Dowling says: 'Since the original teething troubles have been resolved and town centre users and operators have become familiar with the system, much of the initial opposition has waned.'

February 23 – A luxury £200,000 penthouse, thought to be the most expensive flat in Norwich, is sold with an added bonus of its own novel burglar alarm. The police station is downstairs. The apartment, one of 12 on the top floor of Dencora House in Theatre Street, is sold for a rumoured £200,000 plus.

February 26 – An emotional farewell for coxswain Tony Jordan as he leads the launching of Wells lifeboat for the last time. A change in rules forces the 58-year-old fisherman to hand over the wheel after more than 40 years of service to second coxswain and mechanic Graham Walker – the man at the forefront of the successful fight to keep Wells Cottage Hospital open.

March

March 12 – A drilling rig is to be parked off the Wellington Pier at Yarmouth as a tourist attraction. The news is announced at the annual Publicity Association ball. Local businessman Peter Jay says: 'There was a sort of stunned silence. I don't think anyone could quite believe it was going to happen. The tourism possibilities are absolutely enormous. We expect thousands of people to drive to Yarmouth just to see it.'

March 13 – Splendid birthday surprise hatched by Diane and friends Ken and Linda Walton. They have tickets for the Elkie Brooks concert at the Theatre Royal in Norwich. I find mine under the plate as we enjoy a meal before the surprise trip. Elkie says it is her farewell concert and that heightens the sense of occasion as we savour the music.

1989

March 14 – Acle's £7.6 million by-pass is opened by Transport Minister Peter Bottomley to the cheers of villagers besieged by heavy traffic for decades. Mr Bottomley cuts the tape to open the road four months ahead of schedule.

March 18 – The drilling rig at Yarmouth is making its presence felt. Dawn Cotton of Albion Road says 'It is really lovely at night, but in the day it is a bit of an eyesore. The rig has been dubbed by enthusiasts as 'a landmark to equal the Eiffel Tower'.

March 26 – Christmas comes early – or late – for a Yarmouth hotel. Regulars sit down to a full traditional Christmas dinner, complete with turkey, pudding and crackers. The daft dining at the Duke's Head Hotel is in aid of Comic Relief and raises about £500.

March 27 – A chance diversion on the way home from work brings a delightful treat as we pull into Holt Country Park and enjoy a stroll among the trees. Danny collects his first fir cone and has a close-up of a ladybird. We tell him it's really a bishy-barney-bee. Primroses abound and the sun filters through the branches. We promise to return before long for a picnic.

April

April 1 – Afternoon tea and chat at Fakenham with the team who provide *The Talking Times*, the newspaper for the blind and partially sighted in the Dereham and Fakenham area. There's a big gathering of their weekly listeners. Among the guests is Enid Coulson who used to run the riding stables at Holkham House, just up the road from my Beeston homestead. Evening call at Bodham's *A Night of Squit*, deliciously appropriate on this date.

April 2 – The new Broads Authority takes over, giving the area a status on a par with the National Parks, but with much less to protect and much more to restore than when the idea of a Broads National Park was first mooted in 1947.

April 7 – When three-and-a-half-year old Joan Boardman launched a Broads wherry at Reedham in 1905, two white doves were released to bring the vessel luck. Little did the girl know that 84 years later she would come again and set free two more doves to mark the relaunch of the Wherry *Hathor*, now restored to her original grandeur. The ceremony is part of celebrations to herald the Broads' new status.

April 15 – Norwich City's Wembley dreams fade as they lose their FA Cup semi-final 1–0 to Everton at Villa Park. But events here are totally overshadowed by tragedy on the terraces at Hillsborough. Over 90 fans die in a sickening crush that forces the other tie between Liverpool and Nottingham Forest to be abandoned after a few minutes. It is Britain's worst football tragedy.

April 29 – Another Bank Holiday weekend and sure signs of panic among bread-shop customers. They've sold out in Cromer by the middle of the morning, pointing yet again to that strange affliction running through shoppers at holiday time. Most stores will be open on Monday in any event, but people seem scared of running out.

May

May 3 – Hundreds of screaming teenage fans weep tears of joy as Jason Donovan hysteria hits a Norwich nightclub. Twenty-five swooning fans end up in hospital as exhilaration turns to over-excited exhaustion. And 140 more end up in the arms of police and ambulance men being carried out to a makeshift treatment unit outside Ritzy's in Tombland. Supt Terry Maxim of Norwich Police says of scenes around the popstar 'I've never seen anything like this in Norwich before. I suppose it takes me back to the days of Bill Haley and the Comets.'

May 10 – Dersingham Parish Council vote unanimously to complain to the European Commission about the quality of their water. Parish Council vice-chairman Roy Hipkin says many people are taking to bottled water because they are worried about nitrate levels in the tap water.

May 13 – The once-mighty Norfolk Rate Payers Association winds itself up with the battle to reform the rating system complete. The association once had about 500 members, but only four are present for the end of a 15-year era.

May 14 – A spontaneous standing ovation brings to a close a memorable night at the Theatre Royal in Norwich. It is in honour of one of the great writers of the theatre of the twentieth century, America's Arthur Miller. It is a kind of elevated *This Is Your Life* with a celebrated cast to play out scenes from his plays and stories. Timothy West, Prunella Scales, Warren Mitchell, Susannah York and Connie Booth are among stars on parade. Leading names of British, European and American theatre are involved in the weekend seminar at the University of East Anglia, organised to mark the inauguration of the Arthur Miller Centre. For Michael Billington, critic of *The Guardian*, it is a non-starter.

He was to have presented the first paper of the day, but on the way to Norwich he fell ill and, in great pain, drove direct to the Norfolk & Norwich Hospital where he was detained with a kidney stone complaint.

May 27 – Sheringham lifeboat coxswain-mechanic Brian Pegg makes his final launch. His family have traditionally joined the crew and it was more than 40 years ago at the age of 16 that he became a station helper. Since he became coxswain in 1986 he has held the distinction of being the only Salvation Army member at the helm of an RNLI boat.

May 31 – Fire sweeps through shops in the historic heart of Norwich, virtually destroying one of the city's medieval architectural treasures. The early morning blaze severely damages a row of five shops in The Walk, leaving little of the fifteenth-century Curat House at its centre.

June

June 1 – Eveline Noble sits down to a Yarmouth seaside holiday breakfast nearly 90 years after she first visited the town. The south Londoner started her love affair with the resort in 1902 and has holidayed there ever since. The first thing that strikes her as she arrives for her annual holiday this year is just how busy it is. She recalls that when she first visited Yarmouth with her parents she sailed up on a paddle steamer from the Thames. But that stopped in 1908 and she started travelling by train.

June 10 – Memorable afternoon at Beetley to open the Dereham and Swaffham Methodist Circuit summer fête. Years melt away as voices and faces from the past ask for close inspection, including a character from Beeston School, circa 1951. Mr Barton, a teacher there for about 18 months, comes over to renew acquaintance. I didn't know his first name was Douglas – he was just Mr Barton to us in those long-ago days. He moved on to Swanton Morley and then to Cambridgeshire. Now retired, he is so pleased I can remember him. There's also a reunion with Helen and Grace Dye, daughter and widow of former South-West Norfolk Labour MP Sidney Dye.

June 12 – Farewell Norfolk, all roadworks and dog roses, as we head for a break in the Cotswolds. Danny dozes off, appropriately enough at Little Snoring, aware that he has to pace himself over the long journey. Development signs all along the route and it's also clear how traffic and all its anti-social aspects dominate the lives of so many towns and cities. Motorways so noisy and functional, so short of soul on a summer's day.

Final launch for Brian Pegg at Sheringham.

1989

June 22 – Disabled campaigner William Fairbank gives up his five-day hunger strike and goes home claiming victory after British Rail agree to request stops for two lunchtime trains at Harling Road near his home. The move comes after a personal visit from BR production manager Nick Higton to Mr Fairbank's makeshift shelter beside the station.

June 24 – An intriguing evening at Drayton Village Hall for the selection of a local beauty queen. Only two contestants, so diplomacy reigns as we decide to ask them to share the duties in the coming year.

June 25 – The sweltering continues, so it's the perfect afternoon for sitting in a deck-chair watching cricket. I'm at Overstrand Road for the Carter Cup quarter-final between Cromer and Bradenham. I'm due to speak at both club dinners in the autumn, so this is a useful opportunity to take stock. Cromer win comfortably, to revive memories of their successes in the early years of the competition.

July

July 2 – Evening in the sunshine facing Cromer Pier as I'm invited to take part in the annual open-air *Songs of Praise*. Former Sheringham lifeboat coxswain Brian Pegg is one of the others invited to select a favourite hymn and to introduce it. I pick 'Dear Lord and Father of Mankind, Forgive Our Foolish Ways'. Meanwhile, a service which used to be a traditional part of Norfolk is being kept alive by a tiny village near Fakenham. Hospital Sunday used to be recognised at hundreds of churches throughout the county, but now Stanhoe is the only one left. Hospital Sunday was set up 70 years ago to recognise the valuable service of staff in our local hospitals. The first service at Stanhoe took place in the first summer after the end of the first world war and the sequence has continued unbroken ever since.

July 8 – Morning round the shops in North Walsham with my new cricket trousers the main item on the list. They must have that elasticated and generous waist to spell comfort on my occasional outings.

July 13 – The Canaries are back in training and Norwich City claim seven out of ten fans would back a move from Carrow Road. The club reckon it means supporters 'would welcome a move away from the city centre to a new stadium on the outskirts of Norwich'. We've heard it all before. Many years ago a super-stadium and other sports facilities were proposed for the Norfolk Showground at Costessey.

July 18 – A council names a street after a scrap dealer who fought them all the way to the High Court and the European Court of Human Rights. Richard Drake's old scrap yard at Buxton, near Aylsham, has given way to four executive homes, and Broadland District Council is naming the new access road Drake's Loke. But for 12 years the late Mr Drake was locked in a courtroom battle with Broadland over land he owned at Stratton Strawless. It was only in 1986 that the council dropped a High Court action against him. His widow Kathleen says it makes a nice peace gesture.

July 21 – We're told up to 300 jobs could be created in Norwich next year with the launch of a cable television network. There's only one little snag: it will mean three and a half years of disruption for the city as every road in the area is dug up to lay cable. Jimmy Hartley, Norwich Cablevision director, does not regard that as much of a price to pay: 'I find the idea that we have 30 times Anglia's capacity very exciting because we can produce all kinds of exciting, new and different things and extend people's range of choice.' Yet another example of how commercial interests blatantly push aside any social considerations.

August

August 7 – I take my place on stage for the opening night of the fifth Mundesley Festival, the local flavour between rousing sessions from a Bavarian oompah band. I provide home-grown dialect verses to underline my growing affection for this home-grown festival.

August 8 – Gardener Bob Tubby wins an award for the best-kept allotment – but it's a hollow success for the 66-year-old farm worker. Later this year Mr Tubby of Horsford will lose the land which he and his father have tended for more than 70 years. The site is to be used for development.

August 12 – Local entertainment to the fore at Acle Recreation Centre to raise money for the local voluntary aid scheme which does such good work across 23 villages. I share the stage with The Kipper Family, father Henry and the boy Sid, and David 'Muck Carter' Lambert. Local vet Roger Clarke does the introductions. I begin with a tongue-in-cheek *This Is Your Life* for

David 'Muck Carter' Lambert – full of Norfolk squit.

parish council chairman Basil Tibbenham, an old adversary on the local cricket scene.

August 20 – Samuel Powell, Norfolk's oldest resident, dies at the age of 108. Mr Powell, who lived at Corton House retirement home in Lakenham, was born and educated in Leeds. He moved to Norwich in 1913, and in more than 50 years of office work he never had a day off sick. He worked for the same company, Stubbs Mercantile, for 67 years.

August 21 – Hungry woodpeckers have drilled their way through a rare wood-tiled steeple on a Norfolk church. And one of the country's few specialists is called in to repair the damage. St Andrew's Church at Quidenham is visited by the birds in their search for insects. Over the years those special tiles have been lifted and opened up by probing beaks. George Paget from Attleborough, who specialises in repairs to churches and old buildings, is replacing the cleft oak shingle tiles, a painstaking job as each one has to be shaped to fit the octagonal steeple.

September

September 1 – As the month opens we hear Norfolk has basked in one of the sunniest summers this century with more than a thousand hours of sunshine in the last four months. The blazing summer follows the mildest winter on record for 300 years.

September 14 – The big-hitting success of a cricket team starts a row between players and villagers. Angry residents at Aldborough, just inland from Cromer, call for netting to be put up around the picturesque village green to stop a barrage of cricket balls damaging their homes. How is it they didn't weigh up the risks when they moved there?

September 15 – Pleasant duty at Attleborough to open the Bramley Court sheltered housing for the elderly. I unveil a plaque at the entrance and enjoy a mardle with guests and residents. Orbit Housing Association are behind the scheme, flats and bungalows with a homely flavour. All but six properties are let to local people.

September 20 – The summer sunshine has caused £100,000 worth of damage to Norfolk roads. When the roads cool stone chippings sank beneath the surface making them slippery in rain. Now 27 stretches across the county are to be repaired.

September 21 – Danny's third birthday reminds us how time flies. Meanwhile, cheering villagers line the pavements to pass on greetings to their favourite great-great-grandmother, 100 year-old Amy Morton. The sprightly centenarian makes a right royal tour of Great Hockham, near Thetford, in a horse-drawn wagonette. Amy is driven to a party with five generations of her own family after collecting flowers, cards, gifts and good wishes along the way.

September 29 – The final curtain is about to fall on Wells Art Centre following its latest financial crisis. It will close at the end of October with the loss of two full-time and four

Cricket on Aldborough Green.

part-time jobs. The closure of the 10-year-old centre comes as neither of its funders, Eastern Arts and North Norfolk District Council, are prepared to continue to provide cash.

October

Robin James Skipper on his christening day with the rector of Hevingham, Christopher Basil Morgan.

October 2 – Robin James Skipper is born at 4.12p.m., weighing in at 8lb 4oz. So Danny has a little brother, and he says 'Thank you very much!' when I do the round of calls. Again I surprise myself by staying with Diane throughout. Very appropriate timing as this is opening day of the Labour Party conference.

October 3 – Back to work after baby-watch, and a chance to address numerous dignitaries in the county council chamber. I launch a campaign for people to get rid of unwanted medicines after organising a limerick competition on the radio to highlight the dangers. County Council chairman John Birkbeck makes us welcome. He's in the news for making the blunt assertion 'I don't like tourists'. It must be the first time this council chamber has heard limericks with a strong Norfolk flavour.

October 9 – Family outing to have Robin James registered at the Cromer office in North Lodge Park on a windy day. The seas are rolling only a matter of yards away and the bust of Henry Blogg is close enough for a nodding exercise. A delightful setting as we place our latest arrival on the official list.

October 11 – Exciting first for Danny as he joins me on the train journey to and from Norwich on a damp day. He peers out of the window all the way there – and sleeps most of the way back. I hope he remembers some of the details.

October 15 – Can this be true? A gang of willing workers putting up the Christmas lights in Cromer on a wonderfully bright Sunday morning! While one can admire the enthusiasm behind the operation, it is sad to think this is necessary a fortnight before the clocks go back. I object each year to the indecent haste with which we pave the way towards Christmas in the blatant name of commercialism.

October 26 – Campaigner, author and artist Doreen Rash – who wrote more than 50 books under the pen-name of Doreen Wallace – dies at 92 at her Diss home. She gained national recognition in a 40-year campaign to abolish what she described as 'the iniquitous tithe tax'. A former landowner and farmer at

Doreen Wallace – 'a latter-day Boadicea'.

Wortham, she became president of the National Tithe Payers Association before the last war. The *Eastern Daily Press* in a warm tribute calls her a latter-day Boadicea: 'Here was no ordinary Lady of the Manor, and a distinctive era of local life fades with her passing.' Perhaps her novels will now enjoy a revival.

October 28 – As the wind howls and rain threatens I enjoy a warming session with Cromer Cricket Club members and friends for their annual dinner at the Red Lion. Tony Lawes, evergreen all-rounder and groundsman, is the willing victim of my *This Is Your Life* tribute; indeed, he made some telling contributions, including the revelation that his third Christian name is Hebron, and that he was born at Aldermaston, in March, 1941.

November

November 2 – A lifeboat coxswain praises his own crew for rescuing him during a fishing trip. Benny Read, cox of the independent Caister lifeboat, gets into trouble when his fishing vessel is caught in heavy swell with an extra large haul and he is about to founder. Without the Caister crew's help he and two other men 'would have gone down like a bit of lead.'

November 3 – Sad to hear there's but a month left in the life of the Tudor House Restaurant in Cromer. Owner Rita Loynes confirms that the doors to one of the town's longest-established meeting places will close on December 3. Mrs Loynes took over the restaurant 34 years ago. She says illness and the unpredictability of summer staff have led to the sale of the building to Scottish clothiers Mackays.

November 8 – High winds and torrential rain bring down many of the leaves and a few bigger items as well. Hardly the right setting for a harvest supper but that's my destination on a stormy night. The event in Itteringham Village Hall is in aid of this building and the church in a village where some of the old-fashioned virtues remain intact. The community is well away from the mainstream and fully alert to siren voices offering inducements to allow certain developments in this little bit of well-preserved Norfolk. Long may they find strength to resist.

November 12 – Warm sunshine to greet Remembrance Sunday and perfect going for a thoughtful stroll along the beach. The Mayors of East and West Berlin are shaking hands beside the crumbling wall that has divided the city for 28 years. Hopes of old divisions being healed, and suddenly the world looks so different. Danny joins me in our little act of remembrance in front of the bust of lifeboatman Henry Blogg as he peers out to glimmering seas.

December

December 1 – Grand start to the Christmas month with the switching-on of the Cromer festive lights with large crowds in buoyant mood around our splendid Parish Church. I am the official switch-pusher but honours are shared with pensioner Jill Pepler. She celebrates her 77th birthday by joining me on the podium. Town Crier Jason Bell calls the audience to attention. We socialise afterwards in the Tudor Restaurant – for the last time.

December 6 – Happy family evening at Holt for the start of the town's Christmas festivities. Slight change to the programme because the sparklers will not light to give the signal for the rocket to be launched to set the church bells pealing to tell the shopkeepers to turn on their lights! I ask the crowd to join in an impromptu version of *Hev Yew Gotta Loight, Boy?* to act as the launching pad.

December 12 – Dozens of swans meet their death through fog. An estimated 50 Berwick and Hooper swans have died after striking overhead power lines as they return at dusk amid thick fog to the wildfowl and wetland reserve at Welney, near Downham Market.

December 14 – A freak tornado destroys part of a Norfolk village, leaving one woman injured and cars and buildings wrecked. Terrified customers flee shops and pubs after ten seconds of mayhem as the storm smashes the centre of Long Stratton. Buildings shake, a car is rolled over and debris flies through the streets.

December 25 – Robin's first Christmas at the heart of our family considerations. Danny awake at 2.30a.m. and through to our bedroom – but he has a bad cold and that's his concern rather than Father Christmas's visit. We send him back later to find a packed stocking. 'The anti-Christ died on Christmas Day,' says a Bucharest radio announcer following news that deposed Rumanian tyrant Nicolae Ceausecu and his wife Elena have been executed after a secret court martial. The couple who misruled Rumania with megalomanical zeal for almost 25 years were found guilty of the genocide of 60,000 people, stealing a billion dollars from the state and undermining the national economy. So international news of such a dramatic nature creeps into our Christmas lounges to jolt us out of any complacency bred by excessive eating and drinking – and also to remind us that the all-powerful television set is not simply a medium of celluloid adventure.

December 29 – Chad presents his farewell concert on the eve of his move to Gibraltar. One of the great survivors of the local entertainment trade, he has been a regular Friday fixture on the show for eight years. Chad, an alias for Patrick Faux Chadwick, was an art teacher at Gaywood Park in King's Lynn before trying his luck as an entertainer in local pubs and clubs.

Chad – off to Gibraltar to be a rock star!

December 31 – Last day of the 1980s. A decade with the BBC. I have married and helped produce two boys. We have settled at Cromer. I remain deeply concerned at what is happening to my home county. I remain determined to use my platforms on radio and in the local press to continue preaching the only gospel worth extolling – Norfolk must not be sacrificed on the altar of economic expediency.

1990

January

January 6 – Sorry to hear of the death of Ralph Potter, an outstanding character from my days on the local paper. Among his many roles over the years was taking copy over the telephone; his was one of the first voices at the other end of the line in my early reporting career. Later he was on Saturday afternoon duty for my running reports on Norwich City matches. Ralph liked to play a full part with suggestions for new ways of saying 'the ball skimmed over the bar' or 'shot narrowly wide from a difficult angle'. In more recent times he wrote and acted little Norfolk cameos for the radio station. He was 86 and an official city guide. Other jobs included artist, film critic, holiday camp manager, pianist, wood-carver and pottery-maker. If you told a story, Ralph would do his best to top it.

January 12 – A classic entry for the 'I told you so!' file. Plans for a garage complex on Cromer's Holt Road are given the go-ahead. North Norfolk District Council had been opposed to further development of an area of outstanding natural beauty when plans were first put forward last July. But now they have admitted defeat because they had already given themselves planning permission to build new council offices on a large slice of nearby land.

January 18 – End of the line for the Jolly Butchers as another slice of local history bites the concrete. The Ber Street pub in Norwich, with its vibrant memories of landlady Black Anna and her singing sessions, is to be transformed into offices.

January 25 – Stormy going with over 40 people killed as howling winds and torrential rain batter Britain. Force ten gales smash a trail of devastation across Norfolk with police describing the county as in a state of general chaos at the peak of the storm. More than 100 trees are felled, blocking dozens of roads, while trains arrive up to six hours late at Norwich as the London service is reduced to a snail's pace. As the winds rage I mourn the death of my first screen goddess. Ava Gardner, once voted the world's most beautiful woman, dies at 67. It was in the film Showboat that she first caught my eye and sent my tender emotions into a frenzy.

February

February 4 – Hundreds of disco-goers, labelled 'depraved' by a vicar, watch the midnight mock-hanging of a witch. Some 250 people at Rosie's Disco at Yarmouth see a stylised re-enactment of a sixteenth-century execution.. Cabaret act Nightmare, three entertainers who bill themselves as 'Europe's top shock show,' use special effects to recreate other gruesome killings to rock music.

February 7 – Outraged birdwatchers denounce as 'irresponsible' the gunman who shot down the first peregrine falcon seen in East Norfolk for 20 years. And the RSPB warns the shooting could cost the hunter a £2,000 fine in court. The rare peregrine falcon was wintering around Breydon Water.

February 19 – A 'litter snooper' could be sent out onto the streets of Yarmouth to catch people illegally dumping rubbish. The town's policy committee agrees to hire a private detective to spot people leaving bin bags in the town centre.

February 22 – Another village is to lose its only shop. Weasenham St Peter Post Office and Stores, which serves the village and neighbouring parish of Weasenham All Saints, is to close at the end of March. Owner Norman Merrett says the gradual erosion of its business by larger stores in surrounding market towns has prompted his decision to retire.

February 23 – The thermometer on Eastern Counties Newspaper's Prospect House shows 17 degrees Celsius. While Athens can only boast 15, RAF Coltishall records a high spot of 18, the warmest February day on record in Norfolk.

February 26 – Gales batter the region and it's a full-time job walking along the road. The amusement arcade on Cromer Pier is uprooted and carried along the beach. Many locals feel this may be divine intervention and suggest the arcade should not be replaced.

February 28 – More weather problems. A freak whirlwind tears through Thurton, near Loddon, leaving a swathe of destruction in its wake. Part of the thatched roof of the Norman church is ripped off while farm buildings and houses are severely damaged. A tree also crashes down on Starston church, damaging the altar and organ.

KEITH SKIPPER'S NORFOLK DIARIES

March

March 6 – Hundreds of furious protesters force the abandonment of a meeting to set the Norwich Poll Tax when they lay siege to City Hall. About 80 policemen are called in from across Norfolk to hold crowds at bay while officials inside barricade doors. Demonstrators use dustbins, traffic cones and pallets to smash windows and gain entry to basement computer rooms. There are chants of 'Can't pay, won't pay' from a crowded public gallery at Lowestoft Town Hall as councillors set the community charge level for Waveney District Council.

March 7 – The Queen is to pay the poll tax for more than 100 workers on her Sandringham estate, as well as their wives or husbands, at a cost of about £56,000. Buckingham Palace confirms she will pay the tax for staff at Sandringham and Balmoral, her private estates, because she does not want workers to suffer financially. Other major Norfolk landowners praise the Queen's gesture – but say they can't afford to follow suit.

March 9 – The Duke of Edinburgh goes to the top of the class at Wymondham College. He's given the tick of approval by the 820 students at Britain's biggest state boarding school. Science student James Clevelley takes his courage in both hands when Prince Phillip visits the Information Technology Centre computer room. 'I asked him if he would care to sit down and pose for a computerised photograph. He said he would, and it's priceless. I don't think he poses for much other than official photographs.'

March 14 – A royal visitor spotted through the window in Surrey Street. The Duke of Gloucester opens Sentinel House, the new Norwich Union offices opposite the radio station and unveils the city's newest landmark – a bronze sculpture of the Greek goddess Gnea. The 8ft statue, which shows a mother cradling her children, was created by Cley-based artist Colin Miller. Despite the cultural uplift, my long-standing objection to the giant building remains. The sky has gone over Surrey Street.

March 24 – The vexed question of where to put a permanent gipsy site in Norfolk is causing more hackles to rise. Councillors are being recommended to press ahead with plans for a permanent site on the outskirts of Swaffham despite intense local opposition.

March 28 – Brisley Bell, one of my favourite watering-holes, is about to close. Landlady Ada Gricks is pulling her final

Ada and Henry Gricks – my hosts at the old-fashioned Brisley Bell.

It's homely for all in the cosy front room at the Bell.

pints at a pub where fruit machines, disco music and rowdy customers never darkened the door. Parts of the pub date back to 1500 and it was originally a beer house. No spirits were allowed until it secured a full licence and a bar was installed for the first time in 1966. Before that beer was carried from the cellar down a long passage and served in the kitchen. Ada's father, Edward Olley, ran the beer house at Brisley Bell back in 1897. He was there until his death in 1939. When Ada and husband Henry leave to live in a bungalow in North Elmham she will be tearing herself away from the place where she was born in 1900. Apart from 12 years in service as a nursemaid in Hertfordshire, Ada has never been away from The Bell. I recall such a homely welcome on several visits with Caister to play the village cricket team. Over the green and into the pub after the game. The sun dipping as we tasted a rare bit of old Norfolk. We shall never enjoy anything like it again.

March 30 – Lord Fisher pays a call as one of my village guests from Kilverstone. Naturally, he dwells on the wildlife park he and Lady Fisher have built up since the early 1970s. Then, as we chat about village life and community spirit, he claims Kilverstone will soon be part of Thetford –

and he sees nothing strange or unsettling about that. I express surprise at his Lordship's rather bland acceptance of the spread of urbanisation. He says it is a planning business and does not accept my concerns about the erosion of village life. He does not seem alarmed at the prospect of more dormitories and less rounded communities. This is an unusual diversion from the regular pattern, where ardent supporters of traditional parish life bemoan the loss of so many strands. Perhaps this change of tune does remind us that there is another side to the coin. There are some who want to break down what they regard a sentimental barriers. In any event, Sir Arthur South rings after the programme to say he found it fascinating!

April

April 5 – There are claims that Cromer's tourist trade will be hit by a new television commercial being screened for millions of viewers. Councillors, fishermen and hoteliers are angry at the commercial which spotlights sea pollution and was filmed on Cromer Pier. But North Norfolk District Council defends its decision to allow the pier to be used. The commercial earned them a £3,000 fee.

April 10 – Birdwatchers flock to North Norfolk after a rare white stork is spotted on the coast. It's only the fourth time this giant Mediterranean visitor has been seen in the country this century. It is seen drifting high over Cley Marshes.

April 11 – Children are safer on rides at the fair than they are on the car journey there, according to latest research. The findings are welcomed by managers of leisure facilities along the east coast who are preparing for the Easter influx of visitors.

April 19 – Former newspaper colleague Don Urry dies from cancer. He spent nearly 40 years on the local papers. He had just returned to the Dereham office, where I worked with him in the mid-1960s, as chief reporter when he fell ill. He spent most of the last year at home with his family at West Winch. Our last reunion came with a trip to King's Lynn to present a *This Is Your Life* tribute at the Rotary Charter Night.

April 23 – Real warmth in the sun on St George's Day as I enjoy my train trips to and from the city. Colours multiplying along the track and the lilac is waiting to burst into life at the Salhouse stop. Youngsters back to school after the Easter break but still plenty of holiday-makers doing the rounds. Norfolk appears to be increasingly popular.

April 30 – A family hit out at thieves who virtually strip an 84-year-old's allotment at Dereham. Roger Wade has grown vegetables on the patch for more than 20 years and his family cannot believe anyone would steal from him. The allotment is near St Nicholas Church.

May

May 1 – A fourth thatched cottage is hit by fire, bringing to five the number of historic Norfolk homes wrecked by blazes in nine days. The latest is a Thompson, near Watton. The nine-day tally of destruction started when a 400-year-old listed cottage at Rickinghall, near Diss, was destroyed by flames. A farmhouse at Shipdham, a 200-year-old cottage at Hemblington, near Acle, and a Tudor farmhouse at Tibenham are the other victims.

May 2 – Two American airmen escape death as their F111 fighter crashes into a field close to houses at Binham. A massive crater and pieces of burning metal are all that's left of the plane based at RAF Lakenheath after it nosedives into the ground in a huge fireball. The pilot and weapon systems officer eject seconds before the crash.

May 7 – A busy Bank Holiday Monday. I host a radio tribute to Beryl Bryden, the Norwich girl who went on to international acclaim as a jazz and blues singer. She's 70 this week. After the show I head for Little Melton to open the new £180,000 Village Hall, an impressive building in a community they have to fight hard to keep apart from sprawling Norwich influences.

May 9 – How goes the fight to save Norfolk's soul? Well, the mad rush to build more homes has slowed down, at least for the time being, because the rich bottom has dropped out of the market. The roads lobby are being matched in the headline stakes by the alternative transport supporters, and there's a much more honest acceptance that it does matter what sort of environment we live in. Even so, I fear the market forces army are just waiting for the mood to change. They probably feel this 'green' spell will blow itself out.

May 11 – Another old newspaper colleague has gone. Wilfred Bunting, editor of the *Yarmouth Mercury* for 33 years, dies at 81. He retired in 1973 after working on the paper for almost half a century. Pipe-smoking, rather shy and quietly spoken, he ran the office his own way during my years on the *Yarmouth Mercury* in the mid-1960s. He would often have a gentle word about getting in late or horseplay around the typewriters without making the sort of fuss others employed as a matter of course.

May 23 – We enjoy our first family visit to Pensthorpe, the waterfowl park and nature reserve near Fakenham. We mingle with children on educational trips and nature-lovers of more mature years. The lakes have all been created from flooded gravel workings. Gravel extraction took place between 1974 and 1979, and the pits have been carefully restored as a nature reserve of 200 acres. Meanwhile, Prime Minister Margaret Thatcher tells us the Broads are wonderful as she pays a visit to How Hill, at Ludham.

May 29 – More grim warnings about our environmental future. Coastal villages are first in line as a new exhibition unveils glimpses of a seaside settlement almost completely covered by the sea. A church tower is all that remains of the lost village of Eccles and scientists say many other seaside settlements in Norfolk could go the same way within 40 years.

June

June 1 – Children as young as eight are burgling houses in Norwich. Two boys of that age have been interviewed about thefts from a house on the Plumstead estate. The law protects children of this age – evidently under 10 they don't know the difference between right and wrong. But what about their parents? A pensioner is left shaking and

in tears after vandals with air-guns shoot at windows on a sheltered housing estate.

June 5 – A pair of Japanese figures which changed hands in Norfolk for five guineas set a new world auction record in London. The two seventeenth-century Kakiemon models were bought in a house sale in 1914 by a Cromer man. Today they sell for £154,000, triple the amount estimated. The grandfather of the present owner bought the figures during a sale of the home of Sir Edgar Speyer of Overstrand.

June 12 – Developers who want to build a new village south of Norwich meet with a hostile reception. Proposals for 353-acre Mangreen Hall Farm, near Swardeston, include up to 1,500 new homes, a village green, a village centre with shops and a community centre. Also planned are a primary school, parkland, a landscaped retail park, a hotel, a community leisure facility and park-and-ride service into Norwich. London-based developer the Mountleigh Group invite Stoke Holy Cross and Caistor St Edmund parish councillors to a special private meeting. Caistor St Edmund Parish Council chairman Ken Mills says: 'It's a nice piece of countryside and we don't want it spoiled.' Stoke Holy Cross chairman Charles Bussey says there are both benefits and advantages. It would draw development away from

Cliffs under siege at Beeston Regis on the North Norfolk coast.

existing villages but 'it's another area of open countryside which is going to be swallowed up'.

(*The new village got no further than the drawing board.)

June 17 – Norfolk racing driver Martin Brundle pilots his Jaguar to the greatest triumph of his career by winning the Le Mans 24-hour endurance race. Brundle, of Gayton, near King's Lynn, leads the Jaguar 1–2 victory charge in the world's most famous sports car race at his third attempt. His first car broke down after only six hours of the gruelling 3,000-mile race, but he was able to switch to a second Jaguar. He roared to victory with co-drivers Price Cobb and John Neilson. Meanwhile, the Revd David Ainsworth is the toast of Northrepps after plunging from the top of his church tower, watched by scores of cheering parishioners. His sponsored abseil raises money for church repairs. The 61-year-old rector says before his dive: 'Before I launch myself into eternity I want to welcome you to this great occasion, and I hope you find it highly entertaining.'

June 24 – Thurning, between Fakenham and Aylsham, may have only 60 names on the electoral roll. But if the unexpected happens, the village is sure it can cope. Flooding, hurricane damage, 6ft of snow – the small Norfolk community is ready to take up the challenge. This is proved in today's Exercise Gale Force as the villages civil protection organisation is put to the test.

June 25 – A new seal hospital opens with the aims to nurse seals back to the sea and to educate children about dangers these mammals face from marine viruses. The hospital at the Hunstanton Sea Life Centre costs £250,000 and was set up partly in response to the killer virus which two years ago wiped out about half the east coast seal population.

July

July 5 – A Norfolk private school closes its doors for the last time as 125 years of learning comes to an end. The closure of All Hallows' School at Ditchingham, near Bungay, set up by a community of nuns, was announced suddenly at the beginning of the year. Parents were very critical of the way the matter was handled. But the closure is a quiet affair with a number of events and activities being organised with the remaining pupils.

July 7 – Champion fund-raiser Carrie Coleman is reduced to tears as she receives news of a special birthday treat. Carrie, who will be 81 in a few days, will hear the bells of her beloved Gimingham Parish Church peal properly for the first time for over a century. Carrie started fund-raising

six years ago – and now £12,000 later she is ready for a wonderful birthday peal.

July 10 – Dick Condon resigns as general manager of Norwich Theatre Royal after 18 golden years at the helm. He says it is in protest against what he sees as the mishandling by the trust of the theatre's major improvement project. Dick's resignation was in fact submitted to the trust some time ago when he was already deeply unhappy with the management of building work and its financing. A truly sad day even for those who don't go to the theatre. He has made such an impact on the Norfolk scene.

July 13 – I'm not superstitious but my train fails to turn up at Cromer station on this Friday 13. And I have a rotten cold. Things can only get better.

July 14 – Out into the sunshine of Necton Village fête. I do the opening honours, hand out the gardening prizes and judge the children's painting competition in the Village Hall. The majority of people behind this event are newcomers, many with London accents. That suggests the old guard have handed over the village challenges and it is churlish to criticise those prepared to get on with the work. I think a mix works better with native know-how allied to fresh enthusiasm. Perhaps Necton with its sprawling estates has grown too much for its own good, sitting precariously close to the busy A47.

July 25 – Glorious sunshine for a *Dinnertime Show* broadcast from the Sandringham Flower Show. The Queen Mother, as energetic as ever on the eve of her 90th birthday and Prince Charles, his right arm in a sling after breaking it in a polo accident, are the star attractions of the 109th year of the event.

July 30 – A day for rare courage as I go to Cromer Hospital after work to have ingrown toenail problems sorted out. Diane waits outside as I make a few weak jokes and two amiable women make it as painless as possible. I limp home for tea and sympathy.

July 31 – Day off work to rest my foot – and it's just a coincidence that England are winning a record-littered test match at Lord's. Graham Gooch, with 333 in the first innings and a century in the second, leads the way to a comfortable home success.

August

August 2 – Norfolk firemen continue their fierce battle with the elements. Hottest day of the year so far sees the service working at full stretch tackling more than 40 countryside fires as tinder-dry fields and woodland catch light. Firemen join forces with worried farmers to launch a 'Stop Norfolk Burning' poster and leaflet campaign.

August 14 – Plenty of fresh air and exercise as we take a family stroll along one of the walks at Mannington Hall. Down the boardwalk to a patch of the great Norfolk outdoors made available to those who feel inclined. We move on to nearby Corpusty to pay a call on old friends Ivy and Henry West. We round off a pleasant session with afternoon tea at The Chimes in Reepham market-place. A few spots of rain, but hardly enough to stir the dust.

August 16 – Trip to Great Witchingham Wildlife Park as the weather turns. Sudden showers send us scurrying for shelter. Far bigger than expected, the park can tax your staying power as snowy owls and peacocks give way to rabbits and reindeer. I find it hard to feel totally comfortable in places like these, even though the creatures seem happy and well cared for.

August 22 – Bulldozers demolish the once-thriving F.W. Harmer clothing factory in Norwich. The shriek of rending metal replaces the busy whirr of sewing machines which once produced clothing for the whole of Britain. Demolition brings to an end Harmer's 150-year association with the city.

August 28 – Workmen stand in silence as the bones of a mystery family who died more than 500 years ago are reburied in the foundations of a Norwich hotel. The man, woman and child had laid undisturbed for centuries until they were unearthed by men working on the foundations of the Maid's Head in Tombland.

August 31 – Sad end to the month with a call to tell me about vandalism at Roydon Nature Reserve near King's Lynn. I'm due to open it on Sunday. Another grim reminder that Norfolk is catching up with other areas – and in this instance there's no cause to give thanks.

September

September 5 – Councillor Jocelyn Rawlence coins an intriguing new expression during a debate on satellite dishes. 'Hideositics' is how she describes the white discs sprawling on house fronts around South Norfolk. 'The commercial side is going ahead willy-nilly and they didn't realise the impact it was going to have on the countryside,' she tells South Norfolk planning committee.

September 8 – 'Bring back our bobby on the beat!' is the plea of Hethersett residents, who share their village policeman with 12 other parishes. Now the parish council asks Norfolk Chief Constable Peter Ryan to look into the problem after a spate of vandalism. 'It would be nice to see them walking around or even on a bike,' says council chairwoman Elizabeth Capleton.

September 11 – Milestone for the local wireless – Radio Norfolk celebrates a decade on the air. There's a civic reception at County Hall, but I'm busy hosting the *Dinnertime Show*. I do have a part to play in the evening item on television's *Look East*, reflecting on the station's successful ten years and underlining how the word 'parochial' holds so much attraction for me. Success has been achieved despite a small staff and a puny budget. My main hope for the future is that regional radio will not gradually move in to water down the truly local flavour.

September 26 – Family trip on the North Norfolk Railway from Sheringham to Holt. It's all steam and nostalgia and brings back my schooldays on the old Dereham to Swaffham line. When we stop at Weybourne there's a man dressed up as a station master. The guard and others on our train wear boyish smiles as they indulge their passion. Heather in bloom and the mixture of steam and sunshine paints the blackberries and other trackside fruit. No wonder this attraction appeals to all ages.

September 30 – Boaters, blazers and wicker picnic baskets bob in boats on the Broads as 1200 people pay tribute to the memory of Arthur Ransome. Ranworth Broad is transformed into a scene inspired by his classic story *Coot Club* with over 30 pre-war boats assembled. Enthusiasts from The Association of River Thurne Sailors – known as Tarts – even dress up as characters from the book.

October

October 3 – The trials of rail travel continue to prompt a mixture of smiles and groans. It's not unusual for us to be kept waiting in Norwich for a driver or a guard. Nor is it that exceptional for the train to conk out along the way. Now, at alarmingly regular intervals, we are without a guard to collect the fares. That must cost British Rail dear. At a time when support for this mode of transport is growing it is hard to be too enthusiastic just as fares go up again.

October 10 – Books and beer can prove a popular mix. The Lillie Langtry pub in Unthank Road, Norwich is stocking books alongside bottles. Regulars keen on a spot of reading matter with their pint are simply asked to put 10p in a charity collecting bottle.

October 12 – A £2.2 million by-pass built in record-breaking time is opened by South Norfolk MP John MacGregor. The contractors complete the A140 Dickleburgh by-pass 11 months ahead of schedule, bringing relief to the traffic-choked village near Diss where it was impossible for two lorries to pass each other in the main street at the narrowest point.

October 13 – A real country feel to our trip to Skeyton Village Hall for the harvest supper. This little village is far enough removed from the mainstream to keep certain conditions and images intact. For me the occasion is a telling echo of 30–40 years ago and encourages the impression that Village Hall functions are enjoying a revival. Of course, so few people now have anything to do with the harvest they must feel a twinge of conscience when the hymns are sung and the glasses raised.

October 21 – Jim Howard, a retired headmaster at Cawston, has died at 78. He was renowned for entertaining locals with his act in Norfolk dialect. His old friend John Kett, himself a noted performer, says: 'Cawston will not be the same without him. He has entertained practically every-body in the village over the last 30–40 years.'

October 22 – Cricket star Ian Botham is given a rousing welcome to Norfolk as his marathon charity walk enters its final week. Thousands line the 20-mile route from Holbeach to King's Lynn, while the Duke of Kent joins Botham for the first five miles of the day. The East Coast Walk, raising money for leukaemia research, began on October 1st and will end 612 miles later on Friday in Ipswich.

November

November 10 – Huge flocks of hungry waxwings are reported all along the east coast of Britain in a repeat of 1970's spectacular invasion. The starling-sized birds from eastern Europe are arriving in massive numbers, attracted by a rich harvest of wild berries.

November 16 – Foundation stone laid marking the official start of building the Castle Mall shopping precinct in Norwich.

November 21 – Pleasing task at Cromer High School just up the road to do the presentation honours at the annual prize-

Skipper's tour de Norwich as the site for the Castle Mall shopping complex is prepared.

giving and to pass on a few words of wisdom. I relate a few memorable incidents from my schooldays and renew acquaintance with Philip Mindham, PE teacher at the school. He was an established sporting star when I first arrived at Hamond's in Swaffham in 1955 – and he's still in good working trim.

November 22 – End of a political era on a damp and dismal day as Margaret Thatcher resigns as Prime Minister after 11 years at the helm. Now it's a three-cornered fight for the keys to 10, Downing Street between Michael Heseltine, the man whose challenge signalled the end of the Thatcher years, Chancellor John Major and Foreign Secretary Douglas Hurd.

November 24 – Ann Scott of Wymondham runs a competition at her local Women's Institute for members to guess how many gallstones she had removed in a recent operation. She raises £11 for Children in Need. The correct total was 106.

December

December 1 – The Pleasure Beach at Yarmouth is named in the top ten of the nation's tourist attractions for the second year running. Managing director Jimmy

Jones believes the secret of success lies in investing for the future.

December 12 – The Dunkirk spirit on show in Norfolk as an entire community is moved to safety from floodwaters. About 150 people are evacuated from the Bush estate at Eccles on the coast to the Village Hall at Lessingham. Winds peaking at 70 knots and mountainous tides combine to cause a night of panic for thousands of people around the coast and on the Broads. Police with loudhailers tour villages in Broadland areas urging people to stay indoors. Meanwhile, I celebrate a personal triumph inland – addressing members of the Institute of Advanced Motorists! Despite several failures to pass my driving test, I am heard with respect.

December 22 – Yarmouth is in the height of its holiday season for the second time this year. Winter breaks by the sea are booming with holiday camps and hotels fully booked this Christmas. I suppose it does have a certain attraction, although I would have thought most people would prefer the North Norfolk coast!

December 25 – A wild backcloth for the cosiest day of the year. The wind howls and rain lashes against the windows as Christmas activities begin in earnest at about 6.45a.m. as Danny makes an appearance. Robin sleeps on a bit longer and the main present opening waits until Nan and Grandad arrive. Then we brave the elements to take presents and greetings to our dear friends down the Loke. Jo and Gimi Jordan are celebrating their golden wedding.

December 30 – Clear skies and sharp breezes as Danny and I savour our final seafront amble of 1990. The inevitable call at Victor's corner shop for a browse through the books. The lad selects *Skip the Squirrel* while I'm delighted to find a second volume of the diaries of the Dereham vicar Benjamin Armstrong.

◆ ◆ ◆

A bustle of boats on Blakeney Quay.

Letting off steam in North Norfolk.

A jumble sale on the beach at East Runton?

Norfolk's Road to Moowhere!

Intrepid sailor rests after perilous journey through Broadland reedbeds.

Brolly good idea at Narborough. Planting a tree to mark the opening of new houses under the umbrella of Cotman Housing Association. Chairman Antoinette Faulkner provides a spot of shelter.

Sorting out wheat from chaff at Tunstead Trosh.

Autumn frame for Langham Parish Church. Captain Frederick Marryat, author of Children of the New Forest, rests in the churchyard.

A rewarding pastime – puffing out cheeks with real Norfolk pride.

Two scribes who picked up the pen with purpose in Thetford. Thomas Paine, the one in the elevated position, did exert more international influence.

I know all his relatives living in the sea off Cromer.

Time for a few pointed reflections on a Cotswolds holiday. Painswick churchyard offers a resting-place.

The building blocks of family life at Cromer.

Leslie Thomas, one of my favourite authors, stands to attention for an interview on Radio Norfolk.

On parade for a night of Norfolk entertainment at Sheringham Little Theatre. I'm joined by (left to right): Pat Maitland, Maggie Secker, Mike Godfrey, Ian Prettyman, Brian Patrick and David Woodward.

Crab lines dangling – an evocative scene from a painting by old friend Ken Tidd of Brancaster Staithe.

Shrine to the man who found Poppyland. It's on Overstrand Road in Cromer.

Memorial to the Beeston boy who became boxing champion of the world. I pay my respects to Jem Mace in the village churchyard.

Where did all the ink-wells go? Technology rules in the classroom as I return to Beeston Village School for a quick lesson on the keyboard. Nephew Stuart Laws and niece Claire look on.

Blessed companions on a round of local churches with All Preachers Great and Small.

'It gives me great pleasure...' I lead a chorus of praise at Phil and Joan Drackett's golden wedding celebration. The couple made their big mark in Mundesley with tireless work on behalf of the local festival.

Hair-ruffling day in Hunstanton, popularly known as 'Sunny Hunny'. The boys enjoyed their rations of fresh air. (Inset) Skip's off the old block! The lads help me out with a few choice extracts from A Load of Old Squit.

Oar-inspiring character on Barton Broad.

The Skipper boys make a new friend during a family safari into deepest Suffolk.

A Norfolk man at peace with his animals. Arthur Clouting takes a break at a local ploughing match to pose with heavy horses and a light dog.

'I still can't find a damsel in distress...'
On the history trail at Castle Rising.

My favourite whiff of early summer – the lilac bush in full bloom.

Author at work. Book-signing session at Dereham with old friends Colin Chambers (in his shop under the town sign), Peter Whitbread (appearing as Major Egbert Gladstone Pyle of Wanglingham Hall) and publisher Jim Baldwin (my mentor and guide) as I hit the literary trail in the mid-1980s.

Norfolk's very own Dome, sitting like a dumpling on the edge of the old Langham airfield.

Playing it cool as I interview ice-dancing superstars Jayne Torville and Christopher Dean at the Royal Norfolk Show.

My first (and last) stint of reed cutting with expert marshman Eric Edwards at How Hill. He decided he didn't need an apprentice after all.

Inspiration flows down by the riverside at Ringland, just outside Norwich. I took off my shoes and socks a bit later.

'And for all of you listening in stereo, I'm the one in the middle...'
Ready for action in the Radio Norfolk studio.

1991

January

January 2 – Perfect opportunity to debate some of the big issues of local life – traffic and congestion, especially at the heart of Norwich. My guests on the *Dinnertime Show* are Sir Arthur South, influential member of the East Anglian Roads to Prosperity lobby, and architect Edward Skipper, who is proposing a light rail system as a possible answer to the city's chronic traffic problems. Sir Arthur accepts there must be more investment in public transport, especially the railways, but makes no apologies for his support of the roads pressure group. We agree that the crux of the matter is convincing people it is in their own interests to part company with their cars on the outskirts of Norwich.

Sir Arthur South – supports roads pressure group.

January 6 – Death at 77 of Hedley Mitchell, who moved to The Ploughshare pub at Beeston in 1939 and remained landlord for 18 years. I recall tapping at the pub door to buy toffees or a mineral after earning a few pennies by doing jobs on a Saturday morning. Hedley had left the pub by the time I was old enough to call in for a pint. He built up a flourishing insurance business, moving to Necton in 1957.

January 10 – A fierce blaze engulfs Buxton Mill near Aylsham causing damage estimated at up to £1 million. Nearly 80 firemen are called before dawn as flames leap through the roof of the 250-year-old building.

January 16 – Just before midnight, as I watched football on television, war erupts in The Gulf. It's an eerie experience as I watch and listen to the start of hostilities. The boys and Diane are tucked up in bed. The final scheduled tie played this evening, and the draw for the semi-finals of the League Cup, are put on ice as 'We go over to ITN for a news flash'. Very soon we are with two American reporters in a Baghdad hotel. They press their microphones against the window so we can hear the explosions. For countless millions this is the first round of the armchair war. Operation Desert Storm will dominate the news when we awake.

January 29 – The 300-year-old tradition of Mayor of Yarmouth is scrapped. In protest Deputy Mayor Jim Shrimplin pulls off his chain and resigns after Conservative attempts to save the mayoralty fail. The claims are that abolishing the tradition will save money and that a chairman can do just as efficient a job. Sadly, this decision is based on purely political grounds and I feel Yarmouth will live to regret the whole business. How can councillors who have served as mayor vote now to get rid of the office? Does local history and pride count for nothing?

January 31 – Yet another village Post Office and shop bites the dust. As Paul Ross clears the shelves at Northrepps, near Cromer, he says: 'We have had to close the business because no one is using it.' Pensioners drew their pensions – and then went off to the supermarkets in Cromer. A sad trend.

February

February 4 – Hundreds of mourners pack Yarmouth Parish Church for the funeral of Pleasure Beach legend Lottie Botton. The hearse drives though the deserted Yarmouth funfair rides and stalls, including her favourite scenic railway, on the way to the service. It was the same route taken by the funeral cortege of her husband Albert with whom she transformed the Pleasure Beach from duckboards on the sand to a national tourist attraction.

February 9 – Norfolk broadcaster and businessman Ralph Tuck dies at 67. Back in 1959 he was temporarily taken off the air by the BBC because of his Norfolk accent. He was soon back by popular demand. A successful businessman, he turned his talents in later years to training techniques, producing videos and winning a national award a couple of years ago. Perhaps he'll be best remembered as the shrewd operator behind the rise of Allan Smethurst, The Singing Postman.

Ralph Tuck – shrewd operator behind The Singing Postman.

February 12 – Every member of staff at Norwich-based Anglia Television is offered voluntary redundancy. All 711 staff are sent a letter by chief executive David McCall seeking voluntary redundancies and early retirements because of the worst advertising downturn to hit the ITV industry for 17 years.

February 18 – Norwich City put out FA Cup holders Manchester United in a fifth-round tie at Carrow Road. Dale Gordon and Robert Fleck are the Canary marksmen in a 2–1 victory which ends United's 21-game unbeaten run in cup competitions. Alex Ferguson has now visited Norwich five times without a win and United have to look back more than 80 years for their last FA Cup victory against the Canaries.

February 28 – The Gulf War is over after six weeks of fighting. We wait to see how the peace shapes the future. The snow has gone after a sharp taste of winter. This has been one of the coldest Februarys this century.

March

March 7 – Priceless gold and silver discovered by a pensioner in a Norfolk field, one of the most exciting finds in British archaeological history, is declared treasure trove. Retired Squadron Leader Cecil Hodder of South Wootton unearthed treasure worth up to £20 million. A packed inquest at King's Lynn Town Hall hears how 63 torcs, 2000-year-old precious metal and bronze neck rings were found in one field near Snettisham. Cecil tells how he discovered the first of the hoards using a metal detector.

March 8 – Yes, a gold rush is feared as treasure hunters try to find the site of that £20 million hoard. A local historian warns them to stay away. Geoffrey Peach, who lives close to the field where the treasure was founds, has been pestered by telephone callers. He says several people from Kent turned up on his doorstep demanding to know the location.

March 15 – A memorable character to share my train trips today: 83-year-old Ida Watts, one of the guests from Worstead, the *Dinnertime Show* bran-tub village of the week. This former schoolteacher has a fiercely independent streak, cleaning her own chimney, growing her own vegetables and looking back fondly on her years as a motorbike rider. She is not the typical village elder – she says what she thinks too much for that – but she does carry an invigorating air. I walk from the train station to the radio station on arrival in Norwich. She goes off shopping before arriving back to take her place among the Worstead visitors. She chats all the way home as well!

March 19 – Elsie Cole bows out 70 years after joining the parochial church council at Lyng. 'I think the time has come to hand over to a younger person,' says Elsie, who has lived nearly all her 86 years in the village. Mind you, she

likes to see the world and is preparing for her 20th trip to America to see her rector son in Pennsylvania. Her father was a churchwarden in Lyng.

March 22 – The great debate continues! Not for the first time in a long and illustrious career of standing up for Norfolk I am accused of going too far in criticisms of newcomers. In a phone-in on Radio Norfolk, ostensibly to discuss last night's television programme about the problems of village life, one woman suggests that if I said the things in London I say here, I'd be up before the Race Relations Board! Of course, I defend myself vigorously against such charges, but it is a pity that this highly important argument should come down to such a level.

March 25 – Hundreds of people enjoy the sights and sounds of the steam age as the Charles Burrell Museum opens in Thetford. It depicts the history of Thetford engine builders Charles Burrell & Sons, and is based in the former factory paint shop. South-West Norfolk MP Gillian Shephard arrives at the ceremony on an 1877 Century steam engine, the oldest known Burrell engine in existence.

March 26 – Sam Flogdell celebrates his 100th birthday just up the road and is enjoying a well-earned nap when I drop in to pass on congratulations. It must be the first time I've seen a centenarian having a doze as he reaches three figures! Sam is at the British Legion's Halsey House residential home in Cromer. He attended the official opening in 1948 and returned over a decade ago as a resident. Born at West Runton, he owes his long life to keeping busy and being able to put his head on the pillow with a clear conscience each night. Meanwhile, Dr David Dickie believes he is one of the oldest serving GPs in Britain. Changes in the law are forcing him to leave the practice he took on 44 years ago. Dr Dickie, who celebrates his 80th birthday this week, says he'll miss the work and the Shipdham practice he ran single-handed for more than 40 years.

April

April 2 – George Lee, a familiar figure with Norwich City Football Club for three decades dies at 71. He joined the Canaries as trainer when Ron Ashman was manager in the early 1960s and went on to work with five more City managers. I saw a lot of George during the Ron Saunders era. Born in York, George played nearly 350 league games between 1946 and 1957 with York, Nottingham Forest and, most notably, West Bromwich Albion. A speedy outside-left, he featured in West Brom's FA Cup-winning side at Wembley in 1954 when they beat Preston 3–2.

1991

Don Shepherd –
Dad's Favourite Tunes.

April 10 – Sad day at Radio Norfolk as news comes through that colleague Don Shepherd has died peacefully in his sleep at the age of 63. He made a distinctive mark as host of *Dad's Favourite Tunes* on a Sunday lunchtime, mixing music and memories. In fact, the show became the most popular put out by the station, and I sat in for Don several times when he was poorly.

April 13 – Bells ring out across the parish as the Rector of Diss marries his 21-year-old fiancée. Widower, the Revd Jimmy James, 55, marries dental nurse Kelly Evans. Mr James' first wife died tragically after an asthma attack in 1988. This marriage service is conducted by the Rt Revd David Bentley, Bishop of Lynn.

April 15 – I'm asked to comment on a Norwich hotel's idea of a £75.50 weekend break to give guests a quick lesson in Norfolk dialect, followed by an eavesdropping trip into the countryside to hear the accent in everyday use. My verdict? Revolting! 'The county is not a zoo. The next stop will be setting up a Norfolk Wildlife Park full of us peasants so people can come and stare. Peasant hunting is a new blood sport the county can do without.' My quotes are destined for the front page of the *Eastern Daily Press*. There's the irony. The hotel has won far more publicity than it deserves.

April 28 – Day out with a difference at the Fakenham Museum of Gas and Local History. It's their second open day and I'm invited to say a few words as cheerful weather brings out useful support for this worthwhile project. I enjoy chats with several people connected with the gas industry.

May

May 6 – Over a thousand people are evacuated from their homes as a big chemical spillage on the North Norfolk coast sparks a major emergency. About 40 people also need hospital treatment after two tankers leaking chemicals are washed up on the beach near Weybourne in Norfolk's biggest toxic scare. The Army spearheads a massive clean-up operation.

May 10 – The Norfolk Naturalists' Trust awards the county's most prestigious conservation medal to Ken Durrant of Sheringham. He's the third person to receive the Sydney Long medal for services to nature conservation in Norfolk, following in the footsteps of Ted Ellis and Christopher Cadbury. Ken joined the trust in 1949 and the study of insects has been his lifelong passion.

May 18 – Start of our first family holiday week in a chalet at Winterton. It's a comfortable little base, and I intend to do a fair bit of reading. The old scraggy tree, bent in submission to the winds, makes a poor sentry as the chalet park grass runs down to the dunes and the sea. Scarcely a breeze this evening as birds come scavenging at the door. Fresh air and exercise encourage Robin to sleep in a bed for the first time. He has the bottom bunk.

May 19 – Up the road to Caister to watch my old club take on Topcroft in the Norfolk Junior Cup. What a sad scene greets us. The pavilion, vandalised and daubed with graffiti, is an insult to those who use it for sporting occasions. Matters are not helped by the belligerent presence of three uncouth teenagers whose every other utterance is an obscenity. They are playing football round the swings, slides and roundabouts made for little children.

May 21 – Pleasantly surprised at some aspects of Yarmouth gearing up for the new season. For example, pedestrianisation of the market-place area makes a telling difference. Bit of an oasis in the middle of so much traffic. I find plenty to interest in David Ferrow's second-hand bookshop, a spot I haunted regularly during my days on the local newspaper in the 1960s. He has one of the best selections of local books I have come across and I invest a few pounds in a few more volumes.

May 30 – A grand 'Rum Function' in Norwich to salute old colleague Don Shepherd and raise some funds for his widow Vera. Johnny Cleveland is the organising spirit behind the event which is well attended by Don's old friends and colleagues, many of them in the entertainment business.

June

June 8 – Along the coast on a cheerful Saturday morning to do the opening honours at the new BREAK charity shop in Sheringham near the railway station. The town is bustling, with market stalls on the nearby car park, but we find time to drop in and admire the new Sheringham Museum, opening officially next month.

KEITH SKIPPER'S NORFOLK DIARIES

June 11 – My quote of the year so far: 'You can't offer us anything. We have got a beautiful area. We have got peace and quiet – and that is what we want.' That's the way to tell the developers! The quote comes from Graham Green as about 100 people crowd into Stratton Strawless Village Hall to hear more about plans for a five-acre leisure park.

June 16 – Long trip to East Wretham in Breckland for an open day at the Norfolk Naturalists' Trust nature reserve. Rex Hancy and I are asked to do the opening honours. It's no hardship to form a double act with a supreme enthusiast who has been explaining the world of nature to Radio Norfolk listeners for a decade.

Nature man Rex Hancy (left) *and bird man Chris Durdin – wildlife experts on Radio Norfolk's* Dinnertime Show.

June 17 – Some newly-qualified chartered accountants face up to life on the dole as the recession takes its toll on the profession. Recruitment is being cut back and a leading East Anglian accountant says the profession can no longer be regarded as providing a job for life.

June 18 – Kilverstone Wildlife Park is closing this autumn, another victim of the recession. It's an important breeding centre and last year 130,000 people visited the park. Rising overheads of £900,000 and falling attendances are blamed for the decision to close.

June 22 – Evening treat at the opening of *Seaside Special '91* at the end of Cromer Pier. It's another winner – but I can't help wondering how many good shows were poorly supported before that television programme highlighting the Cromer efforts inspired a dramatic revival. Gordon and Bunny Jay are back to pull most of the comedy strings. Good to see Dick Condon on parade despite all his recent health problems. It's not the sparkling Dick of Theatre Royal days, but he draws warmth and affection from many who want to shake hands.

June 30 – Death of Victor Dewing, that marvellous old horseman, Salvation Army stalwart and legendary supporter of the dialect night at the Cromer Festival. Victor was 91 and represented in many ways the old Norfolk of the land with a fierce pride and undimmed passion for the furrows he ploughed. It was a hard life but he recalled it all without a hint of regret but with much good humour and colour.

July

July 1 – Gallyon & Sons, Britain's oldest family gun-maker, falls victim to the recession and stringent shot-gun legislation. The firm, founded in 1784 and with a Royal Warrant, will close both its Norwich base and Peterborough branch in a fortnight. The move leaves Norfolk without a manufacturing gun-maker and a game fishing specialist.

July 6 – Long trek into Breckland to do the honours at Feltwell's big carnival day. It's roasting out of the shade. Old-established families now have to work alongside the newcomers to get shows like this on the road. I denote a little bit of antagonism just below the surface, although I suspect that applies to any bunch of organisers in any kind of community.

July 10 – Airmen from RAF West Raynham leave the airfield for the last time as No.85 Squadron is disbanded. Aircraft flew from the base in the two world wars. Now the Squadron is being put into mothballs, its role operating Bloodhound missiles at an end. The move means a reduction in personnel from 600 to about 350. The station will close completely in two years.

July 13 – I enjoy a ride on a horse-drawn fire engine round North Walsham before opening the 999 Spectacular. Emergency services put on displays and there's a strong anti-crime flavour to this well-attended event. Sad that we need a big shop window like this but there's no point in hiding down a cosy little cul-de-sac of nostalgia.

Norfolk's accident rate and crime statistics give cause for deep concern.

July 17 – Enthralling family day out. The restored County School railway station near North Elmham is a glorious spot, and we enjoy a picnic lunch on a wooden table just beyond the platform. We fulfil a long-standing pledge to take a look at little Gateley nearby. A few houses and the church down a narrow and winding lane in the middle of a bit of Norfolk that time forgot. On to Brisley and Mileham to stir more memory buds, and when we get to the old home village of Beeston I show Danny the house where I was born.

July 22 – One of the most significant rounds in the Battle for Norfolk. The county's High Sheriff, Thomas Cook, launches a scathing attack on 'fly-by-night developers' who, he says, are ruining the place. He describes developers as 'an insidious enemy which masquerades under the name of economic development.' He goes on: 'If it is not stopped now this great trampling, bludgeoning, insensitive, greedy, dinosaur-like juggernaut will destroy rural Norfolk within our generation.' Now perhaps a few more will listen.

July 23 – Predictable response from the growth lobby to Thomas Cook's criticisms. Veteran county councillor Dick Phelan, the Labour group spokesman on planning, says 'He should get his head out of the clouds.' The House Builders' Federation says Mr Cook's comments show 'a total lack of concern for the welfare of those Norfolk residents who need jobs and affordable homes'.

August

August 4 – An exciting day afloat! I take to the North Sea in the Cromer inshore lifeboat which bumps us down to Sheringham. Then we switch to the real Cromer lifeboat for the start of the annual raft race. I surprise myself by enjoying the whole afternoon session with coxswain Richard Davies at the helm. The flotilla of fun looks most impressive as we follow contestants along the route. The coxswain loses his hat as we take a diversion further out to sea, and promptly dives in to retrieve it! The jet-ski brigade, all noise and bravado, are much in evidence testing themselves against the wash of the lifeboat.

August 17 – Norfolk champion Rosemary Tilbrook keeps the great debate going in the *Eastern Daily Press* with a few choice questions... 'What has happened to our beautiful county? The Norfolk of yesterday, and the day before yesterday? The Norfolk of leafy lanes and flowery churchyards, crystal rivers and lilied broads?'

August 18 – Cromer gives hero's reception to the man who rescued the most famous lifeboat in Norfolk history. Hundreds welcome benefactor Peter Cadbury as he arrives to give the legendary *H.F. Bailey III* back to the town. Mr Cadbury, who bought the *Bailey* at auction four months ago, inches his way through the crowds for his first glimpse of the boat, now completely restored, on the promenade. Relatives of several seafarers saved by the *Bailey* are among those acclaiming Mr Cadbury's generosity in paying £15,000 to buy her for Cromer Lifeboat Museum.

August 31 – Sunny day out at Sandringham where I open the fête at Park House, Princess Diana's birthplace and now an impressive country hotel for the disabled. A real pleasure to see a face from my youthful past: Ruth Butcher, a popular figure on the Swaffham Methodist Circuit when I was a lad, strolls over to say hello. She now runs a home for retired preachers in Minehead.

September

September 8 – I head for Italy on a trip organised by Radio Norfolk. A smooth flight all the way to Bologna, but then comes the first hitch as our bus turns up nearly an hour late. First impressions of Florence after dark are of a laid-back community who take noise and speed as necessary ingredients of life at any time.

September 9 – Florence, with so much history and culture, is just made for tourists. It accepts the role with relish, and it makes me wonder if anyone goes to the boring old office for work in an orthodox manner. All ages on those scooters and motorbikes haring up and down the narrow streets. Statues and pigeons abound with camera-clicking tourists all around in the sunshine.

September 11 – From Florence to Sienna and it turns into a real magic roundabout! Our Italian driver makes a few unscheduled diversions so we're late at our hotel. Delightful off-the-cuff remarks to lift laughter above petty moaning on the bus: 'Thass it – he thought the instructions said Vienna!' and 'Talk about spaghetti junction!' vied for top honours.

September 13 – Friday 13 lives up to its reputation with one of the most bizarre episodes I can recall anywhere. We spend most of the day in Assisi in the middle of the massive tourist industry built about St Francis – the man who renounced material wealth and became famous for looking after the natural world. How he would hate this huge bazaar! Down to Lower Assisi in a hotel more like an Army barracks. Centre-piece of our dramatic session is a meal punctuated by thunder, lightening and short power cuts. At the other end of the room monks are busy with their meal – and it's almost a disappointment when they fail to start chanting. Iris Murdoch might have written this scene, although some of our party suggest, rather irreverently, that we're all part of a 'Carry On' film revival.

September 17 – History lessons come to life as we journey deep into Rome's glorious past: St Peter in Chains, with the wonderful sculpture of Moses by Michelangelo; the Coliseum, which defies your imagination not to run riot; St Paul's Basilica, virtually rebuilt after the great fire of 1823.

September 18 – To the papal audience in the Vatican, a spectacle of outstanding proportions, even if it does border on the bizarre and banal at times. As a party we are welcomed as 'pilgrims from Norfolk', and it's good to get a mention among an international gathering of many thousands. Several parties sing in response to the papal greeting, and there's an element of the Eurovision Song Contest about the proceedings. I earn a ticking-off for wondering aloud if we can reply with *Hev Yew Gotta Loight, Papa?*

September 21 – Back home in Norfolk just before 6a.m. and hardly time to catch up with much-needed sleep before a busy day unfolds. It is Danny's fifth birthday and he wakes me to open cards and presents with the expected relish. I catch up with all his news about starting school while I was away in Italy.

September 27 – Presentation time at Yaxham Village Hall. The Best-Run Village Hall stakes winners and finalists are on parade. It's the third competition and I savour the chance to salute those who work so hard and so willingly for their local communities. A total of 66 halls took part. Old Catton, Reedham and Yaxham take main honours this time.

October

October 1 – Cromer Railway Station looks like a bomb-site as work continues on the new supermarket alongside. I watch it rise as I travel each day by train. Currently it's all mess and mayhem in the name of commercial progress – and Norwich continues to be dominated by traffic and the Castle Mall project.

October 3 – A story to sum up the frustrations of rail travel in this area. A commuter who wanted to let the train take the strain says awful service is forcing her back onto the jam-packed roads. When Kathy Swann and her husband Ivor decided to swap city bustle for a country home they thought they could also escape the hassle of traffic congestion. They moved from Costessey to Reedham, right opposite the station, and thought commuting into Norwich would not pose a problem. Now they say delays and cancellations have forced them and other villagers back onto the roads.

October 12 – A happy double on a busy day. First, we head for Banham where I open a fête to mark first birthday celebrations at the village's impressive community centre. We travel home via Kirby Cane, where we drop in for half an hour as Will Baldry greets well-wishers attending his 100th birthday. He sits like some eastern potentate accepting gifts, smiles and congratulations. It is hard not to bow as you step forward. He was a guest on my wireless programme a few days ago.

October 19 – Cromer Cricket Club's centenary dinner at the Cliftonville Hotel on the seafront as rain and wind provide a stormy cocktail. I have the pleasure of proposing a toast to the club, with former captain and fellow Old Hamondian Phil Mindham replying. I look back at what else was happening in 1891, from a horse with bad legs winning the Grand National to controversy caused at Cromer by men being seen near the 'women's portions' of the bathing machines.

October 21 – The Castle Mall in Norwich is a 'once-in-a-century' project which will bring new life to the city, says junior environment minister Robert Key. He says planners and architects have worked together to meet the 'green challenge' of fitting a modern shopping centre into a medieval city without ruining the environment. Well, he's entitled to his opinion!

October 22 – A packed church at Hevingham for the funeral of the Revd Christopher Basil Morgan – and I half expect him to pop up in the pulpit to ask where all these folk had been hiding during his years as rector in the village! A butterfly flutters in the window above our pew as Diane and I pay respects in the church where we were married and our lads christened. We nod agreement when it's claimed Norfolk has lost a true colourful character.

November

November 5 – A soggy Bonfire Night and the rain is needling

down as we walk to Suffield Park School in Cromer for the annual extravaganza. We watch some of it from the shelter of a mobile classroom, but venture out as the wind freshens and the rain relents. Some of my feelings about 'the youngsters of today' are reinforced by the boorish behaviour and unpleasant language of so many as they mill around in the mud. Too many follow similar patterns on the rail trips I take most days.

November 13 – Novelist Salman Rushdie make a surprise appearance at the University of East Anglia. The author, whose book *The Satanic Verses* earned him a sentence of death from Ayatollah Khomeini, is smuggled in half-way into a talk by writer Fay Weldon. The audience gives him a standing ovation as he walks onto the stage to give his first public reading in three years. Tight security surrounds the visit and no one is allowed to leave during his hour-long appearance.

November 23 – Pub bankruptcies are rocketing in Norfolk, leaving a legacy of shuttered pubs and homeless landlords. Big brewers are blamed for charging high rents at a time when demand for beers has dropped.

November 25 – International haulier Norfolk Line is pulling out of Yarmouth after 30 years. It blames bad road and rail links and the unfulfilled promise of an outer harbour for its decision. The biggest operator in the port is moving to Felixstowe, which will mean the loss of more than 140 jobs for Yarmouth and the disappearance of those distinctive blue and white juggernauts from the main roads of Norfolk.

December

December 3 – Local entertainment will never be the same again. The Kipper Family prepare for their final show at Norwich's Maddermarket Theatre. It was on April 1, 1982 when the audience at Norwich Folk Club, then at the York Tavern, were intrigued by the appearance of two odd-looking characters who sidled in and sat at the back during a singers' night. One was a rather unkempt old man with a bushy grey beard, flat cap and walking stick. The other, a menacing figure with a scarred cheek, Brylcreemed hair and an outrageous tie. After listening for a while, the old man asked if he and his boy Sid could sing one of their old songs. They did, and the folk music scene was never the same again. The following year, Henry and Sid were 'discovered' at Sidmouth Folk Festival, and since then they've appeared at clubs and festivals all over Britain, been to Shetland, Jersey and Hong Kong, and made six albums and countless radio appearances. Now Henry is

The Kipper Family, Henry and his boy Sid, take their final bow in harness at Norwich's Maddermarket Theatre.

about to warble his final swansong, leaving Sid to carry on alone in the New Year.

December 14 – Sad news in keeping with the grim weather. John Arlott, the voice of cricket, the voice of summer, dies at 77. He brought the eye and tongue of a poet to the game, and many of my generation still hear him as the most distinctive wireless voice of our time.

December 19 – The new general manager at Norwich Theatre Royal promises that from the start he will be 'on the bowsprit' where the public can see him. Peter Wilson wins the job against 71 other competitors.

December 25 – Danny joins me for a stroll down The Loke to wish Gimi and Jo Jordan a happy 51st wedding anniversary. They have two young ladies from Taiwan staying with them, and we relish the chance to teach them a little bit of Norfolk. International thoughts today dominated by President Gorbachov announcing his resignation after nearly seven years as leader of the Soviet Union. He has changed the course of world history and yet been largely rejected by his own people.

December 27 – Much needed fresh air and exercise after festive excesses. We climb the 'stone mountains' at Salthouse, where the going is bright but bracing. Sad to see so much rubbish along the beach, some of it clearly left behind by seasonal revellers. Back to the car for a gentle run past Cley… twitchers and woolly hats. Blakeney is packed to the rafters with the well-heeled set. Holt is busy and so is Sheringham as we pull in for a cup of tea. Thank goodness we're well away from sales fever and bargain-barmy shoppers!

1992

January

January 2 – The former USAF base at Hardwick, near Long Stratton, is listed as a venue for tourists in a publication by the East Anglian Tourist Board just as Norfolk County Council plans to turn it into a rubbish tip.

January 14 – Norwich Union expects to move about 850 staff from Norwich to Sheffield over the next three years in the biggest relocation programme in Norfolk's history. In terms of sheer numbers, it is the equivalent of transporting the entire workforce of Lawrence Scott & Electromotors out of the city.

William Foster – man of vision.

January 17 – A Norfolk landowner with far-sighted vision for conservation and agriculture dies at 80. William Foster, Lord of the Manor of Litcham and Lexham, was a benefactor in his rural community and strove to maintain employment and social structure in village life. This former High Sheriff of Norfolk bought the Lexham Hall estate in 1946 and set about reviving it. As well as modernising about 40 cottages, Mr Foster planted thousands of trees. He was responsible for leaving Litcham Common to the County Council to become a nature reserve.

January 18 – A fascinating piece of North Norfolk history is discovered in cliffs near Cromer. Experts uncover the bones of an Ice-Age elephant which hold clues to what life was like more than half a million years ago.

January 29 – An evening with the cream of North Norfolk society! I sing for my supper with members of Cromer and Sheringham Rotary Club. I tell of my pride in this county and seek to prove it with Norfolk stories and anecdotes. I'm grateful yet again that a considerable number of people have not heard most of my oldest yarns.

February

February 6 – All eyes on Norfolk as the Queen picks her adopted county for celebrations to mark 40 years as monarch. Sandringham House is a fitting place to remember four decades of rule. As a woman of 25 she succeeded her father George VI who died there on February 6, 1952. More than 500 people cheer the Queen at today's only public appearance at Tapping House in Snettisham, a hospice mainly for people suffering from cancer – the disease that cut short her father's life.

February 8 – Pleasant evening at Aldborough Community Centre as they bid farewell to local doctor Colin Skipper. I am asked to make a surprise appearance with a whimsical *This Is Your Life* item as villagers file in to give thanks. Colin, a distant relative and fellow Old Hamondian, tells his friends that when he went out 18 years ago he didn't lock up his house. 'Tonight I've put on the burglar alarm,' he says as a telling example of how village life has changed since he started his medical rounds.

February 15 – Trip to Dereham and a packed church hall to browse round an exhibition to mark the 50th anniversary of the fall of Singapore. Harrowing memories for many and ghastly images for us all. I can't help playing my own memory game as we stroll around town. Whatever happened to the spruce market town where I spent a couple of years on reporting duty in the 1960s? It's all congestion and rather grubby now. This isn't the first time I've felt like this towards Dereham, a mixture of hostility and sadness.

February 16 – I break new ground as the weather turns wintry, leading a WEA day school at Wensum Lodge in Norwich. *The Norfolk Way* attracts a score of folk anxious to find out more about the county and I feel the session produces some useful results. I look at the obvious development pressures and also size up the value of the dialect and books on local topics. Interruptions and diversions are encouraged, and one woman claims she found it hard to settle in Norwich. I try to avoid too many glib summaries or ready answers to deep-rooted problems, but the use of humour makes it easier to pursue some areas of

George MacBeth – strong Norfolk links.

reasoning. Talking of writers, I note that George MacBeth has died in Ireland at 60. He had strong Norfolk links, living at Oby, near Yarmouth, and latterly in a gaunt Victorian Gothic mansion near King's Lynn.

February 18 – Manny Lake, the man I dubbed 'Lord Mayor of Hockering' dies in a car crash. I first met this colourful character in the early 1960s when I was on the *Dereham and Fakenham Times* and Manny the milkman was a leading light on the local soccer beat with East Tuddenham. We met up again in more recent years on the cricket field. In fact, Manny was one of the umpires for the Neave Plate final at St Andrew's Hospital ground in 1983 when Caister beat Rollesby and I collected the only trophy of my career. I recall a few hearty sessions with Manny as he yarned in the pub in that earthy style which made him notorious.

February 29 – I pick up a copy of *The Countryman* magazine at Norwich railway station, and the latest edition makes some suitably sharp points in its editorial. 'The number of people living in rural areas is rising steadily, but, of course, very few of the newcomers are working on the land or indeed connected to farming in any way at all – except that it makes a nice view from their windows.' Needs to be said!

March

March 10 – An unexpected journey. I thought my trip to Downham Market for a mardle with the local Women's Institute group was booked for my birthday tomorrow – but a telephone call after today's radio programme informs me that all is ready for a session this very evening. It transpires that the error is not on my part, but the sudden news causes a minor panic. I manage to track down my driver Pat Maitland, who just happens to be at home for the afternoon, and he changes his plans to make sure we get there on time.

March 12 – Evening with a difference as I join the bustle at the Hungate Bookshop in Norwich for the launch of D.J. Taylor's latest novel. I chatted to him about *Real Life* on the *Dinnertime Show* yesterday, pointing out that some reviewers were bound to be over-critical in view of his reputation as rather a savage critic. Now the poacher-turned-gamekeeper must put up with acid drops from writers he has lambasted. I have read the book. I have read several reviews. It seems many reviewers regard this whole business as a private game with showing off a priority, rather than give us a reasoned and intelligible summary. There remains an elitist flavour about the book business, although

Taylor is a modest, unassuming chap. One of the guests at this publishing bash is Malcolm Bradbury from the University of East Anglia, the most accessible of academics and keen to talk about Norfolk village life.

March 24 – A woman offers a lift as I leave the house with sharp showers about. She is a truly sensitive soul. 'I won't drop you off at that supermarket you don't like next door to the railway station… I'll leave you near the Methodist church.' Very thoughtful, and it shows how you can get a reputation in this job.

March 25 – Work starts on building the second professional theatre in Norwich. Starved of a large-scale theatrical base for two years, enthusiasts will have the choice of two when the Playhouse opens in 18 months time. The refurbished Theatre Royal is due to reopen at the end of this year.

April

April 9 – Sunshine all the way and the Conservatives sweep to a sensational fourth consecutive general election victory. A high turn-out of over 80 per cent in some constituencies helps John Major back to No.10 Downing Street. The opinion polls are confounded – and that's no bad thing. In Norfolk, John Garrett remains the Labour Party's only MP in the county. He increases his majority in Norwich South.

April 11 – Pilgrims at a world-famous religious shrine are asked to use less holy water as drought hits the eleventh-century holy well at Walsingham. The well has already been deepened after threatening to run dry in the drought.

April 12 – Norfolk boxing legend Ginger Sadd dies at 78. His most famous fight was in 1939 when he narrowly missed winning the British middleweight title in a bout against Jock McAvoy. Ginger lost on points over 15 rounds but was given an emotional reception by a crowd of over 2000 on his return home to Norwich.

April 15 – Another sporting strand is cut with the death of Norwich City Football Club's long-serving groundsman Russell Allison at 68. He tended the Carrow Road pitch for over 40 years. He was head groundsman from 1946 until he officially retired in 1989, but carried on part-time. Before he took over his father Russell completed a 28 year stint which

Russell Allison.

KEITH SKIPPER'S NORFOLK DIARIES

began at The Nest. In March, 1989, Russell retired, leaving his son, Russ to become the fourth member of the family to hold the post. Russell's brother Roy also did the job for 25 years. Russell will be remembered as a rough-and-ready character who touched his forelock to no one and seemed reluctant to let players muck up the pitch it had taken him so much skill and patience to prepare!

April 18 – Tributes to a 150-year nautical life-saving tradition flood in as Sheringham's off-shore lifeboat launches into retirement. Hundreds of spectators wave farewell as the town's relief lifeboat *Lloyds II*, slips into the waves to answer the boom of maroons and sails for Lowestoft. Even as the boat leaves the crowds welcome its replacement, a 21ft Atlantic inshore inflatable.

April 25 – Reflective weekend after the deaths of comedians Frankie Howerd and Benny Hill. And we've lost another much-loved comic with the closure of the *Punch* magazine. In this case, it appears to have been retribution for trying to 'widen appeal' and aim for a younger audience. A lesson, perhaps, to the *Eastern Daily Press* whose circulation figures are down after a prolonged period of trendy competitions and so-called improvements.

May

May 10 – A day to wallow in memories with a Hamond's Grammar School reunion lunch at Swaffham. Before the food, a heady swig of nostalgia, peeking into the old classrooms, opening the door to what used to be Major Besley's study, finding the physics lab just as you left it. Does this clock move as slowly as the one in there over 30 years ago?

May 12 – Now here's a surprise – the county's top planner is worried about the way Norfolk is going. Martin Shaw, director of planning and property, warns that development and population growth has created a 'downward ecological spiral' that is threatening Norfolk's special environment. He says the county council is determined to set a ceiling on future growth. He appeared to dismiss such things as alarmist a few years ago when I chatted with him on Radio Norfolk. Good to know that those at the top eventually see the light!

May 14 – Police reveal that one school in Norfolk is broken into every day. Schools are being urged to be more vigilant to beat intruders who cost them thousands of pounds. This week, four schools in the Dereham area have been raided.

May 20 – The £14.8 million Trowse by-pass is opened to bring peace to a village which has been used to 20,000 vehicles a day pounding past. Delighted residents hold a street party.

May 21 – At last! Someone has the courage and vision to call for curbs on the car. The Countryside Commission reckons they should be banned from East Anglia's traffic-clogged tourist villages and beauty spots. It is to push local authorities to create car-free zones as part of a programme to encourage visitors in rural areas.

May 27 – Veteran Norfolk craftsman Oliver Meek, whose hand-made baskets were bought by people from all over the world, dies at 96. A familiar pipe-smoking figure he spent 60 years at his Swaffham workshop and his death signals the end of an era. The family have been basket makers for eight generations, but Oliver had no children to continue his centuries-old skill.

May 31 – Visit to Sheringham Park for a reminder of Humphrey Repton's glorious handiwork. Rhododendrons are rioting and visitors are swarming along the colourful paths. An enchanting final call on our family holiday rounds.

June

June 3 – Danny joins me in Cromer Parish Hall for a memorable session with the Eastern Angles Theatre Company on their 10th anniversary tour. They present *When The Boats Came In*, the story of the rise and fall of the herring industry along our coast. Four actors cover the years in a whole multitude of characters with great skill and colour. The songs are catchy, the memories vibrant, and it's good to see a big audience for this production. Danny insists on buying a tape to remind him of the songs.

June 9 – Norfolk countryman Ted Eales dies after a lifetime spent sharing his passion with people round the world. He was 73 and best known for his appearances on Anglia Television's *Countryman* series. He was also one of the first wildlife cameramen on Anglia's world-famous *Survival* programmes. He was born in the Coastguard station in Morston, overlooking the Blakeney Point National Trust reserve, and followed in his father's footsteps to work as summer warden for 35 years.

June 10 – What a long, hard day! Down to the casualty department at Cromer Hospital by 6a.m. because of a troubled left eye. Danny accidentally poked his finger in it when

1992

Ted Eales – followed in his father's footsteps.

he stretched up to say goodnight. How pleasant to walk the streets before they are aired. I have a badly scratched cornea and will have to wear a patch over the eye. That gets the 'Nelson' and 'Long John Silver' brigades going at work. I struggle on and then head for St George's Theatre in Yarmouth to host an evening of Norfolk entertainment as part of the town's festival week. The Bolshoi Ballet is playing at the Royalty Theatre on the front – so we have plenty of competition in a town where it is notoriously difficult to attract audiences.

June 27 – Colkirk in the sun for the village fête in the grounds of the old rectory – where a bouncy castle greets those coming out of the house. An appealing old-fashioned flavour with plenty of competitions to join in and stalls scattered around. Danny is thrilled to be involved in a play-off for the junior golf crown with Adam. They both score four, and then, with his last swipe of the decider our boy lands a three – and his first major title on the fête scene.

June 28 – Up at 2.30a.m. to join Danny and friend Pat Maitland on an eagerly-awaited safari to Surlingham. Dawn is breaking as we arrive at the Ted Ellis Nature Reserve, Wheatfen Broad, for a walk of over three miles through the misty world of nature. What a contrast after taking the new road carved through countryside on the outskirts of Norwich. Now we savour the peace, the timeless charm of one of the few remaining areas of the once-extensive Yare Valley

Swamp. David Bellamy says Wheatfen Broad is in its way as important as Mount Everest or the giant redwood forests of North America. Ted's widow Phyllis still lives in Wheatfen Cottage, and she provides us with breakfast at 5.30a.m. after our trek. The queen of nature emerges from her slumbers without teeth and wonders where her glasses are. She chatters constantly without hearing much in return as she fries up new potatoes and mixes scrambled eggs. The sun is starting to find power as we leave Wheatfen, renew acquaintance with those dreadful new roads and reach Cromer before 8a.m.

July

July 2 – Second day of the Norfolk Show. I look at drastic changes being made around the Costessey showground in the name of traffic. I can't raise much beyond a wry smile as I spy this headline in the *Eastern Daily Press*: 'Bypass cuts into lovely countryside.' This refers to work at Narborough, where we are assured 'every effort is being made to ensure the by-pass lives in harmony with its beautiful surroundings.' At least these matters are being discussed these days, even if the feeling persists that the same basic rules apply – it's just useful now to keep the environmental lobby a bit happier.

July 8 – Workmen unearth a time capsule containing coins, documents and newspapers dating back more than 100 years as they demolish a Victorian temperance hall. The finds date back to 1875 and are discovered behind the foundation stone of the hall in Shipdham. A copy of the Norfolk News is among items in a glass bottle. They also include one of the order of service for the opening ceremony and a poster advertising the new hall.

July 15 – An intriguing close-up on the holiday scene as I join friends on a trip to Rosie O'Grady's bar in Yarmouth. We are here to salute entertainer Johnny Cleveland. The bar is part of the Royalty complex, and The Grumbleweeds and Rod Hull and his dastardly Emu are performing in the theatre. Over the road at the Britannia Pier comedians Cannon and Ball are being forced to cancel some shows because of a shortage of ready customers.

July 20 – Solicitors are being made redundant as the chill wind of recession blows through the legal profession in East Anglia. It is the smaller and medium-sized firms where the draught is being felt most. There have been redundancies in the domestic conveyancing department of a number of firms over the last few years.

July 23 – Colmans of Norwich is to shed up to 200 jobs over three years and dispose of about half of its 90-acre Carrow site. The moves are part of a £15 million investment programme which they say will guarantee the company's future. The food and drinks giant hopes to achieve job losses through natural wastage.

July 25 – Long trip to Wortwell for the grand opening of the village's community centre. It has been a long haul to this proud day. Last time we were here it rained on the village fête. Today it is hot and sticky as proud locals congregate in their splendid new building. I snip the ribbon and unveil a plaque.

July 28 – The Queen Mother launches the electrification of the railway to King's Lynn and forecasts it will be 'a great boon' to West Norfolk. She praises the transformation of Lynn station and tells British Rail Chairman Sir Bob Reid she considers BR breakfasts 'the best in the world'.

August

August 2 – I'm back in Bodham to open the village fête at the end if this lively community's week of events. Only blot on a happy rural scene is the constant noise of traffic along the road that cuts the village in two. They have managed to get a speed limit after a vigorous campaign, but it's still unnerving at this time of year.

August 11 – Death at 90 of May Burrell, one of Beeston's most colourful characters of the century. Auntie May was a formidable figure during my childhood with her abrupt and forceful manner, and I gather little changed over the years. A nurse, she returned to the village to look after her mother – and the rest of the community! She laid 'em out, helped bring 'em in and dominated the scene on her sit-up-and-beg bike. I last had a brief mardle with her on a visit to the school fête. It wasn't long after that she took a tumble and had to slow down. May spent her last days in a nursing home at Tittleshall. She was a classic example of someone whose bark was much worse than her bite. She constantly did good turns and passed on useful advice.

August 15 – Start of a family break in the Cotswolds as Cromer braces itself for carnival capers. Our long journey is lit up by news of Norwich City's amazing recovery against Arsenal at Highbury as the new season kicks off. The Canaries are 2–0 down at half-time, but they win 4–2 to provide the biggest shock of opening day.

August 16 – One of the best lines to savour for a long time in an Alan Bennett play on television. Talking about a woman with no sense of humour: 'She could only see a joke by appointment!' Must make a note of these little gems as they crop up. You can't remember them all.

August 17 – Pleasant session in Gloucester looking round the cathedral as it prepares for the famous *Three Choirs Festival.* On to an Arthurian exhibition with brass rubbings, moody music and Celtic mists. Gloucester seems in reasonable shape with few empty shops. I'm surprised at the vigour of this place after so many depressing strolls through Norwich in recent months. Our holiday cottage in Randwick on the edge of Painswick, affords splendid views and we all perch in front of the bedroom window to enjoy them. Even after dark the Cotswold world continues to call, twinkling lights strung out across your imagination and a near-silence you wish you could wrap up and take home.

August 19 – Day of contrasts along the tourist trail. We take narrow and winding roads to the Roman villa at Chedworth. Onwards to Bourton-on-the-Water, with a veritable babel of holiday-makers. It's like one large picnic site ringed by shops, blatantly geared to the tourist trade. I wonder how on earth the locals can stand it. This is the perfect example of what Norfolk must avoid, and I wish those who keep on shoving the bandwagon would size up this sort of extremism.

August 24 – Back in Norfolk to learn that colonies of bats are invading churches across the county. They are leaving trails of droppings and urine across pews, hymn books, Bibles and altars. One congregation comes up with the idea of a decoy owl to scare them away. Norwich Castle Museum bat specialist John Goldsmith says: 'It is all very well to say they should go elsewhere, but bats are running out of places to go.'

August 26 – Grand day out at Gressenhall at the Norfolk Rural Life Museum. We take a long walk around Union Farm, with sheep, pigs, cattle, rabbits, turkeys, hens, goats and heavy horses all on parade. We watch a wagonload of straw being carted home the old-fashioned way. I'm transported back to childhood when all fields looked and felt like this. Over to the impressive museum packed with exhibits and memories of a farming scene all but swept away by mechanisation. There's an eerie quality about all this... I can recognise so much mothballed here from my past.

August 28 – Our final expedition of this family holiday – and another big contrast. A call at Burnham Thorpe, Nelson's birthplace, to take a look round the Parish Church where his father was rector. Serene, restful, a delightful corner –

1992

An old-fashioned harvest.

all these come to mind as wind rustles the trees outside and local women prepare for the flower festival indoors. Back to the modern mainstream for a late lunch in Hunstanton, followed by a paddle and a spot of shell collecting before the tide comes in. We have bought some plums on our way through the Burnhams and the hedgerows are dripping with ripening blackberries. Just needs a mist or two to bring early autumn on stage.

September

September 1 – September dawns brightly – but British Rail is off colour. I stroll to catch my train in Cromer and resume normal service only to be told it's been cancelled. A Sander's coach is on the way. A long trip in the sun, following all the railway stops into Norwich. Not so easy to read or to concentrate on anything while travelling by bus, so I satisfy myself with a constant gaze over the country-side. Fields yawning with stubble, cattle minding their own business and villages wearing largely contented looks. Home by train, though, to be met by Diane and the lads.

September 13 – Long Stratton pensioner Dolly Howard refuses to let a broken ankle prevent her celebrating her 60th anniversary as organist at St Michael's Church. She is pushed down the aisle in a wheelchair, her leg encased in plaster, to take her familiar place at the organ. She is presented with a framed painting of the church.

September 14 – Memorable evening at the Old Tyme Music Hall at the end of Cromer Pier. Roy Hudd, one of the most

amiable and talented fellows in the business, leads a sell-out week after the summer show season. He pays cheerful tribute to some of the great characters of music hall such as Max Miller and his love of that era shines through a programme that deserves such support.

September 19 – Final family trek of the summer to Gayton, near King's Lynn. I open the two-day fair organised to raise money for a new Village Hall. After yesterday's storms and a flooded car park, they make some alterations but the weather cheers up sufficiently to bring encouragement. Jenny is the only entrant for the fancy dress competition – and collects £10 worth of book tokens for turning up as Wee Willie Winkie.

September 23 – The water shortage continues despite heavy rain. Water chiefs say the downfall, hard on the heels of last week's storms, will replenish rivers and reservoirs but will not make much impression on the shortage caused by three years of below-average rainfall.

October

October 7 – A dramatic and welcome breakthrough. I have a call from Granada Television to help with a script for a programme featuring Norfolk characters. I am so pleased to show them the difference between the way we talk and how our friends in the West Country do it! Could this spell the beginning of the end for the dastardly 'Mummerzet' to which we have been subjected so often in national productions on radio and television?

October 13 – This is what autumn should be like. Frost overnight soon disappears on a bright, crisp morning. It stays like this all day. Such a pity to waste it indoors in the city. How much better it would be to head for Cley marshes or the Burnhams or anywhere in the countryside where changing colours can be lit by autumn sunshine.

October 14 – Actress Joanna Lumley breezes into the Dolphin pub in Cromer and hands over a cheque for £1.5 million to a ten-strong pools syndicate. They all say the windfall will not affect their lives, and most of them put a new car at the top of the wish list.

October 16 – A late stint in Norwich for a Radio 2 arts programme from Blackfriars Hall spotlighting the city festival. I chat with playwright Arnold Wesker, who is writing the play to open the new Norwich Playhouse. We examine his close links with Norfolk and the sad lack of authentic local accents whenever *Roots* or other plays with a Norfolk flavour are staged. Author Malcolm Bradbury and Theatre Royal manager Peter Wilson are among other guests – but undoubted star of the show is Sid Kipper with his rural repartee and stirring anthems such as *Norfolk 'n' Good*.

October 22 – Another national appearance, this time on a Radio 4 programme being broadcast from the Waterfront Music Centre in Norwich. I try to make a few salient points in the minute or so allowed. I am one of several invited to talk about the city's traffic problems, with special reference to current plans to rip out more of Norwich's historic heart.

October 28 – Is this the eve of a *Poppyland* revival? Well, Clement Scott's book from over a century ago is being reprinted along with *Poppyland* postcards from the early days of the North Norfolk cult. I'll put the book on my festive list, but the postcards do seem a trifle too garish, too crimson to be true. It would be a fascinating exercise to place Scott in the area as it is today and ask him what influence he might have had in shaping it!

November

November 8 – Remembrance Sunday. Morning stroll with Danny along the seafront. The pier is having a face-lift but there's still access. An old man with a limp, a stick and a poppy sits with his wife, their hands entwined on a day full of memories. At the coming in of the tide, we shall remember them.

November 16 – The new look Theatre Royal in Norwich reopens after more than two years in the dark. It has taken £3.75 million to transform the fading star into a glittering lady. This week acts as an overture for the grand official opening on November 24. This evening the Syd Lawrence Orchestra strikes up with a special appearance from Syd himself. Tomorrow marks the 25th anniversary of the founding of the band.

November 20 – Death of Jim Smellie, the Norfolk public health officer who gained national acclaim for having such an apt name for the job. A native of Lancashire, he gained recognition in the national press, in *Punch* and on Esther Rantzen's *That's Life* show because of his name. He moved to East Anglia in 1949 and became chief public health officer for Norfolk in 1960. After his retirement he went into partnership with son Richard – raising pigs in Costessey.

November 21 – The statue of Norfolk nursing heroine Edith Cavell takes up its new resting place next to Norwich cathedral, where she was buried in 1919. The bronze bust of the Swardeston-born nurse was originally unveiled by Queen Alexandra, in Tombland, but years of fumes and city grime left it unrecognisable and the memorial plaque unreadable. It has taken just two weeks for stonemasons Andrew Bygrave and Alistair Aitken to restore the bust and stone plinth to its former glory.

November 27 – The Queen reveals Norfolk is her favourite county as she meets a party of local schoolchildren. Speaking to pupils from Dereham Neatherd High School as they receive a national award for environment work, she asks if they are from Dereham in Norfolk. On learning that they were, she said she was delighted as it was her favourite place, especially with Sandringham being there. One pupil, 16-year-old Helen Williams says: 'I was really surprised when she let it slip about Norfolk – but I agree with her!'

December

December 7 – Parish councils in Norfolk back a move to force district and county councils to consult them on more issues. And they want the more powerful councils to have to set down their reasons whenever they go against the parish view. They also want a ban on councillors sitting on more than one authority, saying they have fears of divided loyalties under the present system. It all makes sense, but I doubt if it will come to anything.

December 10 – Norfolk's bluebell-carpeted woodlands are

under threat from gangs of poachers who have turned the region into a million-pound centre for the illegal sale of stolen wild flower bulbs. Hundreds of thousands of them, including bluebells, snowdrops and rare orchids, are sold illegally in the region each year.

December 12 – Chance to catch a whiff of the festive season with a visit to Ashwellthorpe Parish Church for a Midwinter Festival of Words and Music. Radio Norfolk colleagues Tony Cleary and Lynn McKinney, along with the Taverham Singers and Ashwellthorpe Ensemble, join me for an evening concert followed by coffee and mince pies. A cold setting but a warm glow.

December 15 – Strange, but whenever I utter any criticisms of Norwich I'm told invariably that this is unfair; the city remains much better than most others. I can't accept that as a reasonable argument. I am not making comparisons with Leeds, Derby, Stoke or Cambridge. I am drawing attention to the way Norwich has changed and is changing – and it's all too fast for comfort.

December 24 – Christmas Eve begins with an extra journey along the North Norfolk coast after heavy overnight frost. I board the train at Cromer – but it's behind schedule and so we have to go to Sheringham first before heading for the city. Norfolk is like a giant Christmas pudding as the sun draws the frost and it all mixes with smoke curling from homes huddling together for warmth.

December 25 – The boys defy all traditions by letting us sleep until 8 o'clock – but there's not much rest for the remainder of Christmas Day! Danny gets his big globe and microscope and both boys are overwhelmed by the number of presents to unravel after breakfast. I am perched comfortably in a new study chair as I write these notes. The best-kept secret of the season was the storing away upstairs of my main present.

December 27 – Sad news – death of my old press colleague and mentor Ted Bell. He was sports editor when I joined the sports staff in the late 1960s and a leading light in Rackheath Players when he persuaded me to join up and tread the boards again. Ted was a very gentle man, invariably smiling, softly spoken and ready to think the best of everyone. He was a fine craftsman, an editor who could set a grand example with his writing and able to coax the best out of colleagues simply because we liked him so much.

Ted Bell – a fine craftsman.

◆　◆　◆

January

January 4 – Real winter arrives with heavy snow spreading from the west to blanket Cromer as I crunch and sink my way to the railway halt. Troubles with points, especially at Wroxham, add an hour to the journey. Much of the snow has turned to a grey, messy pulp by the time I head for home.

January 14 – Chance to preach the Norfolk gospel to a 'live' audience with a talk to the Fakenham Society. Their president Sir Harry Tuzo is stung by my comments about the Norfolk Society 'coming down from the mountain to attract ordinary mortals'. After my chat and coffee, there's a lively debating session with several newcomers leading the way. A woman who moved from Essex tells me she 'wakes up with joy in her heart every morning'. Most agree that what they left behind must not be allowed to move on and spoil the best remaining parts of this country.

January 24 – Windows rattle and dustbin lids go bowling down the street as gale force gusts persist all night and provide several reminders throughout the day. As we head for the 40th anniversary of the great east coast floods disaster, this wind brings a lot of grim memories.

January 25 – Villagers at Stiffkey celebrate as their red phone box is saved from the BT axe. A chorus of complaints persuaded them the box should be preserved – and it will get a facelift into the bargain.

January 27 – A modest American hero of the 1953 floods looks across at the sea at Hunstanton and exclaims: 'Boy, it's so cold here!' Reis Leming left four-and-a-half feet of snow when he set off from Oregon. He's remembered by many for saying 'Shucks, it wasn't much' after saving 27 lives. Now he concentrates on talking about the weather and changes in Hunstanton since 1953 rather than his heroics in the town during the floods.

February

February 2 – Now and again a letter leaps out of the *Eastern Daily Press* to demand close attention. Today, K. Sorensen of Foulsham gives me food for thought about the way our county has changed since I was a boy. He says we are now reaping what we sowed in the 1950s… 'Soil became drenched in artificial fertilisers and poisonous sprays to give quicker and ever-increasing yields. Farmers became chemists and forgot what real living soil is like. Village communities were decimated by so-called progress. Big business and greed took over while farming communities disappeared into urban housing estates, commuted every day to new industrial estates created by local authorities. I do not remember many voices then crying: 'Halt, we must preserve our rural life and communities!' Oh yes, we could have preserved it, if we had wanted to. If we had gone for a way of life, rather than quick profits, by going for smallholdings, small farms, smaller machines, less mechanisation, fewer poisons and more working of the soil, we could have accommodated our people on the land.' A letter packed with pertinent points.

February 14 – I compere *Hello Chatterbox* at the Norwich Theatre Royal as Doreen Donnelly's reign as producer ends amid hearts and flowers on St Valentine's Day. She has organised the show for 13 years and helped make a lot of money for the Norwich talking newspaper for the blind.

February 18 – A strange day, but a satisfying one. An American journalist, Tony Horwitz of the *Wall Street Journal*, telephones me at work. He's over here doing a story about villages where the pub is shut – and he's calling from Beeston. We chat about the Plough and other aspects of village life in that area. Eventually he decides to drive to Cromer to have a look at my old Norfolk directories. I find myself considering matters I hadn't thought about in years. It takes a stranger and his pointed questions to draw attention to important aspects of the Norfolk debate.

February 20 – Another host of memories surface as we head for a splendid exhibition of old photographs put on by Litcham Historical Society. We join Ron and Brenda Shaw at their grand little village museum. As I gaze and mardle, representatives from several villages call in to pay their rural respects.

February 23 – Mileham baker Frank Minister is being forced to close his family-run business because he cannot afford to modernise the traditional bakery. New European Community regulations spell the end of an era for the family, which has been baking bread for locals for more than half a century.

Plenty to enjoy in the village museum at Litcham.

March

March 3 – Hints that the recession could be ending come with the news that Norwich-based joinery firm Bolton & Paul has returned to a five-day week. The company, which supplies joinery for new housing developments, has suffered badly from the downturn in the building industry and has had to make hundreds of staff redundant. The Lowestoft factory went on a four-day week in November, but now an increase in sales puts the 350 workers back on full-time.

March 11 – My 49th birthday celebrations begin with a visit to the doctor's surgery in Cromer as my ears continue to give trouble. My attendance is eagerly seized upon by a nurse who gives me a tetanus injection and a general MOT before I see Dr Ding about my lugs!

March 16 – I find a tonic in the annual Norfolk dialect get-together in the WI Hall in Cromer. Danny makes his debut, but I ask organiser Jason Bell to sort out comments and a certificate for him. Can't have too many cries of 'nepotism!'

March 22 – Hooray! Public pressure kills off a flock of stone sheep earmarked for Norwich's Castle Mall park. They were to have provided a target for youngsters to clamber over and slide down as part of a specially built play area. But the developers admit they have dropped the idea following a spate of complaints from the public.

March 28 – Family outing to Salhouse Broad. A packed car park tells us this is a popular spot to exercise the dog or just take the air. A black swan is one of the takers as bread rations come out.

March 30 – Danny joins me for another outing to see Eastern Angles touring theatre company in *Beneath The Waves*, a new play about the 1953 floods along the east coast. Mummerzet accents the only disappointment for a full house at Cromer High School.

April

April 2 – Long haul to Wisbech for a dinner with the town's Rotary Club. We are housed in a large marquee at the rear of the Queen's Hotel, and I keep waiting for the bride's father to get to his feet to propose a toast! Former *Eastern Daily Press* reporter George Wells, who looked after this patch with distinction, has furnished me with background details about leading local luminaries, and my mardle seems to be well received. As we journey into Fenland, I notice how scruffy King's Lynn is around the edges. And where there are no hedges or trees, where the wind runs free and cold, a feeling of grim survival is paramount.

April 13 – After more than 500 years the whole of historic Dragon Hall in Norwich is open to the public for the first time. Builders and craftsmen have been busy restoring old cellars and vaulted undercroft in the way they must have looked in the fifteenth century. Work still has to be done on the great cloth trading hall upstairs.

April 15 – The auctioneer's hammer falls on the final lot at Acle market to mark the end of an era. Waters & Son, a weekly feature there since 1921, hold their last sale, leaving rivals Howlett & Edrich to carry on the tradition alone. The two firms have been a focus for thousands of buyers and sellers over the past 70 years, turning Acle into a thriving commercial centre every Thursday. But now Andrew Waters, owner of Waters & Son, is selling off the remaining two and a half acres of his land for building. He says: 'The EC restrictions mean we can no longer sell foam furniture or certain sorts of electrical goods and our trade has been affected'.

April 26 – A treat at the Theatre Royal in Norwich with a production of Sean O'Casey's *Juno and the Paycock*, a potent mixture of comedy and tragedy and terrible echoes of family, community and country being torn apart. This is our first 'proper' visit since the theatre's transformation. The authentic Irish cast are outstanding, with Mark Lambert as the conniving, scruffy, scheming Joxer, a clear winner for me in the personality stakes.

April 27 – Mark Lambert, alias Joxer Daly, joins me on the radio. He likes cricket and books – so there's no real hardship in having a chat! Both his grandfather and father played cricket for Ireland, grandfather coming up against W.G. Grace. His father also played rugby for Ireland and was a rugby referee at international level. Mark points out he is not able to play the game because actors are not allowed to put their profession in such dire dangers.

April 30 – That eerie fog has gone. Wonder what the bank holiday tourists would have made of that! Rural crime very much in the news. It's being claimed that many are frightened to complain too loud in case reprisals are swift and nasty. I take up these points with a couple of retired police officers on my radio programme from King's Lynn. I find little comfort in assurances that Norfolk remains one of the safest places in which to live. I still make my comparisons with the Norfolk I knew 30 or 40 years ago.

May

May 10 – Norfolk dialect lives! The *Eastern Daily Press* has conducted one of its occasional surveys to show many adults have a strong command of our distinctive local vocabulary. Children fared better than expected with Thetford pupil Amy Chrystal scoring 17 out of 20. International language expert Professor Peter Trudgill, who hails from Norwich, says the survey confirms there is a future for the Norfolk dialect. 'Norfolk people will always be speaking in a way which distinguishes them from London and the Midlands.' This is a timely boost to the campaign to keep our vernacular vibrant, especially in the face of dire liberties taken with it on national television and radio.

May 14 – Brenda, Doris and Maureen put the smile back on Mileham's face, even though Joyce can't make it because she's covering a local funeral for the paper. Yes, the country's most unwelcoming village – according to *Country Life* a few months ago – has been in the spotlight this week on my *Dinnertime Show*. The girls who come in emphasise how the place has changed and grown with newcomers from Kent, Essex and London. A pity they are not represented here although it's agreed many of them have made an effort to join in various activities. That hideous local

label stuck on Mileham by a magazine intent on making wild generalisations to inspire outrageous headlines can hardly have helped the Norfolk cause.

May 22 – Down sunswept lanes to open little Suffield's first festival of arts and crafts, exhibits shared between the Village Hall and Parish Church. After the opening ceremony conducted on a trailer carefully covered to hide the creosote, I take a lift on a lovely old steam engine to the church. 'If we all travelled at this speed, there wouldn't be any accidents,' chuckles the driver. Teas are served in the churchyard where you can enjoy glorious views of the rolling countryside. Suffield is well spread out, but there's an obvious closeness about this small community and its aims.

May 27 – Norfolk's first alterative energy site has become a top tourist attraction. Coachloads of trippers are flocking to see the 30m high white turbines set up last December. But villagers living close to the windfarm at Somerton claim sightseers are jamming the narrow country lanes and ruining their peaceful weekends. One local asks: 'How long before there'll be hot dog stalls and ice cream stands?'

June

June 1 – Former Chief Constable of Norfolk Peter Ryan launched a fierce attack on the judicial system, claiming some lawyers 'could not prosecute their way out of a paper bag'. On his last official engagement in the county he rounds on the 'bureaucratic judicial system' which he says encourages lawyers to created defences for their clients based on technicalities.

June 2 – Rain right on cue to go with a flood of memories about the coronation 40 years ago today. It rained then – and we heard it on the wireless!

June 11 – Archie Macaulay, the manager who inspired Norwich City's greatest FA Cup feats, dies at 77. He took over at Carrow Road in April, 1957, with the task of breathing new life into a club which had finished bottom of the Third Division South and was forced to apply for re-election to the Football League. In the 1957/58 season, City finished eighth to earn a place in the new Third Division. The following season remains the most famous in Canary history as Macaulay's giant killers achieved national recognition by reaching the FA Cup semi-finals. He completed his transformation of Canary fortunes the following year when the club finished second in the table to gain promotion to the Second Division.

June 12 – Flying off to Southern Ireland for a few days, joining a 40-strong party on a gardening tour. Smooth flight to Cork and then we travel westwards to Bantry Bay via Kinsale. This is the heart of Cork tourist country but they still know how to use space.

June 13 – Relentless rain as we visit the Creagh Gardens of Skibbereen, where the owner, Peter Harold Barry, has been working since 1945. Over 80, his wife and daughter gone, this tall old man wonders out loud about the future as we trudge past him through woodlands sloping down to the sea estuary. Ireland does not have a National Trust, and he's clearly concerned about a world of change and theme parks. Rain still falling as we clamber aboard the boat for Garnish Island, a delightful spot I first visited on a trip here in 1965.

June 17 – Back to Norfolk basics. An evening meeting in Cromer WI Hall to discuss the future of the Sheringham–Norwich railway line. No guarantees as privatisation looms, but a brave bid to make sense of the present by regional manager Barrie Thomas.

June 19 – Saturday outing to Morley, near Wymondham, to officially open the new Village Hall amid cries of anguish over another break-in during the week. It's the second recent spate of trouble, costing nearly £1000 altogether. We shake our heads, recall Norfolk times when such things simply did not happen and salute those who have worked so hard to bring this scheme to reality. Last night, chairman Tony Finon slept in the hall, the sort of protective role that sends more despair than admiration through a community.

June 26 – Death at 78 of Jack Gaskin of Hindringham, local preacher, baker and raconteur. Jack lit up countless chapels with his humour and uncluttered faith, while I got to know him best when he took part in the annual dialect celebration at Cromer. Jack invariable ambled over the time limit, but no one minded. He told stories rich in anecdote, many of them collected on his bread delivery rounds. I marvelled that he managed to get home at all!

June 28 – The curtain falls on the Wymondham Regal Cinema after nearly 60 years. Film-lovers and town residents flock to the 276-seat building to watch its grand finale. Manager Les King says he could no longer compete with Norwich cinemas. It was still using the same projection equipment as in 1937 when the first picture show starred Ginger Rogers in *Springtime*.

July

July 1 – Television personality David Bellamy is shunting home his views on railways at Sheringham. The bubbling botanist marks a local line's centenary, standing in front of a hissing steam engine and enthusing: 'What an amazing smell! If they could bottle it as aftershave I might well start using a razor again!' He unveils a specially painted engine and a museum coach, both celebrating the centenary of the founding of the Midland & Great Northern Railway.

July 3 – Evening in a Norfolk paradise to celebrate the award of an honorary MA degree to Charles Roberts, literary and arts editor of the *Eastern Daily Press*. A well-attended capping-out party down Cut-throat Lane in Yaxham is blessed with perfect weather. The setting is beautiful at all times with the village's round-tower church nestling in greenery over the way. Charles, also celebrating 25 years with the *Eastern Daily Press*, has become a fiery convert to the Norfolk survival cause. I spotlight those qualities in particular on being asked to say a few words of thanks on behalf of his guests.

July 7 – Ruth, Lady Fermoy, grandmother of the Princess of Wales and a close friend of the Queen Mother, dies at 84. She founded King's Lynn Festival and was made an honorary freeman of the town for her outstanding contribution to its cultural life. Lady Fermoy organised the first Lynn Festival 43 years ago and her friendship with the Queen Mother led to it enjoying royal patronage. She was a lady-in-waiting for well over 30 years and spent much of her time in the royal circle.

July 14 – A lengthy chat with Radio Norfolk boss Keith Salmon. I ask for a personal hearing after yesterday's staff meeting held while I was on air. There are cuts and changes in the offing. I never cease to be amazed at the way local radio is asked to make more sacrifices even though it is obvious there's no meat left on the bone.

July 18 – A busy weekend. Old Catton Scouts fête yesterday and the opening of Hockering's new playing-field this afternoon. I bowl the first over in a cricket match organised to mark the occasion – and give away just one run to prove the old magic has not dried up completely.

July 31 – Last day of a difficult month, although I am finding useful solace poring over books and jottings in the library at 25 St Mary's Road. What a sanctuary it is proving to be and even the boys are reluctant to break the spell. The sun comes through again in mid-afternoon after another sharp

KEITH SKIPPER'S NORFOLK DIARIES

shower, and I take that as a useful July summary. Life has always been a mixture and you realise how selective memory can be after a prolonged spell of anxiety. Exploitation was going on in Norfolk long before I noticed, and dilution of precious characteristics probably began before the last war. This was the ideal time to read George Orwell's *Coming Up For Air* with its basic text that thou must not seek automatic refuge in the past because the present is rather unpalatable.

August

August 5 – More like November as I make my annual pilgrimage in search of culture at the Mundesley Festival. The wind is howling, white horses are making a cavalry charge out in the North Sea and the general scene is a bleak one. Local entertainment to the fore with a new version of the *Hound of the Baskervilles* going down well. More like a night for Black Shuck.

August 11 – A giant gas tap switched Norfolk and the nation into an undersea energy revolution 25 years ago this week. With the turn of a valve Bacton turned from being a quiet holiday village into Britain's biggest new terminal for North Sea Gas, capable of supplying nearly half of the nation's gas needs. Millions of cubic feet of natural gas now flow daily into homes, hospitals, shops and factories, having been landed and 'cleaned' in Norfolk.

August 14 – Off to the Cotswolds again, this time to Slad and a delightful cottage just a few doors away from *Cider With Rosie* author Laurie Lee. It's an evocative setting down a twisting lane – and is there salad still for tea prepared by a thoughtful Aunt Freda!

August 16 – The Wildfowl and Wetlands Trust haven at Slimbridge is the focal point of today's rounds. A sort of Pensthorpe with bells on, the flamingo taking top spot on the interest list. The lads enjoy feeding time although Danny almost loses his whole supply in one fowl swoop. An over-anxious swan makes sharp inroads into his bag.

August 27 – A packed Norfolk programme to wind up our family holiday fortnight. County School Station at North Elmham our first stop for refreshments and souvenirs. Round and down the lanes through Beetley, Bittering and Beeston before we decide to take a stroll on Litcham Common, now a lovely nature reserve. Guess who is sitting in the car park? Only Aunt Margaret and Uncle Cyril, taking the air before their ruby wedding anniversary. We chuckle at the coincidence, enjoy a mardle and then head

off to seek out more of Norfolk's rural delights.

September

September 4 – A rewarding day. The Nat West cricket final between Sussex and Warwickshire provides rich television entertainment. Well over 600 runs scored – and Warwickshire win on the last ball. I sample the highlights after a grand Norfolk night at the Thursford Collection. We take to the stage to raise money for repairs to the roof of St Andrew's Church in the village.

September 6 – Radio Norfolk boss Keith Salmon tells me my contract is ready for another year – so that's a relief after all the speculation about saving money and cuts. The *Dinnertime Show* carries an extra bounce, and then it's off to the grand opening of Barker's Herne, an Orbit Housing Association development of 30 sheltered flats on the site of the old North Norfolk District Council offices on Holt Road in Cromer. I am billed as 'principal guest', and use the occasion to remind councillors and officers that those lovely old buildings over the road at the railway station must be preserved.

September 12 – A long stint at the Theatre Royal in Norwich to help with a special production of *An Evening with Gary Lineker* in aid of Bryan Gunn's appeal for leukaemia research. Norwich City chairman Robert Chase and manager Mike Walker lead the walk-on parade, while radio colleague Roy Waller and I have commentary roles as substitutions are made to the cast. Over £30,000 is raised.

September 19 – We take advantage of the September sunshine to go blackberry-picking. Where the hedgerows are allowed to blossom there's fruit in good supply, with hips and haws adding to the colour. We are busy round Beckham, Bodham and Gresham, and the juices of childhood run strong as brambles bite and fingers become stained. Traffic is by no means scarce even in remote country lanes these days and we take care to keep Robin well in from the road.

September 21 – A woman who left £80,000 to a Norfolk crematorium is remembered at a special ceremony. Marie Novak was born in Bohemia in 1916 but moved to Norfolk with her husband in 1939 when war broke out. She died in 1984 and left her entire estate to the Mintlyn Crematorium at Lynn.

September 24 – Norwich's Castle Mall shopping complex is open and 40,000 people pile in. The £145 million centre has risen in three and a half years from a huge muddy crater. Only a handful of shops are open to cash in on first-day sales. I'm in no hurry to join the throng – and it's off to the little hall at Cranworth, near Shipdham for the harvest supper.

October

October 1 – The September monsoon carries over into the new month as we head to Sporle for a harvest festival thanksgiving service at the village church. We smile at all references to 'gentle rain' and it lashes down while children sing and recite home-made verses and prayers. I go into the pulpit to share items by George Edwards, Colin Riches and John Kett.

October 2 – Happy day at the old homestead. The boys have a joint birthday party with over a dozen of their young friends piling in for fun and games. Ollie Day, Radio Norfolk colleague and a useful lad to have on your side at such times, puts on his magic show to keep them amused after tea.

October 5 – Tom Cable, one of the Broad's most colourful champions, has died at 82. He was a water bailiff in the area for more than three decades, and in retirement at Ludham he continued his mission to safeguard the waterways through books and letters. An outspoken opponent of speedboats, careless tourists and even the water authorities themselves, he warned constantly that his beloved Broads faced desecration and destruction.

October 9 – Down memory lane to Rackheath Village Hall. Rackheath Players are 40 years old and this is the last of a three-night run of drama, variety and old tyme music hall. I accept an invitation to take the chair on an evening dedicated to the memory of Ted Bell, who did so much to keep the group to the fore. Proceeds tonight go to Ted's favourite charity: Save the Children.

October 12 – Incessant rain lashes down, causing flooding in many areas. If painting were my forte, I'd have a grand time looking across the eerie landscape from my railway seat – lakes on fields and roads turned into gushing rivers. Expanses of water near Wroxham suggest a passion to join the Broads Club, while birds circling above seem unsure where to land.

October 19 – 'Wunderbar!' says the *Eastern Daily Press* front page headline, a tribute to Norwich City's stunning victory in Europe. They become the first English team to beat Bayern Munich on their own ground in European competition. City win the first leg in this UEFA Cup-tie 2–1 with goals from Jeremy Goss and Mark Bowen.

October 30 – On the road to Burnham Market to open the new kitchen at the Village Hall, £20,000 of impressive facilities. Gloomy skies but the autumn colours are glorious and they help to cheer us on our family outing.

November

November 3 – The Canaries taste more European glory. They draw 1–1 with Bayern Munich in the return leg and so go through to the next round. Manager Mike Walker exclaims 'That was one hell of a result! This is the biggest night in the club's history.'

November 6 – Daylight doesn't seem to last long. Leaves are piling up along The Loke and a quick trip to the seafront has as much to do with bravery as habit. Some of the local shops wear a rather sullen look despite early attempts at festive trimmings. Perhaps the recession will hold back the inevitable commercial tide a little longer this year. I like the winter Saturday format; extra time in bed and then most of the day in the library sorting out bits and pieces while keeping in touch with sporting news on radio.

November 7 – Hanworth Post Office, on the road into Cromer, closes after 80 years in the same family. Avril Turner gives up the business after 28 years. Her father moved there in 1931 and then her mother ran it. The building which houses the Post Office was a toll-house in about 1840 and it used to be a school.

November 13 – Another of those unwarranted attacks on Norfolk, this time by television presenter and motoring journalist Jeremy Clarkson. He dismisses the county as flat and featureless, peopled by yokels, perverts and cretins. 'They spend millions telling us that it is foolish to smoke but not a penny telling us not to go to Norfolk – unless you like orgies and the ritual slaying of farmyard animals.' Perhaps we'll do well just to ignore him and he might disappear up his own exhaust pipe.

November 14 – The wind howls and rain lashes down. I fight my way to Cromer front, confronting an angry white sea with a bravery hitherto kept under wraps since our arrival in town. I have the place to myself for this Sunday safari. I feel rather pleased with myself on reaching home in one refreshed piece. Then comes dramatic news: Cromer Pier has been sliced in two by a runaway rig! The end of pier theatre and lifeboat shed are marooned at sea, severed from the prom by a gaping hole. We learn later that a bailey bridge will be slung across the gap to allow lifeboatmen to reach their craft. There's an immediate pledge that the pier will be fully repaired in time for next summer's season.

November 15 – Bright day dawns to mock the weekend storms. Sightseers flock to Cromer to see the stricken pier. I pay my respects as darkness falls. You just look and feel regret.

November 26 – Big night out at St Andrew's Hall in Norwich as one of the speakers at the Insurance Institute of Norwich annual dinner. I'm in illustrious company sitting next to Norfolk fire chief Brian Smith and one of the other speakers, Major Gen. Sir David Thorne KBE. An audience of over 500 and an after dinner collection of over £2,600 for Children in Need. Chance to chat with many notables including the new Chief Constable of Norfolk Ken Williams; Norwich Lord Mayor Roy Durrant; County Council chairman John Donaldson and Norwich North MP Patrick Thompson.

December

December 5 – Sunday morning tears as I hear of the death of Marjorie Tann, head teacher at Beeston village school when I was a boy. She had retired with husband Frank to their bungalow in the village and had been in poor health for several years. Happily, I managed a couple of visits to pass on personal thanks for helping me on the way. She kept a firm but purposeful rein on her mixed family in our little seat of learning. I recall with relish her reading to us at the end of each day, her stirring attempts to woo me into the country dancing fold and her smiling permission to listen to test match cricket on the school wireless during the dinner break. The school is still open, a fitting memorial to the likes of her and Mrs Webdale, the infants' teacher.

December 8 – Norwich City's great European adventure is over, but they and their supporters earn great credit in Italy. The Canaries lose the return leg 1–0 in the San Siro stadium, but they had enough chances to see off Inter Milan in the UEFA Cup. As it is, the Italian giants go through to the quarter-finals 2–0 on aggregate.

December 10 – Homeward trail for the funeral at Beeston church for Marjorie Norah Tann on a cold, blustery morning.

I am invited to stand in front of the village class to say a few words of tribute to the woman who fashioned the direction we should follow. Plenty of familiar names and faces to recall, albeit from over 30 years ago in many cases.

December 17 – Novelist, critic and lecturer Malcolm Bradbury spends nearly an hour with me on the wireless talking about books. His latest, *The Modern British Novel*, has just been published and forms the basis of our chat. He is no dry, dusty professor but a cheerful, persuasive companion, a friendly guide along the shelves. I chide him gently not having read Mary Mann, the outstanding Norfolk writer from the turn of the century. Saul Bellow's *Hertzog* is his choice as book of the century. He shares my admiration of George Orwell and Graham Greene and has plenty to say in support of the new generation of British writers. Hardly surprising when you consider Professor Bradbury's leading role in the UEA Creative Writing course.

December 18 – Danny and his Suffield Park Infants School colleagues present their nativity play at Sheringham as part of the Little Theatre's 20th annual Christmas concert. My boy makes a fine job of his part as narrator, even though he did forget his plimsolls and has to parade in black shoes! Danny sorted out the script for himself and clearly enjoys life on stage.

December 19 – Out in the wind and rain to Booton's outstanding church for a service with children to the fore. We've been invited to this special event, one of few held in the church, after I mentioned on radio that we had paid a visit to the Cathedral of the Fields during the summer.

December 25 – So civilised! Danny and Robin let us rest until 8a.m., although the elder lad did pay a brief call at 3.40a.m. to check the time. A long present-opening adventure topped by appearances of Stretch Armstrong and Action Man, natural successors to Roy Rogers and Hopalong Cassidy.

December 27 – Holiday weather on the depressing side, but we risk a run-out by car round the muddy back lanes of North Norfolk. We saw most of these in better shape during the blackberry-picking season. A lone cyclist in Baconsthorpe leads us through the village where that precious sense of timelessness manages to cling on through the rain. A few strollers in other parishes draw a happy contrast with crowds converging on shops for the sales spree.

1994

January

January 3 – A simple blessing service in a Norfolk churchyard honours the memory of ten wartime airmen whose plane fell from the sky half a century ago. Parishioners at Upper Sheringham bow heads as a priest blesses the memorial outside All Saints' Church honouring the crew of an American Liberator bomber which crashed nearby.

January 6 – Metal detector thieves plunder Norfolk's ancient Roman capital, destroying vital parts of the county's heritage. The gang dig about 400 holes in the site at Caistor St Edmund, stealing coins and broaches and disturbing the 2,000-year-old town known as *Venta Icenorum*.

January 15 – Four Attleborough youngsters can hardly believe their eyes when they stumble on a box filled with jewellery while making a den. It has been hidden in a peat sack and covered with leaves by a burglar who broke into homes on the town's Springfield estate three weeks ago. Delighted owner Hilary Hunter gives each of the lads a £5 reward. 'It does restore your faith in young people,' she says.

January 23 – Broadcasting loses two outstanding characters. Tony Scase, one of East Anglia's leading journalists, dies at 56. In a career which spanned 40 years he became widely known as a freelance reporter for newspapers, radio and television. Brian Redhead, the early morning scourge of politicians on Radio 4's *Today* programme, dies at 64.

January 24 – One of the great moments on British Rail. We run out of juice on the way home! Yes, the diesel has all gone and we have to wait at North Walsham for another train to complete our run to the coast. Plenty of smiles amid the 'you-must-be-joking!' comments. One passenger calls for a meeting with the Fat Controller.

January 26 – The Singing Postman comes out of the shadows. A bedtime drink proves the ideal tonic for Allan Smethurst, who has been living for several years in a Salvation Army hostel in Grimsby. His most famous song, *Hev Yew Gotta Loight, Boy?*, has been adapted for a TV advert for Ovaltine Lite, leaving him with a nice little earner in royalties. He admits: 'I haven't done much since 1970. My fingers curled up and I couldn't play the guitar.'

January 27 – A rich winter mixture, with a rainbow in the morning and thunder and lightening with fierce snow showers after dark. Sunshine makes a brave appearance in between. A strange cocktail, luring me and the lads to the top floor to size up the little drama after dark. Robin takes top prize for imagination with cries of 'Frankenstein!'

January 31 – I'm sifting through hundreds of ideas for Norfolk pub names, the first *Dinnertime Show* competition of the year. I like The Truculent Tractor, The Dew Yew Come Inn, The Good Ole Boy and The Samphire Gatherer. It all began with my affection for The Eradicated Coypu.

February

February 4 – Discovery of the year so far is a sample of *Melinda Twaddle's Notions* in the *Yarmouth Mercury*. They were penned by Arthur Patterson, the famous naturalist who wrote under the pseudonym John Knowlittle. His great-granddaughter Beryl Tooley provides me with an example from October, 1927 as I continue to build a collection of writings with the aim of compiling an anthology in the name of Norfolk dialect. I have more Melinda Twaddle material promised by my old friend Ken Jary at Caister. He's a compulsive hoarder and just the sort of chap to know in matters such as these.

Arthur Patterson

February 5 – Down the runway of memories thanks to an article in the *Eastern Daily Press* by Keith Roberts, a former USAAF Liberator crewman now living in California. He recalls 'England, a place of flat green fields, country lanes and bicycles.' His station 118 was an airfield carved out of farmland between two small villages, Wendling and Beeston. He recalls the children hanging round the airfield, watching them over farm fences, counting the planes that left in the morning for the day's mission, and counting them back.

February 15 – We awake to the whiteness – swift retribution for those who dared to mutter spring-like thoughts last week. Rubber boots come out of hiding as I trudge through a couple of inches of snow to the station. Train warm and on time. Thaw soon sets in. But the day will be remembered for an earthquake! The earth moves for thousands as the tremor measuring at 4 on the Richter scale strikes at 10.16a.m. Even so, apart from a few cracked ceilings and broken crockery there's little damage from the biggest quake to hit the area for more than a century. Shock waves from the epicentre just south of Swaffham are felt more than 100 miles away, reaching as far at Nottingham and Kettering.

February 19 – One of Norfolk's most famous landlords, Les Winter, finds a buyer for his historic pub, but the Lord Nelson spirit will live on. The new publicans of the Lord Nelson at Burnham Thorpe promise to retain the shrine to Norfolk's naval son when they take over in March. After 28 years as hosts, Les and his wife Dorothy will use the pub as their own local as they are moving into a cottage just down the road.

March

March 8 – Villagers at Ludham are busy preserving their community's past and present for future generations in the form of a television documentary with the aid of a £500 arts grant. Schoolchildren are working closely with elderly villagers and bringing to life memories of bygone experiences in the form of animation. The wartime plane crash in the high street and the legend of the Ludham Serpent, a dragon said to have terrorised the community until vanquished by a local, are among topics on parade.

March 11 – My 50th birthday. The big day dawns with pleasant sunshine and ends in a major surprise at my regular Friday watering-hole. I make my way to the Horse and Dray in Norwich's Ber Street for what I think will be a celebration along 'have-a-half' lines. But waiting round the corner with a surprise spread are Diane, Danny and Robin. They launch a memorable evening as several old friends and colleagues file in for a munch, a sip and a mardle.

March 18 – A memorable night at Weston Longville Village Hall marked by torrential rain hammering on the roof. Our Norfolk Night helps raise money for the Parish Church where Parson James Woodforde preached 200 years ago.

March 23 – Complaints about noise are soaring in Norfolk as neighbours fall out over everything from late-night DIY to rowdy lawnmowers. Council officials say they are facing hundreds of moans from angry residents. Norwich City Council dealt with a record 440 noise complaints last year, while in neighbouring Broadland complaints have doubled in two years.

Charming thatched cottages in the Broadland village of Ludham.

1994

March 27 – Palm Sunday celebrations don't quite follow Biblical lines in Attleborough as Jesus swaps his four-legged mount for two wheels. The lack of a donkey means there are a few smiles and raised eyebrows as Christ – alias church lay-reader Russell Davies – rides his bike at the head of a procession to St Mary's Parish Church. The rector, Revd John Aves, explains that the donkey which usually led their procession had retired and the intended replacement died.

March 29 – Birdsong is louder. Flowers and trees are warming up for summer. There's some strength in the sun. I enjoy the morning stroll to catch my train, accepting the sharper edge of the breeze as refreshment rather than warning. I'm still an autumn man, but I can find much to savour at this time of the year. Sadly, I feel rather depressed after England's cricketers are humiliated in the West Indies.

April

April 1 – Stormy start to April but at least the weather gives Good Friday a chance to breathe. Heavy rain and high winds continue into the afternoon, by which time many people must have decided to stay at home. Still there are crowds in the city around the shops as I leave for Cromer after the traditional Good Friday reflections and music on the air. Among my offerings is an essay by Eric Fowler – who wrote as Jonathan Mardle – on the funeral of Sidney Grapes (the Boy John) in April, 1958. A wonderful article full of colour, hope and Norfolk virtues.

April 3 – Late decision to visit Hevingham church pays dividends. A lively Easter Sunday service and a chance to renew old acquaintants. Danny tells the vicar: 'Dad says you shouldn't return to the scene of the crime.' I remind Danny that he and his brother were christened here in the church where his parents were married. We take a look at the former rector's grave – Christopher Basil Morgan rests in the churchyard. His tribute reads 'Heaven is a more colourful place and Norfolk blander.'

April 16 – Busy day in Fakenham to unveil the plaque on the town sign and to open a spring fayre at the High School. Over 1,400 pupils at this seat of learning, one of the biggest in the county, and I can't help wondering if it matters to pupils, teachers and parents that some will remain strangers to each other.

April 21 – Showbiz stars are helping to kill off the traditional British seaside show by asking for too much money. So says Yarmouth entertainment boss Peter Jay as he shelves his summer season for the first time in 12 years. Mr Jay, who runs the Royalty Theatre, says he's been negotiating with several big names but none had been available at the right price for a season at Yarmouth.

April 29 – An anxious sort of April wends home. We've had a lot of weather from that bizarre Easter cocktail of snow, sleet, hail, rain and wind to the recent burst of warm sunshine. My moods have varied as well, not least as a new holiday season gets under way amid the usual calls for more visitors and more tourist attractions.

May

May 3 – I enjoy my regular trains of thought between coast and city. Letters to the *Dinnertime Show* continue to provide genuine delight – like a batch on the subject of Norfolk treacle mines. These must rank in significance alongside those dealing with the fascinating subject of belly-button fluff several years ago.

May 5 – A couple of hours after leaving town, I hear at Radio Norfolk there has been an armed robbery at a Cromer building society. It hurts to weigh up the implications and I decide not to tell the boys this sort of thing is happening in our home town.

May 8 – Showbiz calls! I compere a concert in the Pavilion Theatre on Cromer Pier to raise money for the RNLI, with Cromer Smugglers singing their way to the top of the bill. There's a full house. Afternoon rehearsals are followed by a teatime thunderstorm, but the weather is kind as crowds stroll along the pier for Sunday evening entertainment.

May 26 – Anglia Television wins praise from TV watchdogs – and then announce plans to cut 171 staff. Union chiefs warn programme quality will suffer as a third of the staff lose their jobs. The cuts follow the take-over of the Norwich-based station earlier this year by a media group which controls south of England broadcaster Meridian. Anglia say the job cuts are 'sad but necessary' and the station has to stay competitive.

June

June 1 – RAF West Raynham closes today with parades and fly-pasts. Nearby residents are losing more than just an air force presence. The number of service personnel and civilian workers has been dwindling since the closure was confirmed in 1991. The loss to local business caused by its closure and that of nearby RAF Sculthorpe has been estimated at millions of pounds. West Raynham opened in 1939 as part of a rapid pre-war expansion in the number of airfields. At the outbreak of war it was home to Blenheim bombers with Mosquitoes of the top-secret 100 Group moving in later. After the war the base became a testing ground for new fighter aircraft. In later years it was home to Bloodhound missiles.

June 17 – A visit to the University of East Anglia's film archives department to do the commentary for a video on old Norwich. I answer the call from David Cleveland, who has built a strong reputation in this field, rescuing old local films and giving them new life.

June 25 – Two derelict wind pumps in the heart of the Broads grazing marshes have been restored. More than £10,000 has been spent to revive Tunstall Smock Mill and Tunstall Dyke Power Mill. The work has been carried out through the Norfolk Mills and Pumps Trust, grant-aided by the Broads Authority. The two pumps stand within 50m of each other on Halvergate Marshes near the village of Tunstall.

June 29 – No need for an alarm clock to be ready for the first day of the Royal Norfolk Show… thunder rolls and lightning flashes in the early hours. However, weather is back in the summer groove as I set out a little after 7 o'clock.

July

July 1 – End of the road for colourful Bessie Carter, a mid-Norfolk legend behind the wheel of a bus. She has died at 84 and first took control of a 14-seat charabanc in 1929 at the age of 21. She remained a driving force for the next 40 years. Bessie and her late husband Gordon founded Carter's Coaches at Litcham. The firm remains there today, now run by their son and grandson. In the war Bessie's coach was used to take prisoners of war to work from their camps to surrounding farms. She also showed great skills on the piano accordion and played in a band.

July 12 – Big day out in London. Morning sightseeing on a tourist bus, although I'm forced to take refuge from the top deck through fears of sunstroke. I buy a floppy hat for future expeditions. Then it's on with our new outfits and off to Buckingham Palace for the eagerly-awaited royal garden party. Thousands join us in the sizzling heat, many in Ascot-style garb. Suddenly, we spy a familiar figure, Charles Roberts of the *Eastern Daily Press*. Another familiar face from King's Lynn, former Norfolk County Council chairman John Donaldson. A man from Thorpe St Andrew recognises my voice as we line up for refresh-

ments. A few lines away is magician Paul Daniels. He can't make the hordes disappear. We stroll and chat in the gardens and wonder how the Beefeaters and other over-dressed characters can bear the heat.

July 13 – Thunder, lightning and rain provide a rare cocktail at 3.30a.m., and I'm moved to look out across the London skyline. Still sultry when we rise officially after 8a.m., but it turns out to be a dull and much cooler day. We take a walk through Belgravia and stride on to Harrods, where the sale has just started. Inevitable comparisons to be made as we embark on the bus trip home, moving slowly through Whitechapel, Stratford, Stepney and other seedy sprawling suburbs. I'm glad when we find the open road – even if it is a motorway.

July 24 – Danny insists we embark on a bird watching expedition with book and binoculars at the ready. While England's batting collapses against South Africa, and Mike Atherton is landing in hot water for tampering with the ball, we find a little countryside refuge on the road out of Cromer. Looks like a bumper blackberry crop on the way among the nettles and butterflies. The odd pigeon flutters across to the woods, but there are few chances for Danny to consult his new book.

July 26 – *The Winslow Boy* opens at Norwich Theatre Royal and draws praise from the critics. I chat with actor Peter Barkworth on my radio show and recall memories of a production in the 1950s at Hamond's Grammar School, starring John Needle. His father Jack died recently. We met him last Christmas when he narrated the Nativity story at Booton church, a beautiful setting. I was prompted to write to John. He answered. Jack has gone. *The Winslow Boy* keeps going…

July 27 – Ladybirds on the march. Such an invasion at Wells that tourists and locals are driven inside.

July 29 – Three generations of the same family join me on the *Dinnertime Show* to fly the flag for Bodney, our bran-tub village of the week. Mary Butters (84) has lived there for 70 years – but still has a strong Somerset accent. She pops back to Taunton occasionally to tell them we don't talk like them! Her daughter Ann works for the Ministry of Defence in the Battle Area and has plenty of wartime and harvest memories to share. Her son Cedric is a teacher at a primary school in King's Lynn, but retains warm affection for the small community in which he was raised. This golden thread of continuity is warming in a fast-changing and cynical world.

1994

August

August 1 – Fire rips through Norwich Central Library, causing millions of pounds of damage and destroying priceless relics from the city's past. I get a glimpse of the extent of the damage as I walk to work. Much of the city's lending and reference library, as well as the USAAF Memorial Library is lost in the blaze. Memories of another city centre fire are revived. It destroyed a Norwich department store 24 years ago to the day. On August 1, 1970 Garlands store in London Street was gutted by fire.

August 10 – An unusual setting for my latest after-dinner speech: the new £1 million service centre for Duffields of East Anglia on Gapton Hall industrial estate at Yarmouth. I'm invited to mardle on a night dominated by serious talk on big trucks and roads. Former MEP Paul Howell is my 'warm-up man' with a serious look at the economic picture. I keep my contribution on the light side, although I seize the opportunity to emphasise the need to protect Norfolk from thundering juggernauts and damaging road 'improvements'.

August 13 – We take the busy road to the Cotswolds again, voting for the same cottage as last year down the twisting trail to Slad Valley. Within ten minutes of arriving, Robin's blue shoes turn to black as he finds the duck pond.

August 20 – Farewell Cotswolds, hello motorways and the outskirts of London! Such a contrast as we head for Middlesex and a couple of days with Diane's brother, Tim, and his wife, Carole.

August 21 – While the boys get an early birthday treat in the shape of a trip to Chessington Theme Park, Diane and I head for Hampton Court, all royal history on the Thames. A gem to visit and wonderful gardens and walks to go with the palatial buildings. Diane gets strange vibes on the way round, especially in the Long Gallery with its stories of Catherine Howard pleading for her life after being threatened by Henry VIII.

August 22 – Home to Norfolk and what relief to get off those motorways! The M25 and M11 provide me with ample ammunition to keep the battle going against these grotesque veins running through the land. Poor Hertfordshire! All we see of it is lane upon lane of thundering traffic mocking the stubble fields and cowering farms on either side.

August 31 – Another view of Norfolk from my bus seat and a dramatic insight into the twilight world of the coast. A lad in his early 20s is on the way back to Sheringham and his two-room flat after visiting his 'future wife' in hospital. She's expecting a baby any time. Chatting to a busker friend, who gets off at Aylsham, our Sheringham lad talks of drugs, another child in London and a lodger in his flat who is a junkie. And so the catalogue of problems and pressures continues. I'm amazed at the way so many details are put on public parade. There's no shame in being on social security, but why does he advertise his drug problems and crime-sodden acquaintances with such relish?

September

September 4 – Sheringham's seafaring traditions are marked with a costume celebration of the town's part in saving hundreds of lives. The lifeboat *Henry Ramey Upcher* is honoured one hundred years to the hour of its launch by enthusiastic onlookers. The craft was launched 60 times in 41 years and saved the lives of more than 200 people.

September 7 – A happy evening at the Old Rectory at Bawdeswell on the occasion of Dereham Antiquarian Society's 41st annual dinner. I sing for my supper after being greeted by a sudden thunderstorm and flickering lights. Society president Jonathan Boston is Rector of Horsford. His father, Canon Noel Boston, was Vicar of Dereham and one of Norfolk's most colourful personalities as I plied my trade on the local newspaper. Jonathan is a grand supporter of the Norfolk dialect and enjoys doing his party piece.

September 9 – Drama as Danny starts the next stage of his education at Cromer's brand new Junior School. Angry head teacher Tony Brown criticises County Hall officials for failing to complete their summer homework on time and then shows them the way. Work has not even started on promised road safety measures, so Mr Brown marches into the busy Norwich Road armed with PE cones and rounders markers. Soon traffic-slowing islands appear and a safe haven is created for the lollipop lady. As young mums arrive, Mr Brown encourages them to contact County Hall to protest about lack of action on a promised £60,000 scheme.

September 12 – Day after Radio Norfolk's 14th birthday, and I can't help feeling the station has gone rather stale. Perhaps I can make too many comparisons, having been there from the start, but recent emphasis on news and current affairs has tended to cast a cloud over what was a successful outfit for both entertainment and information.

KEITH SKIPPER'S NORFOLK DIARIES

September 14 – Soggy chaos as torrential rain sets in, and my journey home by double-decker bus has a touch of farce about it. I'm well soaked by the time I reach Surrey Street bus station to catch the 3.15. Then it transpires our vehicle has a bit of a leak near the front, water gushing up to soak passengers. One woman on the Aylsham Road complains that her bus shelter afforded no protection whatsoever. Her criticisms are still reverberating when water rises to soak her feet. We have the undignified sight of female passengers lifting their feet when they hear trouble bubbling, and one goes so far as to drape them over the rails of the luggage section at the front.

September 22 – Heavy rain of the past few weeks is a mere drop in the ocean compared to what will be the water needs of East Anglia in the twenty-first century. The population of Britain's fastest-growing region is set to soar by a million in the next 30 years. That means a far-reaching strategy for water management is needed now. The National Rivers Authority calls on everyone to care more for the environment. The message to water users is use it wisely.

October

October 6 – Afternoon tea in The Swallow tearoom at Walsingham. A few visitors wandering the streets but the peak season for pilgrims is over. I find this spot with all its religious trappings easier to take when it is quiet – but there's still a sense of wonder at finding such a place in Norfolk after ambling down narrow lanes.

October 7 – Trip to Dragon Hall in Norwich's King Street as one of the 76 personalities featured in a new exhibition of men and women who have helped shape the city of today. The portraits, including the one of me with Danny and Robin on Cromer beach, have all been taken by Norwich photographer Andrew Coe. *Faces of Norwich* aims to raise funds for the unique hall, and it ties in with Norwich 800 and the Norfolk and Norwich Festival.

October 9 – Back in the city to lead a WEA day school on Norfolk writers and writings at Wensum Lodge. It is well received by the dozen or so fellow enthusiasts, and it's

The Skipper lads feature in a exhibition staged at Dragon Hall in Norwich.

particularly encouraging to find more interest in the works of Mary Mann. I look at the explosion in 'little' local books, the use of dialect over the years, size up some recent novels and select my top ten. The 'class' provides an opening 150 words for that Norfolk novel they've been threatening to write for years.

October 15 – A night of sporting nostalgia at the Old Brewery House in Reepham. Former Norfolk, Middlesex and England cricketer Peter Parfitt comes home to help raise money for Foxley church tower. I introduce one of the county's most famous sporting sons and he treats us to a session of rich anecdotes from his playing days. The Parfitt family are out in force along with plenty of sports personalities, most notably from the Dereham area.

Cyril Jolly – champion of the Norfolk dialect.

October 17 – Death at 83 of Cyril Jolly, author, preacher and champion of the Norfolk dialect. I first heard him in the pulpit at Beeston Methodist Chapel when I was a boy and a service of song was a big attraction. We enjoyed reunions in recent years when he presented a series about local lifeboats on my radio show. Cyril will be best remembered for the definitive biography of Henry Blogg of Cromer, the most decorated lifeboatman in history.

October 29 – Final Norfolk Night of the 1994 season at Burnham Market Village Hall. It's a rousing session in front of an enthusiastic audience made up of hardened locals with a fair sprinkling of recent arrivals. We have a guest artist. Geoff Smith of Happisburgh is planning enforcement officer for North Norfolk District Council. He presents Nathaniel Titlark to give the programme more variety.

November

November 2 – Norwich pub The Freemason's Arms is to be rechristened in honour of one of the city's most colourful characters – Billy Bluelight. An appeal by owners Woodforde's Brewery for a new name for the Hall Road hostelry ends with Billy Bluelight, flower-seller, pedlar and runner. Billy, who died in 1949 aged 90, was famous in his younger days for racing against wherries and steamboats from Norwich to Bramerton. His nickname is thought to have come from an article in Colman's

Carrow Works magazine in 1907, which praised his 'blue light of eloquence.'

November 13 – The Parish Church bells toll, and my solo stroll before 11 o'clock is marked by a stunning fly-past of seagulls. They soar and scatter from the churchyard when the bells pause. Fairly quiet along the front, with a few youngsters swigging cans of drink and wearing peaked caps the wrong way round – a fashion that causes me more annoyance than perhaps it should. I buy two small dressed crabs for tea.

November 14 – To Letheringsett King's Head to push over a pile of coins in aid of the RNIB. A neat way of raising over £250 but what goes down has to be picked up and counted. The task has some of us on our hands and knees. I'm joined for this happy pub occasion by former Norwich City goalkeeper Sandy Kennon, one of the stars of the FA Cup run of 1958/59. The big South African reflects on his years in Norfolk and says how much he enjoys being a grandfather.

November 15 – Danny demonstrates a good sense of humour as he returns from football action after school. 'I scored my first goal...' – a clenched fist in triumph – 'but trouble was it went in at the wrong end!' Still, his team won 5–4. He's coming on.

November 16 – Our Indian summer may be over but the month continues to follow bright lines. I watch a congregation of rooks form a wavering black tassel over bare branches as I wait for the train at Cromer. The noises rise above the traffic's roar as Holt Road goes about its hasty business. How that avenue has changed since we moved to Cromer!

November 25 – Evening visit to High Kelling Social Club, down a long, unmade road for supper and a mardle with a gathering of predominantly retired folk getting used to Norfolk ways. One has to accept there are several colonies like this in North Norfolk. I enjoy preaching the Norfolk gospel to newcomers, most of whom are sympathetic to the preservation cause.

December

December 1 – Now it's official... I'm off on safari around Norfolk in the New Year to feel the pulse of the county towards the end of the twentieth century. The news coincides with Radio Norfolk boss Keith Salmon's announcement that he will be retiring next Easter. I'll soon be formulating my programme for the first three months of 1995, but first I have to explain the project to *Dinnertime* regulars. Some of my colleagues suggest I may not return to full-time broadcasting, although I have no clear picture in mind. In any event, I am looking forward to renewing acquaintance with familiar corners and taking a closer look at others.

December 6 – Another chapter full of comedy for the memoirs. I travel to East Harling for a Victorian evening at the Women's Institute with driving instructor friend Pat Maitland at the wheel. Mindful of finishing up in Thetford on the way home after our last visit, Pat asks for clear instructions on how to get back on the A11 for Norwich. Suddenly, we are off the beaten track and evidently heading for the beauties of Roudham Heath. We spot lights round a sharp corner and discover a police car. The lone officer tells us we are indeed going the wrong way and invites us to turn round and follow him back to the land of the living. He asks where we've been in our smart dinner jackets. We say a WI meeting. He says 'Of course – I should have guessed.' Then he admits he recognises me and suggests I look better in the paper than I do in the flesh. He points us towards the A11 and we are back in Cromer just before midnight.

December 23 – My last *Dinnertime Show* until April, with many regulars dropping in to do a little turn and pass on season's greetings. End-of-term climate is inevitable and some are interpreting it as possibly the end of an era.

December 24 – A chilly Christmas Eve. Another sharp frost covers the county and we wrap up well for shopping. 'Collect the cockerel' is top of the list. The boys find it hard to walk away from the toy shelves and I can scarcely complain when I think of all the time I spend in book departments.

December 25 – The frost has gone during the night. Rain arrives with the milder weather as Christmas Day dawns. Most items on order duly arrive. The cockerel is tasty and what I laughingly describe as the most expensive Christmas pudding in the world comes up trumps. I paid nearly £8 for it at a farm shop a few weeks ago. I didn't check the price tag before buying. My new diary for 1995, a present from the lads, has a blue cover after a succession of black ones since 1984. I'm tempted to read deep significance into that.

December 31 – I tune into the third Test match at midnight. England start in familiar fashion by losing their first three wickets for 20 runs to the Aussies. What have I achieved during 1994? I've done my bit towards keeping public transport in the spotlight, regularly using trains and buses to and from the city. I've kept the Norfolk faith, attacking excesses and exploitation where possible and championing small village schools despite considerable odds against survival in some cases. I have read prodigiously, talked to numerous writers of all levels and intensified my urge to write more myself. I have fought my corner with vigour where needed and tried to keep humour near the front as well. I have betrayed intolerance on occasions – but that's because I care so much.

◆ ◆ ◆

January

January 1 – Invigorating start to the New Year with a bracing stroll to Cromer Lighthouse and back. Snow flurries on the trek home. Evening delight is a new TV version of *Cold Comfort Farm*, one of my favourite novels. This adaptation from Stella Gibbons' satire is by Malcolm Bradbury from the University of East Anglia. Sort of D.H. Lawrence meets H.E. Bates as it sends up every countryside cliché in the book.

January 9 – So how am I coping with drastic changes in my lifestyle as I prepare for a three-month absence from the airwaves? I relish the chance to rise later, especially on mornings full of bad weather, but I am not the best when it comes to setting myself a routine. I need a deadline to get me going. Still, brisk walks can stir the imagination and get me stoked up for bursts of activity.

January 23 – We're off! My first recording trip for the special series of programmes about Norfolk at the end of the twentieth century. I join up with producer Nick Patrick and we head for a chat with Sir Arthur South at Drayton. He looks well as he squares up to the challenges of his ninth decade

and we enjoy a wide-ranging discussion as he reflects on 60 years in local political and social life. Then it's on to South Norfolk District Council's pagoda-style headquarters at Long Stratton for a mardle with chief planning officer Mike Haslam. He's been in the county 20 years and talks with refreshing candour about planning problems, with special reference to the professional middle classes that move into villages and want to keep everything else out.

January 24 – Interviews with John Ayton, former head of planning at Norfolk County Council, and Paul Howell, Norfolk's MEP for 15 years. John repeats his familiar claim that Norfolk owes a lot to its planners and emphasises that more houses were built in the county in the 1960s than in the 1980s. He also suggests that, in planning terms, Thetford's overspill development worked. Paul, down the lane in his farmhouse on the outskirts of Scarning, puts up some convincing arguments for the county to look outwards.

January 30 – Blessed day! England win a test match in Australia and Beeston is waiting in sunshine for my return. To the village school for a mixture of romance and hard

Beeston School – still open with 38 pupils after standing on the village crossroads since 1879.

111

KEITH SKIPPER'S NORFOLK DIARIES

work in the name of the Norfolk Project. It's still open with 38 pupils after standing on the crossroads since 1879. Head teacher Myra Street is a doughty fighter and there are good feelings as we chat about the precarious future and golden past. Our afternoon destination is pretty little Hempstead, near Holt, to record a chat with Malcolm Freeguard, one of the moving spirits behind the East Anglian Film Archive at the UEA. He looks at Norfolk through a settler's eyes, although he was stationed here in the war, visited as a child and became determined to live and work in the county.

February

February 6 – Weather puts on a springtime smile as we embark on another chapter of the Norfolk Project. To Hingham and Norfolk Rural Community Council headquarters for a chat with field officer Geoffrey Leigh. Then he spearheads our look at examples of what he's been talking about – Itteringham and its village shop run by locals, Beachamwell School with 14 pupils and a battle plan to keep going and Foulden where a housing association project gives local families affordable property in the village where they want to live.

February 7 – I take the train from Cromer to Diss for a visit to Alan Bloom's gardens and steam museum at Bressingham. Alan, with flowing grey locks and earrings, is a pioneer along the local tourism trail. He's concerned about its future and his views will make good listening in our series. We make a tour of the loco sheds to see some of his wonderful engines and other exhibits.

February 13 – Danny and Robin busy making Valentine cards for the morrow. Robin reckons the object of your desires can work out from whence the message comes by the number of dots that make up your Christian name, such as ….. He is rather crestfallen when we point out Danny, Keith and Diane also have five letters!

February 14 – Day out in the bright sunshine. To Sennowe Park first for a recording stint with former High Sheriff of Norfolk Tom Cook. He unfurled the 'Save Our County!' banner during his year of office and inspired many to think they are not alone and helpless. Logs smoulder in a room dominated by paintings and books as he outlines his hopes and fears. He's clearly passionate about retaining Norfolk's credibility as a largely rural county. After lunch at Blakeney, we head for Stiffkey to meet countryside campaigner Robin Page. A Cambridgeshire man, he has borrowed a bungalow to use for writing and as a base for uplifting

walks. He fears the worst from urban thinking and reckons this part of Norfolk will be spoilt just like his native county by the middle of the next century.

February 28 – Busy day to end the month. First stop, County Hall and the countryside team. After a general mardle we join Steve Harris on the road at Strumpshaw with the Yare Valley glistening beyond, and then on to Litcham for lunch at The Bull and a stroll round Tho Common nature reserve. We complete our recording session with a visit to the University of East Anglia. Richard Crum at the Economics Research Centre follows the 'popular' line of Norfolk having to face up to the realities of the modern high-tech world. He appears to have little time for those who want to preserve the character of the county.

March

March 6 – Morning trip to the *Diss Express* newspaper office for a chat with editor Amanda Hadfield. The office overlooks the Mere – a real tonic as the sun sparkles on the water. Amanda talks of the boom that never came to Diss after electrification of the rail line to London. Diss hasn't changed much, she says, and is not likely to do so in the next half century. Comforting words as we head for much-maligned Thetford, where I started my newspaper career in 1962. Mayor Colin Armes, born in the town, claims overspill saved it from withering away. Thelma Paines, town, district and county councillor, arrived from Clapham Junction in 1962, and is a real Thetford champion. Good to hear such loud backing, but the general look of the place leaves me cold and disenchanted.

March 7 – To the heart of Broadland to meet reed cutter Eric Edwards at How Hill, a real jewel in Norfolk's crown. The wind blows cold among the reeds, windmills stand guard over precious acres and Eric shows why he must be one of the most contented people in the county. We record in his hut crammed with old Broadland tools.. By boat to the mill where he's been photographed so many times since taking his job with the Broads Authority in 1967. He shows how to use the scythe as we spy his little amphibious vehicle, the old and the new together. I stand and feel the silence, the cold, the beauty. On to the city for a session with *Eastern Daily Press* stalwarts Colin Chinery and Charles Roberts at Prospect House. They live up to all expectations with eloquent dissections of the Norfolk identity.

March 10 – Former newspaper man Tim Bishop is the new managing editor of Radio Norfolk. We wait to see how he'll steer the ship. In the meantime, a 'battle of the airwaves'

Eric Edwards – the reedcutter of How Hill.

is on the way. Two more local FM stations are set to be on the air by summer next year, with radio rivals from Yarmouth and Lowestoft unveiling competing plans for a coastline pop station.

March 11 – My 51st birthday and an evening celebration at the Poacher's Pocket pub at Bacton. Folk singers take the stage, with 11-year-old Thomas showing skills on the fiddle with a bluegrass group. A wet night makes it splashing all the way along the coast road.

March 13 – Engrossing day on the recording beat. Nine pupils at Fakenham College share their hopes and fears about Norfolk, and we are duly impressed by their honesty in giving opinions on difficult matters. All appear to be ready to leave Norfolk to pursue further education and their careers. Two boys from North Norfolk are anxious to head for America, but it's heartening to hear youngsters say they'd like to come back sometime. One boy sums up the dilemma: 'You can't have Manchester and Sheringham. They don't mix.' Next stop Swaffham for a chat with old newspaper colleague John Kitson, who spent over 30 years watching Thetford trying to come to terms with dramatic growth. He underlines one of Thetford's biggest problems as a lack of understanding on the part of people in other areas of Norfolk.

March 14 – I relish this one... from Shipp to Shaw. First port of call on our recording trail is Diana Shipp, information and tourism officer for the Broads Authority. She outlines projects being undertaken to tackle problems caused by over-exploitation. Then it's on to County Hall to see Martin Shaw, the county council's chief of planning and transportation. He comes close to admitting mistakes were made in recent years, especially over roads and out-of-town supermarkets.

March 15 – A real feel of history as Diane and I pay a call on Blickling. The hall is closed so we seek a few minutes of refuge from the wind in the Parish Church of St Andrew next door. It stands on a slight rise overlooking its grand neighbour, proudly sharing in the long and colourful history of the local manor, reaching back to the days when King Harold was Earl of East Anglia. Primroses scattered triumphantly round the gravestones on the path to the porch. Snow and sleet are our companions back to the coast.

March 19 – Robin provides one of the biggest laughs of the year so far with 'not necesscelery'. We'll take to the trenches when we remind him about that in years to come.

March 20 – Recording visit to Jonathon Sissons, president of Norfolk and Waveney Chamber of Commerce and Industry. He's anxious for the drawbridge to come down to help the economy. A Yarmouth lad, he accepts some of the dangers in ending the 'backwater' era. I argue that Norfolk has thrived through many centuries despite being out of the mainstream. On to Yarmouth itself for a chat with Tony King, former head of tourism for the borough. He agrees the town has a tatty edge but reckons more money has to be spent on the holiday trade. Last call of the day at Lowestoft to meet Jimmy Hoseason, at the heart of the holiday business for over 40 years. I take the train from Lowestoft to Norwich for the first time in many years, enjoying the scenery around Somerleyton and Haddiscoe.

March 27 – Last lap of the great Norfolk Project with producer Nick Patrick – and the journey ends in Cambridge on a day of snow, hail and sleet showers. We pay a call on Dr Bob Crichton, director of the Home Office Partnership. It believes passionately that rural economies and rural life can be revived by technology. People working from home provide one of the best answers to Norfolk's problems, he claims, and I cast off my 'luddite' feelings to embrace some of his images and ideas. It's an uplifting end to our travels and now Nick will get busy with the editing. Over 20 hours of tapes to pick from with six half-hour programmes the target for airing.

March 31 – Country life dominates my thinking after all my travels during the first part of 1995. I do have romantic feelings, but how can you survive without them? And why shouldn't some of the dreams, the images persist?

April

April 3 – Back to work to launch *The Norfolk File* from 1.30p.m. until 3p.m. It's so strange sitting in front of a microphone and twiddling all the knobs after three months away. A bit like starting at a new school. Cards in the post and messages by phone make me feel welcome.

April 7 – End of an era at Radio Norfolk as managing editor Keith Salmon retires. He's been in charge since 1982 and there's genuine regret that this largely self-effacing gentle sort of man is leaving Norfolk Tower. He inherited a successful station although the finances were in some disorder. He has cultivated a real affection for the county and appreciates its desire – and need – to remain different.

Keith Salmon – leaving Radio Norfolk.

I owe him thanks for arranging my three-month safari at the start of this year and I hope the results give him an autumnal glow. I have a farewell chat with him on today's programme and there's a grand turn-out at the Hotel Nelson in the evening to see him off in some style. A string quartet provides a civilised background to the merrymaking.

April 10 – I'm relishing what is likely to be one of my literary treats of the year, *Green Fields and Pavements*, published to celebrate the centenary of the birth of Henry Williamson. This is a collection of his contributions to the *Eastern Daily Press* between 1941 and 1944. This from May 1943: 'I cycled along the coast road, free with a delightful sense of solitude, and I came to an area which probably was painted in peacetime more often than any other East Anglian district. Wide marshes and reedy dykes, villages

of pantiled roofs and crumbling flint walls – many broken by traffic – corn barns with their tall, black double doors, cattle yards, an old windmill, fields, green with barley, distant sea and low, ragged lines of sandhills under an azure sky of a clarity unsurpassed in any other English coastal landscape.'

April 12 – Birdsong and blossom cheer the path to Easter, although the wind carries a keen edge today – and not just on the coast. Fire tears through the heart of Norwich's historic Assembly House, the second major blaze to scar the city within a year.

April 21 – Another Norfolk Night triumph, this time at Yaxham Village Hall where an audience of well over 150 let themselves go. Laughter can be so infectious. Local mawthers Flo and Rose join my regulars to do their little turn.

April 24 – Some relief as Radio Norfolk's new managing editor Tim Bishop tells a staff meeting that the future of local radio seems fairly secure. He hints at more changes to come, and there appears to be an ambivalent attitude towards more 'local' programmes. My main concern is that the passion to go for 'a younger audience' will undermine much of the good work since 1980.

April 29 – Full house at Potter Heigham Village Hall for a Norfolk Night. I feel moved to concentrate on a tribute to Sidney Grapes, alias the Boy John, this village's most famous son. The majority of the audience have heard of him and several will have copies of his famous dialect letters. But how do we ensure he is known to the next generation? Schools pay little heed to local characters and local books, so it is up to groups such as ours to spread the word.

May

May 7 – Roy's of Wroxham superstore gutted by fire, causing millions of pounds worth of damage. And there's tragedy at the seaside as the body of a Leicester schoolboy is found entombed in a 6ft tunnel on the beach at Hunstanton. He'd been playing with other children on holiday.

May 8 – Small is beautiful for the folk of Great Hockham. The village becomes the smallest in England to elect its own mayor. Postmaster Jane Dalton wins after 213 of the 300 or so villagers turn out to vote.

May 10 – Purple lilac gives off its annual greeting at Salhouse halt on the railway trip into Norwich. Lovely scent and sight before the mundane last lap into the city with Dussindale sprawling by the day and asking serious questions about development and community.

May 12 – There are occasions touched by magic and a visit to Wells Maritime Museum is one of them. Friend Pat Maitland collects me from home after tea and we take the coast road to dispense a bit of squit and *bonhomie* to Friends of the Museum. It's cold and windy, with racing clouds charging overhead. Once we've passed the undignified piles of caravans between Cromer and Sheringham the mood picks up. I'm reminded of the words from *A Norfolk Notebook* first published by Lilias Rider Haggard in 1946: 'Some enchantment lies upon the coast of North Norfolk which leaves it in memory, not just an impression of peculiar beauty, but a series of pictures standing out as vividly as if you had opened a book…' Anything that moves bends away from the windswept coast.. It's gloomy and blustery as we park on Wells Quay and head for the warmth of the harbour office and the impressive museum. Lifeboat coxswain Graham Shaw is leading light on this busy little scene. It's soon squeezing room only as an evening of seafood and squit gathers pace.

May 26 – Norfolk's 'Insect man', Ken Durrant from Sheringham, calls in for a mardle on my programme, reinforcing the belief that there are still many unsung personalities waiting in the wings. Ken loves to pass on his natural knowledge to youngsters. I bumped into him recently when I was giving a talk to the District Scouts at their annual meeting in Holt.

May 29 – Ian Wallace, with over 50 years in show business behind him, is my Bank Holiday guest. Now 75 with a home near Cromer, he reflects on a career packed with twists from opera to pantomime. He's an exceptional all-rounder. Asthma causes him problems, but the old fire is still burning.

May 31 – The rust is on the lilac and May bids an unsettled farewell. A month that always brings me problems as summer's promises are tied up with too many questions and misgivings. I jot down a few notes: 'I don't gloat over the quality of life we still enjoy in parts of Norfolk. Rather I despair at the number of places where it is being eroded or completely destroyed. I don't count Norfolk's bonus marks; instead I listen carefully to those who move in with dark tales of misery left behind. They teach us lessons. We tell them the price for seeking sanctuary is to help preserve those characteristics which enticed them in the first place.'

June

June 4 – Rain spoils the Norfolk Internal Combustion Engine Rally at Hoveton. Within minutes of my official opening, thunder and lightning send spectators scurrying for cover. We find shelter in Harry Roper's delightful vintage car, but it soon becomes clear there will be an early finish. Ironically, Cromer is dry and fine when we return home.

June 9 – An unusual early-evening 'cabaret' at County Hall before many of Norfolk's great and good and a party of former Ulster policemen and their wives. Several of the visitors are invalids, victims of the troubles. I try to make the cultural leap from Norfolk to Northern Ireland in a light-hearted way. The event is organised by the Norfolk Police Federation and I'm delighted to provide 40 of my Norfolk Companion books as presents.

June 23 – My regular support for our local railway service in particular and public transport in general, leads to an invitation to talk at the annual meeting of the North East Norfolk Travellers Association (NENTA). Andy Cooper, regional boss of Anglia Railways, makes predictable confident noises, but he and his colleagues still ignore the blatant difference between rail fares and what it costs to travel by bus. So much cheaper by road and if there's any trouble along the line, coach operators immediately cash in.

June 24 – Drizzle with occasional heavier squalls as we make our way to Bawburgh Green for the fair. They are raising money to build a new Village Hall. We have to leave earlier than planned when Robin is struck by the dreaded peanut allergy. He comes out in a horrible rash after a pony ride, and we reckon the hat he wears is cause of the trouble with peanut traces in the horse food.

June 27 – Long journey to work as the sun beats down. Brakes failure halts our train at North Walsham so a Sanders bus is called up to take us into Norwich. As usual in these circumstances we follow the railway route and so travelling time is extended considerably. The countryside, with corn turning, poppies blooming and hedges in full cry, is most appealing, especially when we head down back lanes around Worsted. A free trip in and only £1 to travel home in an Eastern Counties bus. Sunshine and savings all the way.

July

July 4 – One of those sad little incidents that throw a dark shadow over life in Norfolk today. A postwoman's mailbag and bicycle are stolen during her round in Cromer as she delivers letters to flats in our road about 9.30a.m. – an hour after my stroll to the station to catch the train to the wicked city.

July 6 – A happy evening of music and mardling in St Nicholas Parish Church at East Dereham. Full house to hear the East Anglian Stompers traditional jazz musicians brought together by Colin Burleigh. They join me, David Woodward and Brian Patrick for this production specially designed for the Withburga Festival. David has the role of Parson James Woodforde from Weston Longville while Brian is on home territory as the Revd Benjamin Armstrong, vicar in this town from 1850 until 1888. Both kept diaries and they turn the pages to good effect as the sun dips beyond the glorious stained glass window.

July 17 – Diane goes bargain hunting at the Runton and Sutherland School's closing-down sale. A guitar for Danny, a recorder for Robin and a big typewriter for me. More like a garden party than a funeral as hundreds of visitors mingle in tree-lined school grounds. End of an era on the cliff tops.

July 19 – A woman who cooked meals for the 'Prostitutes' Padre', the Revd Harold Davidson of Stiffkey, dies at 98. Norah Bayfield was employed by the rector to cook for the family. She was loyal to her former master and kept in touch with his family after he died in 1937. Mrs Bayfield, daughter of Stiffkey sailor Thomas Jordan, left school at 13 and served as a maid before joining the Davidson household. She tended the rector's grave in Stiffkey churchyard and maintained he was 'the perfect gentleman'.

July 27 – Day out at Lakenham in the sun to watch cricket and present *The Norfolk File* programme on the first day of the host county's game against Bedfordshire. Old colleague Bryan Stevens shares his memories. Man-of-the-match adjudicator Barry Battelley, county coach Roger Finney, manager John Shepherd and Minor Counties secretary David Armstrong among other guests. The ground has changed considerably in recent years with the 'Disneyland' tennis-courts covering the trees on the far side. There's a strong commercial feel now and traditionalists like me find it hard to accept the new face of Lakenham.

July 31 – Celebrations and tragedy at Cromer. The town impresses judges in the Norfolk Best Kept Village competition and carries off the crown in the small towns section for the third time. There's tragedy as a teenage boy dies after being hoisted from the surf near Cromer Pier by a rescue helicopter following an hour-long search. I sense the ripples of sadness as I walk through town on my way home.

August

August 4 – A long chat with Radio Norfolk boss Tim Bishop, our first serious session since he took over in April. He stops short of issuing a clear ultimatum but it's obvious he wants me to come up with something fresh and exciting if I want to stay on the full-time payroll. I listen carefully. He does stress my good points but I get the feeling he would risk all the flak if it came to the crunch. He emphasises my stubborn nature, and reckons my dislike of authority might be put to better broadcasting use. He claims all points raised are entirely his own, although I have heard some criticisms many times before.

August 7 – Another successful stint at Mundesley Festival, this time introducing the Cromer Smugglers. In the audience is my Uncle Herbert on holiday in Sheringham from the Midlands. He settles for a cultural evening at the Coronation Hall and we enjoy a chat before and after the show.

August 8 – Not quite paranoia at work, but there's a lot of unease about the future. I catch the opening 20 minutes of a staff meeting and I sense my discomfort is shared by several others on the station. It's a good time to take a break and take stock.

August 11 – I clear my desk and make jokes about how dangerous it can be to be absent from Norfolk Tower these days. Changes are coming in the autumn. Some are sorely needed, but the fear is too much of value will be swept away. New boss Tim Bishop keeps on saying he's no butcher but I'm not alone in smelling pork chops in his office. I'm off for two weeks in the countryside.

August 17 – Visits to Beccles and Halesworth for holiday provisions and bookshop browsing. Pedestrianised areas pleasant in both towns as shoppers slow down. A man from Shropshire causes mild amusement in the supermarket car park at Beccles – he can't find his car! Perhaps he left it in another park… He scratches his head and continues his search as we depart.

August 19 – We find a parking space at last in Southwold! The place seems able to cope with crowds. Like a maiden aunt suddenly asked to entertain all her relatives, she remains unflustered and gets on with the task. A refreshing breeze to take some of the sting out of the continuing heatwave.

1995

August 21 – I'm most impressed by the shape and flavour of many Suffolk villages away from the main roads, but one is left to wonder what substance remains beneath a pretty surface.

August 23 – A brief call at Dunwich to visit the museum. I buy *Dunwich – Time, Wind and Sea*, an anthology of poems from 1173 to 1981. As the introduction points out it is unusual for a remote village of no more than 120 inhabitants to boast a literature as extensive as this.

August 25 – Our last full day at Owles Hall and the wind gets up to stir the trees and mark an apparent chance in the weather. We feel the first tinge of autumn as our final family test match gets under way in an orchard weighed down by apples, plums and pears.

August 28 – Back in the old routine as the Bank Holiday weather strikes a typical pose – blustery with sharp showers. I return to the microphone to share the stage with former *Eastern Evening News* writer Neville Miller. We size up life immediately after the end of the last war with emphasis on local events. I play records made by stars of the era.

September

September 20 – A fateful letter from Radio Norfolk which looks like spelling the end of my weekday broadcasting career. Boss Tim Bishop says that in both the interests of the station and my own career it is time to do different. He proposed programmes on Saturdays and Sundays as well as taking a role in a number of special projects and outside broadcasts. My initial reaction is a mixture of anger and sadness. I get the feeling my future had been mapped out before any recent chats and I remain doubtful about the amount of time Mr Bishop has listened to my broadcasting output.

September 25 – A rude start to the week. Train fares go up again – and there's no warning. Our guard on the Sheringham–Norwich line says he didn't know till he started work. My return ticket goes up 20p to £5.70. That's £3.50 more than a bus ticket for the same journey. Usual mealy-mouthed responses when I ring up customer relations in Ipswich, although there is an apology in our new bulletins. Sadly, today will put off even more potential customers.

September 27 – Clouds of uncertainty still hanging over my future after another lengthy meeting with Tim Bishop. He's still insisting I need a change. I maintain that my contributions round about midday for the past decade are

still well received. I stress the vital importance of keeping the real Norfolk in Radio Norfolk. I tell him my talents and loyalty deserve a better result than being shunted into weekend sidings. How strange that at a time calling out for so much self-examination I should receive a letter from another Keith Skipper living in Wales! Keith Arthur Skipper of Dyfed tells me all his grandparents were Skippers and originated from the Norwich area.

September 29 – Decision day at Radio Norfolk. I reluctantly accept to move to weekends as other changes are announced to the staff. The local press make the most of it all and give me the chance to emphasise my fears that the station could lose its essential Norfolkness. I am sad. The *Eastern Daily Press* calls it 'the end of an era' and no doubt I'll receive plenty of messages of sympathy. Colleagues say little.

September 30 – A Norfolk outing to help ease the tension. Diane and I head for Westacre Village Hall and the harvest supper in aid of church funds. I introduce myself as 'the man who knocked Will Carling off the front page of the *Eastern Daily Press*' and present an after-meal mixture of verses and yarns.

October

October 1 – Britain wakes up to a whole new 'weigh' of life. Metrication Day marks the beginning of the end for traditional pounds and ounces and heralds a new dawn for kilos, metres and litres. I'm reminded of the reaction from a Norfolk stalwart when the currency was changed back in the early 1970s: 'they might have waited until all the old people had died!'

October 6 – Much-needed diversion as letters about me and Radio Norfolk start dominating the local papers. They all bemoan my demise at *Dinnertime*, and I'm grateful for the support. But it's all becoming rather oppressive at work where colleagues do their best to pretend nothing has happened. I fear this saga has a few chapters to run. Meanwhile, it's off to Carrow Road in the wind and rain to sing for my supper at the Norfolk Cricket League's annual dinner. Over 300 on parade, so it's a long night especially when it comes to presentations. I present a *This Is Your Life* feature on league sponsor Les King, and he takes all the squit very well.

October 7 – Smile time! Publisher Terry Davy calls with the first copies of *Squit, Wit and... Shifty Tales*, my 11th book. I'm at pains to point out in press releases that publication at this time of high public interest in my broadcasting career is a coincidence.

October 10 – Back in the fold! *Eastern Daily Press* editor Peter Franzen phones to invite me to resume as a regular columnist for the paper. He admits it is a case of media opportunism but sincerely wants to give *The Norfolk File* shunned by Radio Norfolk a platform in the local press. He promises this is no quick-fire booking merely to take advantage of all the publicity. He wants me on a regular basis – and I jump at the offer.

October 22 – A day bathed in autumn sunshine as I open the apple orchard at Norfolk Rural Life Museum at Gressenhall. Queues to have fruit identified are considerable.

October 26 – Family trip to Yarmouth underlines the way the resort has gone downhill. Wet weather may play a part as I stand on the Golden Mile and weep for the past. Straggling visitors nip in and out of leisure dives with rows upon rows of mechanical money-eaters, flashing, winking and pouting as provocatively as any tart trying to catch your attention. The whole area is dominated by them. Our meal on Regent Road is pleasant enough, although the arrival of a drunken Scot gives the outing an uneasy edge. He keeps on apologising for his state and at least shows no aggression.

November

November 5 – I walk with the lads for a date with destiny. Well, Robin and I are on the touchline as Danny plays for Cromer Under-9s against the Under-10s. The older boys rampage home about 21–0 and it's a meaningless display of predictable superiority. Danny is substituted at half-time. Robin gives up writing down the score once it gets past the dozen mark. Sadly, the tracksuited supremo behind the Under-10s has a habit of imitating the professionals with his constant cries of 'Shape!' and 'Support!' and other telling instructions culled from *Match of the Day* pundits. Happily, most of the lads seem oblivious to them.

November 6 – Here beginneth the final chapter in my career of midday mardling on the wireless. I play a couple of recordings made over a decade ago with Roy Hudd, when he was starring as Fagin in *Oliver!* at Norwich Theatre Royal, and Arnold Wesker when he and his nephew Keith put our voices together for the world premiere of *Sugar Beet*, a dialect piece Wesker wrote in 1953 while working in the county.

November 9 – An astounding day. I am sent home from Norfolk Tower by managing editor Tim Bishop following my article in the *Eastern Daily Press* criticising the way the BBC is taking the 'local' out of local radio. As I prepare for my final live weekday programme, I am summoned to his office. He has come straight from home where his wife has just given birth to a daughter. He calls my article 'a kick in the teeth for your colleagues' and reckons I'm not in the right frame of mind to carry out my final show. I defend the article and my aptitude for broadcasting – but he insists I go home. I call at the *Eastern Daily Press* office to break the news to old colleague Colin Chinery, who handled my offending article for the centre spread in today's paper. I have my picture taken at the train station waiting for an early journey home. The phone rings for the rest of the day and evening. Anglia Television send a crew round to feature the story on their 6.30 programme. My head is buzzing. My heart is pounding. My future is so uncertain. And all because I wave the Norfolk flag with vigour. Diane and the boys provide quiet but solid support.

Tim Bishop

November 11 – Wet and dull on the Norfolk beat, but I find plenty of warmth at book-signing sessions in Wymondham and Dereham. The centre of Wymondham is an absolute mess, all dug up and full of obstacles, but we enjoy a good turn-out at George Reeve's shop. Fred Wigby, the Grand Old Mardler of *Dinnertime* fame, and Bob Bagshaw, a more recent recruit to the programme help keep me company.

November 14 – Still waiting for news from Norfolk Tower. It's through the damp and mist to meet up with Nick Patrick at Norwich railway station for a trip to sunny Southwold. We record some items for a Radio 2 arts programme.

November 15 – End of my Radio Norfolk career. Sad but predictable conclusion to my long-running clash with Tim Bishop. After just over 15 years on air, my voice is silenced following that article in the *Eastern Daily Press* I will not apologise for expressing my views and he says I cannot continue working for the BBC while I hold them. A few tears round the office when he announces the news. I head for the Horse and Dray pub and within minutes a reporter and photographer are in attendance. They have Mr Bishop's statement and I give my side of the story. I do well to make constructive statements considering the jumble of emotions around. The picture for the morning paper will show me supping a pint while reading farewell letters.

November 16 – A day of abject loneliness after all the drama. Diane goes to work in the pharmacy at Hellesdon. The boys go to school. I am home alone. A few phone calls but it seems most old friends want to give me a breathing space before asking for a closer examination of the reasons behind my farewell. I sit and find it hard to do anything but drink tea and run through events of the past few weeks. My £100-a-day broadcasting fee from Radio Norfolk has dried up completely, and I have only a few lucrative engagements lined up. So I'll have to cast my writing and talking nets wider.

November 17 – The weather turns wintry as I clear my desk at Radio Norfolk, some items stretching back to the early days of 1980. Mr Bishop is away and so the climate is not as tense as it might have been. Pleasant exchanges with several colleagues although it's clear some are too embarrassed to talk. I thought a few of the older friends would have been louder and quicker in their support.

November 23 – My first official engagement since leaving Radio Norfolk is a Round Table dinner at the Castle Hotel in Downham Market. I answer a request to outline events leading up to my exit and invite comments and questions after. A lively debate ensues with the rapidly changing face of Norfolk at the heart of it. Some see changes as inevitable, while others, particularly home-grown supporters, see my predicament as another nail in Norfolk's coffin.

November 25 – I'm gradually accepting that my life has to change radically. I have had a few days to weigh up various implications and to push aside as much of the bitterness as possible. I dislike being on my own at present for any length of time, although I accept that may well have to be the case in the coming months. Little reaction from former colleagues although letters continue to flood into the *Eastern Daily Press*. All sing my praises and criticise the manner of my departure. Sadly, adulation and sympathy can't pay the mortgage. Even so, I have been genuinely lifted by the public response; some of it from people I didn't know were there when I was in full cry over the airwaves.

November 27 – Pleasing diversion in the shape of Jarrold's Literary Lunch with a Norfolk flavour at the Hotel Norwich. Over 150 guests enjoy the meal and mardling at this the first completely home-grown production. Chairman John Timpson introduces Mary Barnard, Jean Turner, Bob

Bagshaw and me and we're all kept busy signing copies of our books.

November 30 – Long haul to Watton and the Richmond Park Golf Club to take part in an event with former Norwich City football manager Mike Walker. He has recently put money into

Bob Bagshaw

a skip-hire firm, a point with no little irony as we sit in front of a lively audience to discuss football in general and Mr Walker's career in particular. I also underline that this must be the first time two out-of-work *Eastern Daily Press* columnists have appeared together on the same stage!

December

December 1 – Intriguing start to the month with an eye on tomorrow. I make the trip down the lane to Holt Hall Residential and Field Study Centre, an impressive Victorian building built in the Elizabethan style. It is set in over 80 acres of ancient woodland, lakes and gardens. George Carrick is the amiable warden with Theo Fanthorpe, of Dereham renown, as his deputy. We talk over plans for a Norfolk-flavoured weekend next October. I'll send an outline on my proposed programme with the accent on humour.

December 8 – We make the long, frosty haul to Southwold. Christmas lights go on, and I'm judging the best-dressed shop window and fancy dress competition in the town I love. We book in at Links Cottage Hotel overlooking the common and head for the packed streets after a tasty fish and chip supper. Santa Claus arrives to do the lighting-up honours on a wonderfully made space shuttle.

December 10 – Lunchtime drink and chat at the refurbished Cliftonville Hotel on Cromer front with retired journalist Bill Hicks. He's taking a fatherly interest in my plight after events at Radio Norfolk and in a letter to Mr Bishop even offered to act as a mediator. The offer was declined. But I do appreciate Bill's efforts.

December 12 – Uplifting morning at Anglia Television. News editor David Jennings and producer Mike Read chew over a few ideas for a short series of programmes they want me to make next March. I'm enthused by the project and not just because of the money! They want me to look beyond the county boundaries although they are at pains to point

KEITH SKIPPER'S NORFOLK DIARIES

out I'm not being asked to compromise my Norfolkness in any way.

December 25 – We wake to the sight of snow – a white Christmas! The boys hold fire until 7.30a.m. and then we all rise to start on the parcel-unwrapping marathon. Danny is delighted with his Mega Drive equipment while Robin's eyes light up at the sight of X-Men.

December 26 – A winter wonderland for Boxing Day. Heavy snow overnight ensures a quiet time indoors keeping warm and busy, although other parts of the country have escaped the whitewash. Climate reaches boiling point at Carrow Road after the Canaries lose 1–0 to Southend. Three people are arrested and two policemen hurt amid ugly scenes. There are calls for the resignation of embattled club chairman Robert Chase. Martin O'Neill left earlier this week to take over as manager of Leicester with Gary Megson returning as boss at Carrow Road.

December 27 – How strange to hear my voice featuring so prominently on Radio Norfolk over the festive period. *A Norfolk Journey*, my series of documentaries and two instalments of *Should the Team Think?* are served up as leading delicacies. Not bad for someone shown the door six weeks ago. I smile at the irony and wonder how many listeners will chuckle.

December 31 – I sit down to take stock of the year and to work out what good might have come from my change of direction. I have my regular column in the *Eastern Daily Press* with the prospect of more support from Prospect House. I have an appointment to sort out ideas for a series with Anglia Television. I have several useful bookings on the social scene as well as a weekend of spreading the Norfolk word at Holt Hall. I have a great fund of public goodwill to back me up as I seek out other openings. I have strong family support and so much to be grateful for as the snow melts away as suddenly as it came. Such a rich symbol of how quickly life can change.

Boxing Day's winter wonderland.

January

January 1 – Snow disappears as a new year dawns. I find time for a stroll around Cromer. Vandalism scars the Melbourne Hotel, wearing an ugly frown as it looks down on the sea and a pier shrouded in mist. Other signs of commonplace anti-social behaviour with broken windows and ugly graffiti inevitable results of shops closing down.

January 10 – Prospects are generally bright with a better looking programme for the year than seemed likely only a few days ago. The *Eastern Daily Press* has agreed to place our Norfolk Night concerts under their umbrella while plans for Anglia TV programmes gather pace. There are also plans for a local concert at the Theatre Royal in Norwich with Sid Kipper starring in his home county.

January 16 – A morning in North Walsham as persistent fog hangs around. Young unemployed sit listlessly around the town centre or drift down the street with no apparent aim. I call in at the Parish Church for a few minutes of meditation and to read the introduction to the book I've just bought at The Angel Bookshop. I've been looking for a copy of Augustus Jessopp's *Arcady For Better For Worse* for some time.

January 19 – A significant day in my plans for a busier programme. I visit Prospect House for a meeting with Peter Franzen, editor of the *Eastern Daily Press*, and a couple of members of the promotions department. There's a warm welcome for my package of ideas, including *Eastern Daily Press* backing for the Press Gang concerts as they continue round the area.

February

February 1 – Visit to Norwich reinforces my feelings about the old fabric being torn away. Streets full of buskers, beggars and *Big Issue* salesmen. At least the latter are cheerful and attempting to make a social mark. Knots of aggressive youngsters, some of them with fierce looking dogs in front, dare anyone to get in their way or complain about their behaviour. Down-and-outs at the back of the market seem to multiply and overall this part of the city has a seedy, sorry flavour. No wonder I race to hide in bookshops. When I moved to Norwich to work on the Press in the late 1960s it was a cheerful, safe place by night or day. Now there's an obvious unease after dark – and even

concern at times about antics in broad daylight. It can't be raging nostalgia that tells me life used to be more pleasant.

February 13 – I take stock. I still feel hurt at my dismissal from Radio Norfolk. There's no chance to put it all behind me as people continue to greet me with words of sympathy, invariable coupled with remarks about not listening any more. Even so, I have all but accepted that my future rests in other directions and the sooner I get really busy the better.

February 17 – Busy day at Wensum Lodge in Norwich for my WEA session called *The Norfolk Way*. Over 20 enthusiasts share their views on the county as I provide a variety of readings, reflections and amusing yarns. It is well received although there's one rather jarring note sounded by a woman who has returned to Norfolk. She complains about being kept waiting in shops because people are talking!

February 26 – Memorable family day out on the fresh-air trail. Holt Country Park exercises our lungs and legs before we make a wonderful 'discovery' – Baconsthorpe Castle. Down a farm track to the remains of the English Heritage gem. Two flint-faced gate-houses and parts of the original curtain wall indicate it was once a handsome building. The castle, essentially a moated and fortified manor house, was started in the 1480s by Sir John Heydon, a cunning lawyer who made his money during the Wars of the Roses. Geese in the moat honk displeasure at human intrusion. Snowdrops, like harbingers of spring, are far more welcome. Sun breaks through to brighten the courtyard and you have to use imagination in this history lesson in the open air. Water towers and farm silos over the way, rubbing shoulders with telegraph poles, seem out of place. Coincidentally, we hear that Norfolk landowner and former High Sheriff Captain William Bulwer-Long has died at 59. He lived at Heydon Hall and was instrumental in conserving the pretty village of Heydon near the hall.

March

March 1 – St David's Day visit to Gresham's School at Holt for a literary dinner with the *Eastern Daily Press*'s Charles Roberts in the chair. The other two speakers keeping me company are Juliet Barker, who has written a handsome new tome on the Brontës, and Mary Mackie, a prolific novelist who also spent seven years looking after Felbrigg Hall with her husband Chris. I concentrate on

KEITH SKIPPER'S NORFOLK DIARIES

Norfolk writers and writings, culminating in a Boy John letter written on March 1, 1958.

March 5 – One of the most productive days of my new life. Rain in the air as I catch the train from Cromer – yes, they're still running – and head for a chat with producer Mike Hill at Anglia Television. We sort out plans for filming next week.

March 12 – On the road with Anglia Television. First day of shooting for a short series on topics close to my heart – schools, farming, shops and the search for solitude. My journey begins at Beeston Primary School and continues into Suffolk with a look at a community shop at Rattlesden.

*Filming series for Anglia Television
begins at Beeston School.*

March 14 – Return to How Hill for a mardle with reedcutter Eric Edwards. Cold but satisfying Broadland scene before we move on to Attleborough to meet a couple who have left the rat-race to take up pottery.

March 15 – Last day on the road with the TV cameras. We head for Brian and Liz Allen's 1000-acre farm at Hempnall to size up the changing face of agriculture. Chilly going across the fields where giant tractors now have the horse-power to rule. New-born lambs near the house point the way to spring. Brian's parents ruled here before him. He's planting trees to break up the prairie pattern, but European

form-filling soon takes a satisfied smile off your face. Still four men employed on the farm, a veritable crowd in these days of mechanisation.

March 22 – A wonderful start to the Press Gang season at Dilham Village Hall in aid of the local football club, who are rooted to the bottom of Division 4 of the Anglian Combination. A big audience and local reporter Chris Stokes joins me on stage at half-time for a chat about his work and to draw the raffle. It's a rousing opener now that these evenings of Norfolk entertainment have come under the *Eastern Daily Press* umbrella.

March 27 – *Skipper's World* hits the Anglia Television screens as I take that journey back to Beeston School to launch a series of four programmes. I owe much to the camerawork and editing, but I mustn't be too modest as praise comes in. I can't help thinking how much work goes into just a few minutes on the box – such a contrast with the world of radio.

March 30 – Uplifting concert at Aslacton and Great Moulton Coronation Hall with the regular Press Gang cast on parade. Former village headmaster Brian Patrick is accompanied by his wife Biddy, who was evacuated to Aslacton during the second world war. She joins us on stage with home-spun verses recalling that diversion.

April

April 12 – Happy return to Sheringham Little Theatre for a Norfolk concert. We were on stage here two years ago for the *Henry Ramey Upcher* lifeboat centenary. This time we are invited to help the theatre's reseating appeal. Our guest artist is Tony Hall, *Eastern Daily Press* cartoonist for the past 17 years. He's a dab hand on the melodeon, but arrives late after breaking down on his motorbike at Roughton.

*Tony Hall – fine cartoonist
and dab hand on
the melodeon.*

April 16 – A breath of spring. I have a slightly sore forehead to prove it. I sat outside the back door yesterday afternoon and caught the sun. I'll be ready for the next dynamic burst. Sunny memories as I read *David Copperfield* again and wonder why Yarmouth has made so little of the upturned boat house on the beach and the Peggotty connections.

1996

April 20 – Warming trip home to Beeston Ploughshare for an evening of poetry and mardling. Peter Tyler of Litcham is the moving spirit and his family and friends are out in force. Jenny Cunningham, singer and storyteller, from North Elmham, joins me on the entertaining list. I did wonder if this would work on a busy Saturday night in a popular village pub, but the reception is pleasantly surprising. I read some of my own verses including those I penned after a previous visit.

April 24 – Anglia Television, my most recent employers, receive a 'good, but could do better' verdict from broadcasting watchdog the Independent Television Commission. They say Anglia should be praised for the range and quality of its programmes. But there's strong criticism for reduction in its drama production and for 'losing its regional identity.' I have often wondered how this can be maintained in so vast a concern, although the news has been split into east and west bulletins. Of course, my public disagreements with the BBC were based largely on a matter of local identity. I sense we are on the verge of a new acceptance that local pride could be a solid virtue after all.

May

May 7 – A packed day. Morning date in Norwich for my industrial tribunal preliminary hearing. It decides my claims of unfair dismissal and for compensation from the BBC cannot go ahead because I was a freelance and not employee at the time of my departure. I'm sorry there's no chance to tell the full story. BBC representatives, including BBC Radio Norfolk managing editor Tim Bishop and Head of Centre (East) Arnold Miller are clearly relieved at the verdict. I talk to the local press afterwards, expressing my disappointment at the way a firm can dispense with you at a whim after 15 years of loyal service. At the hearing a lot is made of my opportunities to make extra money as a result of being a 'personality' on the wireless, but there's a failure as usual to recognise the way presenters can do an excellent public relations job for the station, often for little financial reward. My evening fixture is a real pleasure, my 14th successive stint as adjudicator at the Dialect section of the Cromer Festival. Old colleague Stewart Orr records part of the proceedings for a Radio 5 series on 'tribalism'. How ironic that we should be involved only hours after my clash with BBC bosses who don't like my brand of parochialism!

May 18 – Last Press Gang outing of the spring season at the Lakeside Country Club in Lyng to help raise money for the Foxley Parish Church roof restoration fund. Singer Ian

Prettyman has to call off with illness, but the rest of the regular crew are on parade to provide the perfect alternative to television's *Eurovision Song Contest*.

May 26 – A cultural triumph! Nearly a full house at Norwich Theatre Royal as I compere *Norfolk 'n' Good*, with Sid Kipper starring in his inimitable way. At last he is being afforded some of the adulation he deserves in his native county. Cromer Smugglers, Muck-Carter Lambert, Keith Loads, Olly Day, Bobby Benton, Nigel Boy Syer, Damien Barber and the WI Mawthers are also on stage. Theatre bosses seem surprised at the size of our audience and the enthusiastic reception for all things Norfolk. I did tell them squit is a commercial commodity.

Keith Loads

May 28 – It pains me to admit it, but there's no chance of taking my battle with the BBC any further. I don't have the resources, financial or emotional, to carry on and it is unfair to ask my family to make any more sacrifices.

May 31 – Big night at Potter Heigham as the Broads Museum dream turns into reality. I'm invited to say a few words as 'a champion of Norfolk heritage'. This museum will be the only one to chronicle the influence of man upon the Broads. At this early stage they have an enormous variety of exhibits including boats, tools, books and photographs.

June

June 2 – A truly crowning achievement for Coronation Day. I walk the eight miles in the Kelling Hospital Trail and Rail event – and live to tell the tale. Warm sunshine means an all-over tan – that's all over my head – but my legs stand up well to the challenging stroll from the hospital grounds down to Weybourne cliffs and on to Sheringham Park.

June 7 – Thunderstorms across the county signal the end of our blazing little summer. Can't say I'm sorry, although at least I don't have to endure the city stifle after many years of inside suffering.

June 15 – Devotion to one of Norfolk's beautiful corners wins old friend Phyllis Ellis an MBE in the Queen's birthday honours. Typically, the widow of naturalist Ted

Ellis immediately dedicates her award to everyone who works to safeguard Wheatfen Broad, Surlingham.

June 21 – I enjoy a visit to Lexham Hall with friend Pat Maitland. We sing for our supper in a big marquee as the boss Neil Foster hosts a special event for the estate workers 50 years after his father moved in to revive the whole place. A whiff of timelessness about the scene as we amble through Litcham towards the parkland and impressive hall. Sadly, there's no cricket team at present to take advantage of one of the best settings in the county. Happily, there's an obvious family spirit among the workers, some of whom have been there for over 30 years. A real mixture of accents around the tables, and a chap from Leicester says I'm the first Norfolk person he's met with a sense of humour!

June 29 – Rain starts as I open the Suffield Park Infants School Fun Day at Cromer – and refuses to stop. So stalls are moved inside after a couple of dances round the Maypole. Former head teacher Mary Luh is there to receive presents and praise on her retirement.

July

July 3 – My vegetable plot flourishes – it's a bit rich to call it a garden – and the rain is extremely welcome. Some holiday-makers will disagree about that but all the talk of drought means we need much more.

July 13 – Late afternoon safari to Swanton Morley for the opening of their new Village Hall, an impressive testament to six years of community spirit in the name of fund-raising. I judge the carnival floats before festivities begin at the hall. A growing village – the old hall was too small – Swanton Morley does seem to have a heart. The RAF connection used to be its best-advertised asset. Now the Army's moving in on the old base.

July 16 – A Norfolk livestock market becomes the region's first major casualty of the BSE crisis, closing because falling beef sales have ruined business. After 136 years, King's Lynn cattle market will stage its last auction next week.

July 19 – Prestigious appointment at Norwich Cathedral to open the Norfolk and Norwich Art Circle's 149th exhibition. I meet president Delphine Dickson by the South Door and we tiptoe past the last strains of Evensong for a preview of the paintings.

July 22 – Delightful evening at Narborough church presenting *All Preachers Great and Small* as the last event in their festival called Norfolk Glory. A full house as I dip into my memories and the diaries of Parson James Woodforde of Weston Longville and the Revd Benjamin Armstrong of East Dereham. Before we start there's a surprise visit from Winnie Chapman of Sporle, my old school cook and ardent supporter. She gets into her wheelchair to take a look at the church's floral offerings.

July 23 – Busy outings continue and sultry weather gives way to thunder and lightning while I'm addressing an illustrious gathering at Pensthorpe Wildfowl Park. It's the 10th anniversary of the Norfolk Rural Community Council. President Sir Timothy Colman bids me a warm welcome and shows a keen interest in Norfolk squit. Harvest has started so we were bound to get rain.

August

August 1 – A sure sign of approaching maturity – I'm interviewed about Norwich City's epic FA Cup run of 1958/1959! Peter Slater of Radio 5 pays a call to record my impressions of what the Canaries' feats did for Norfolk when I was a lad at school. The programme is due out in the New Year and he's been busy chatting to some of the characters of that memorable saga, Ron Ashman, Terry Bly and Terry Allcock among them.

August 9 – A wonderful diversion at teatime. We accept a family invitation to join friends Pat Maitland and Geoffrey Peake for a sail on Hickling Broad. We meet them at Stalham and follow them down twisting roads to the Whispering Reeds boatyard as the weather puts on its best face of the day. Fairly calm going. 'There's artist Roland Hill's old studio in the reeds!' is typical of the spotting exercise. There's real serenity and room to think out here.

August 26 – Bank Holiday Monday 'at home' – and I applaud the fact that I don't see a moving vehicle all day!

August 27 – Our Suffolk safari plans take a knock as the weather turns sour. Dramatic thunderstorms confine us to the car in front of Framlingham Castle. The boys are none too impressed by the instant *son et lumière* production with lightning and thunder across the ramparts.

August 29 – We batten down the hatches as August is visited by the wettest and wildest day I can recall. Rain lashes down, trees heave and crash, windows rattle and the world is dark. For all that, there's a strange sort of comfort at being confined to barracks in conditions like these in such a pleasant setting. We gather Cromer's end of the pier show has to be cancelled as cross-winds make it dangerous to even walk on the pier.

September

September 7 – I launch Heath Week in Norfolk at Buxton Heath near our old stamping ground at Hevingham. We take a family stroll in bright weather through the bracken and heather. In the evening it's off to sing for my supper at the Norfolk Rural Life Museum at Gressenhall in the restored chapel. The Society of Folk Life Studies members have been taking a close look at our villages and they ask for a spot of local entertainment. The society last visited Norfolk over a decade ago. It was founded in 1961 to 'further the study of the traditional ways of life in Great Britain and Ireland.'

September 18 – Happy evening at Trunch Village Hall for the local harvest supper. I have to sing for mine but it's a warm and receptive climate. I sit next to 'Mr Trunch', Arthur Amis, born in the village in 1907 and author of the delightful memoirs *From Dawn to Dusk*. He recalls the hall being built in 1912 for just under £500 and regales me with countless incidents, sad and amusing. They've named a road after him in the village, and two newcomers from Buckinghamshire sitting opposite tell us they live there.

September 21 – Danny's 10th birthday – and a memorable one as he joins me on the Norfolk cultural trail at Gressenhall. An evening of local music, verses, stories and squit is well supported in the old chapel, refurbished as an art centre, and Danny does his bit with a couple of John Kett's Norfolk poems. Tony Hall, the *Eastern Daily Press* cartoonist, plays his melodeon while poet Peter Tyler and storyteller Jenny Cunningham are the other performers on the stage where I stepped forward to mardle a fortnight ago.

September 24 – What a busy spell! I'm out again, this time at Hamond's High School in Swaffham presenting *Norfolk Voices* at the town's arts festival. I select some of my favourite writers and read extracts interspersing with reflections on my life and times. I follow folk singer Julie Felix, who was here last night.

October

October 2 – Robin's seventh birthday but he doesn't play ball as we mark the occasion with a family outing. A magic lantern show in Cromer Parish Hall attracts a big and enthu-siastic crowd and we reckon the lad may care to have this as his special occasion. It's not long before Robin is curled up asleep on Mum's lap! The show is fascinating, comparing old to new and underlining the way folk entertained them-selves before cinema and television took over. Another milestone today; my *Eastern Daily Press* Wednesday article, restored a year ago, features in the last broadsheet edition of our local paper. It's smaller from tomorrow.

October 4 – Off to the Victorian mansion they call Holt Hall for a mardling weekend entitled *The Heart of Norfolk*. We meet each other before a log fire, and I outline my programme. After a meal we enjoy a wide-ranging chat from the impact of two world wars to the influx of newcomers and holiday-makers in recent years. We debate ways of keeping dialect to the fore without being too self-conscious about it. Grey squirrels leap and bound in the beautiful parkland outside. Sounds of nature in harmony with voices singing Norfolk's praises.

October 5 – More mardling around the big log fire. It becomes clear that the growing number of old folk concen-trated in coastal areas will be a key debating point. We express our sadness at the obvious decline of Yarmouth as an attractive holiday spot. Other worries include Village Halls in small communities and the need for the County Council to adopt a meaningful strategy over growing numbers of older residents. Our evening session is the Holt Hall Horkey, a showpiece of local humour. John Ford, heavy horse enthusiast from Claxton, is the winner.

November

November 4 – I share a speaking spotlight with Lancashire captain Mike Watkinson at the Norfolk Cricket Alliance dinner at Pinebanks in Norwich. I strike a serious note with a warning about dangers of abuse towards umpires threat-ening a big disciplinary crisis in the local game. Sadly, there's no one present from the local press to give the warning big headlines.

November 9 – Happy return to Hevingham Village Hall to compere a Press Gang concert to raise funds for a memo-rial in the village church to the Revd Christopher Basil Morgan. His son, Tim sets the scene for a packed congre-gation, and over £550 is raised towards the memorial. This could have been a difficult day for me marking the first anniversary of my being sent home from Radio Norfolk after that article in the local paper. But I'm able to reflect and find a smile at such a local celebration. Tony Hall plays the old *Dinnertime Show* signature tune 'Primrose' on his melodeon, and even that sets my foot tapping rather than my heart pounding.

November 11 – Evening trip to County Hall where the work of people dedicated to preserving Norfolk's beauty is honoured. The Norfolk Society's annual awards are so well attended there's standing room only.

November 28 – Television cook Delia Smith is installed as the first woman director in Norwich City's history as the Canaries unveil a new eight-strong boardroom team. Delia is joined on the board by three more new directors and between them they're expected to pump more than £2 million worth of vital loan capital into the club. Meanwhile, the gate closes this evening on 110 years of chocolate making in Norwich. The last Rolo comes off the production line at Nestlé. The closure of the factory that had 900 workers when the Swiss food giant announced its closure two years ago will be marked tomorrow with a march and a disco at the Labour Club.

November 29 – Yarmouth is blessed. The Bishop of Thetford goes to the top of Havenbridge House to pray for the port and its prosperity. High above the Yare, the Rt Revd Hugo de Waal blesses the town and its people during a week-long fact-finding mission.

December

December 6 – Drama in Norwich as Danny and I pursue the shopping trail. We're in Jarrolds enjoying a cup of coffee and scones when shoppers run screaming for their lives as a car careers out of control down the sloping cobbled streets of Pottergate, Lobster Lane and Bedford Street. A 60-year-old woman is killed instantly and shoppers are scattered 'like human skittles'.

December 21 – Evening date at Foulsham, the large village earning a glowing reputation for lighting up in grand festive style. Visitors from many miles away are attracted, especially after television coverage, and it must be difficult for anyone here to stay apart from this Christmas campaign.

As I make the raffle draw I express the hope that Foulsham does not strive to make it 'bigger and better' every year, so surrendering that vital local feel.

December 23 – Death of former Hamond's Grammar School maths master George More revives an outstanding yarn from my schooldays. I spent an entire day in the toilet at Fransham railway station because I hadn't done my geometry homework. I was scared of 'Mickey' More, who allowed no levity in his lessons and put fear into those for whom his subject didn't come easy. He sneered rather than smiled, and yet seemed a rather benign character as we met several times in recent years.

December 25 – Morning rain at Cromer on Christmas Day, although there are dustings of snow in Norwich and other places. I'm delighted by a selection of new reading material including a wonderful anthology of East Anglian writers. My dip becomes a plunge before lunch.

December 26 – Intriguing Boxing Day diversion in the shape of an evening mardle to a house party of festive guests at the Blakeney Hotel. A journey into the relative unknown but it turns out to be a pleasant experience. Guests assemble in the lounge, many of them just returned from an afternoon trip to Norwich Theatre Royal for the panto *Jack and the Beanstalk*. I call my talk 'Country Christmas', readings from a variety of books interspaced with reflections and yarns.

December 27 – 'It's a white Christmas after all!' enthuses Robin as he charges into our bedroom and tugs open the curtains to reveal a few inches of snow. A truly festive scene but it soon turns to slush as he joins me for an amble into town. His feet are cold – 'They won't co-operate!' he exclaims – and it's clear the big change in weather has sharpened his taste for language.

December 31 – Diane's birthday as we bid farewell to a dramatic year. There have been difficulties but we have proved we can do without some of the things we once took for granted. It gives you a bit of a self-righteous glow to admit it.

◆ ◆ ◆

January

January 1 – It is with a fair degree of anticipation that I bound over the threshold into 1997 after a year of change and challenge. Norfolk has been good to me – and all the signs are of more goodness to come. I have been forced to diversify although writing still affords me most pleasure.

January 3 – The bitter weather bites again as icy winds and pavements make getting about a real chore. It's remarkable that a place like Cromer with so many old folk allows walking areas to stay like skating rinks. No wonder it's fairly quiet in town and there's only one stall on the car park usually given over to a busy Friday market.

January 27 – I go to Dunstan Hall through the mists to launch Age Concern's special year to mark its 50th anniversary in Norfolk. This coincides with an invitation to the county's retired workers to join a major project to revive rural communities. Help the Aged has been given nearly £2.5 million from the Millennium Commission which it plans to use to release the huge potential of pensioners living in country areas.

January 31 – Shadow Home Secretary Jack Straw put his 'zero tolerance' policy into action as he cleans graffiti off a Norwich city centre wall. Mr Straw has championed a successful New York-style attack on crime involving a crackdown on minor offences as part of the campaign against more serious ones. He puts on protective clothing to launch his 'Get Tough on Graffiti' message on the streets of Norwich.

February

February 18 – Norwich Castle has been plunged into darkness after vandals smash £23,000 worth of floodlights. It will be some weeks before the complete lighting is back to full working order. What will it take to spark an outcry by public and media against such senseless and expensive vandalism? We heard the other day how a mother and toddler group at Martham were left stunned after their store shed was broken into and all toys smashed. There's been hideous vandalism in Yarmouth churchyard… and the sickening list continues day after day.

February 20 – Town clerk Ron Nash is to retire after clocking up one of the longest local government careers in Britain. Ron, 71, steps down from his post at North Walsham next month after a career in council work spanning 56 years. He was 16 when he took a job as a junior council clerk in his home town of Leighton Buzzard. He came to North Walsham in 1956 as clerk of the urban district council, becoming part-time town clerk in the 1974 local government shake up.

February 21 – Snowdrops wave at our front door. Other signs of spring round the corner but experience teaches you to be wary of suggestions that winter has called it a day.

Signs of spring.

February 23 – Only hours after their Norwich theatre is wrecked in an arson attack, trustees vow 'we'll be back'. This defiant message follows the blaze at Sewell Barn Theatre in the grounds of Blyth Jex Upper School.

February 25 – An historic Broads pub is badly damaged as flames rip through the first floor. Staff and drinkers in the bar of the 300-year-old King's Head at Coltishall only realise the building is on fire when a passer-by raises the alarm.

February 28 – Early start for the long trip to Lancashire to speak at a sporting function organised by Chorley Football

Club of the Northern Premier League. How did this fixture come my way? Well, the club's commercial manager is Ernie Howe, a Beeston contemporary who got in touch a few months ago to see if I'd make the journey. Ernie's there as I arrive and there's plenty to chat about in our first meeting for over 20 years. It's not easy singing for your supper in 'foreign' parts but my mixture of yarns and reflections of my soccer reporting years goes down well. I take a look at the Chorley ground; meet chairman and directors, sponsors and supporters. Plenty of local pride involved even if the going is tough.

March

March 3 – Lotus Cars – made in Norfolk by women in hairnets! That's the latest insult from motoring writer and broadcaster Jeremy Clarkson. Asked to explain the preference for a Ferrari over Lotus, he replies: 'Because a Ferrari is built by supreme craftsmen in Italy and a Lotus is built in Norfolk by women in hairnets.' Clarkson's weird impressions are thought to have been formed during a trip to Hethel two years ago. His self-styled role as a bumpkin-basher is gaining notoriety. We'd do well to ignore him.

March 12 – I have treated myself to a John Arlott double cassette for my birthday. I listen with affection to his radio cricket commentaries from the 1940s and 1950s. He truly was the voice of summer.

March 15 – Memorable evening at Bradenham Village Hall for a Press Gang concert to raise over £400 for a local play area. Baked potatoes, sausages and beans are on the menu before we entertain a full house. This is community life at its most vibrant and we can hardly fail in the face of such determination to have a good time. Travelling through Toftwood and Shipdham, long and characterless places full of houses and frowns; it's a pleasure to see the lights shine out across Bradenham green.

March 22 – Another long haul on the Press Gang trail to Carleton Rode where they are raising money to get the church bells ringing again in time for a Millennium peal. A large gathering, more appreciative than rumbustious, but still, all shows are different and we don't take these mood swings too seriously.

March 24 – I behave myself in the classroom at Great Dunham Primary School. I'm invited to open an £80,000 extension, a new library and inside toilets. This is a warm, welcoming place and Diane joins me for a school dinner. I know it's going to be a good day as we leave Fakenham's straggle behind and find that refreshingly open run to Tittleshall and Litcham. Past Litcham Common on the road into Dunham, and the banks are packed with primroses.

March 31 – Last day of the month and we could do with some hefty downpours rather than April showers. Talk of a summer drought takes the shine off the lovely Easter weather. We're told hosepipe bans are inevitable.

April

April 2 – A new era dawns as the first woman High Sheriff of Norfolk is sworn in. Lady Marilyn Evans-Lombe is the seventh member of the Lombe family to hold the ancient title which dates back more than a thousand years.

April 12 – A pulsating Press Gang concert in a crowded Village Hall at Hanworth, a few miles from Cromer but a world away in many respects. Down twisting lanes to this picturesque parish and a splendid reception. The performers respond and we have no hesitation in voting it one of the best outings in a decade. Laughter shakes the small but homely building.

April 13 – How goes the battle for Norfolk's soul? A day to ponder as the weather turns cooler and the general election campaign still fails to rouse any deep passions. Perhaps my feelings are being influenced by my rural rides taking precedence over regular visits to the city, but I do sense village life is holding its own against the rising tide of uniformity. There remains a danger, however, of a new building boom eating into more of our country areas as well as spreading our towns into an ugly sprawl. There's no doubting the different flavours in different parts of the county. Yarmouth and King's Lynn can be so depressing. Thetford continues its grind towards urban decay. South Norfolk has to put up with so much commuter traffic. Mid Norfolk, my old patch, still boasts plenty of open country. North Norfolk remains the most attractive area in many ways, but retirement-led immigration and more holiday-makers make it hard to see that essential character properly safeguarded.

April 25 – Another dinner date, this time with the Norwich Society of Chartered Accountants. My mardle goes down well and the bonus is to be seated alongside a charming couple from Dublin, the national vice-president and his wife. We compare notes on Norfolk and the Emerald Isle, where they're also glad of today's rain to get rid of 40 shades of rust

April 29 – My 15th successive year handing out comments and certificates on dialect night at the Cromer Festival. Danny and Robin are thrilled to collect distinction certificates – and Diane springs a surprise by taking to the stage with a poem of her own. This is the festival's 50th anniversary and we're proud to make it a real family affair.

May

May 3 – Back on my home beat, opening the new Village Hall at Mileham and then enjoying a session at Litcham's own village museum with Ron and Brenda Shaw. There's also a five-acre sanctuary for birds and animals. Mileham's new hall comes three years after the old one was burnt down.

May 5 – Another family affair – at home in the garden. We sort out the vegetable patch at the side of the house, leaving a small portion at the end for Danny's hollyhocks and sunflowers. Rain arrives right on cue as our efforts are completed. Now I can make my daily inspections. Did I hear that? The skyline at Yarmouth is dramatically changed with an earth-shaking double explosion. The South Denes power station chimney has been a landmark for 40 years. But today the county's tallest structure, at 360ft, 45ft higher than Norwich cathedral's spire, bites the dust in spectacular fashion.

May 23 – A big boost as a letter arrives from Countryside Books asking me to consider the idea of writing *Hidden Norfolk* for them. Right up my street! I have so much material to put to use and my knowledge of our villages should give me a head start. We celebrate with a family outing to Mundesley's Coronation Hall for an evening of Gilbert and Sullivan delights with the Sheringham Savoyards. It's a little bit embarrassing to win a basket of fruit in the raffle during the interval.

June

June 1 – What an exhausting start to the month! I step out again for the North Norfolk by Trail and Rail event in aid of the Kelling Hospital appeal, this time with Danny on parade. A tour of the hospital wards brings inevitable jokes about saving a bed for me when we get back – and then it's best feet forward for an eight-mile safari. A lively breeze is transformed into half a gale on Weybourne cliffs.

June 6 – Intriguing meal out – in Cromer. A curry supper with Professor Peter Trudgill, his wife and two friends. Peter, who works in a Swiss university, returns to his native Norfolk on a regular basis. He's an expert in linguistics, a keen supporter of our dialect – and an admirer of entertainer Sid Kipper.

June 13 – It was 17 years ago today that I met Diane at a disco in Yarmouth. No wonder I have serious misgivings about the music industry. Seriously though, time flies and we share a few memories and chuckles. The lads join in with good healthy banter to mark the anniversary. Lights go out as we experience a power cut just before tea. Thank goodness for gas and good company. The poetic style of Edmund Blunden continues to light up my bedtime reading. A book published over 60 years ago, and costing 50p from the second-hand shelves, has marvels in every line as he takes the reader through the months.

June 15 – Father's Day treats. Robin brings up my tray for breakfast in bed. Danny pays the man at the Rocket House Café for our refreshments later in the morning. I'm touched… even though Mum did supply the means.

June 29 – North Elmham's water-mill, dating back to the Middle Ages, is being converted into 11 self-contained flats.

July

July 7 – Trip to Ashill for *Hidden Norfolk* material. The village church is notable for the remarkable record of the Revd Bartholomew Edwards. He was rector here for 76 years and died nine days short of his 100th birthday. He never retired, never went away for a holiday and hardly missed a service. He died in 1889.

July 11 – An evening out with a difference. Mist rolls in to challenge the steam at Weybourne halt on the North Norfolk railway line as I join Sheringham Salvation Army followers and their friends on a fund-raising drive. We board the train at Sheringham, chug along to Kelling and then make a stop at Weybourne. Chairs on the platform to listen to the jazz band opposite next door to the waiting room. I cross the line to stand at the microphone and deliver a selection of Norfolk yarns. Many in the audience are dressed as tramps. Well, Norfolk humour can stand up in any setting.

July 18 – Old football reporting colleague Bruce Robinson revives a host of memories from the 1970s in sending me a copy of his latest book, *Passing Seasons*, in which he reflects on 50 years' links with the game. He mentions our exploits several times and I feel a nostalgic tug or two back towards the game I left for good over a decade ago. Bruce is publishing his own books from his Wicklewood home. He's a fine writer as well as a pleasant chap.

July 27 – It is a 55th birthday tinged with sadness for Graham Walker as he retires after 34 years with Wells Lifeboat, the last eight as coxswain. RNLI rules require crew members to retire at 55, so Graham goes on his last trip from Wells towards the Wash and meets up with boats from Skegness and Hunstanton who present him with a framed picture of a rescue.

July 28 – Off to a giant marquee in a countryside setting at Ketteringham for a strawberries and squit evening to raise money for the local church. Weather is perfect for the event in a parish holding on to its rural soul amid a sea of roads, traffic, supermarkets and concrete just beyond Norwich. I sing for my strawberry supper.

July 30 – Robin stars in a bizarre incident on Cromer front. Despite warnings, he will insist on reading a book as he walks. A jogger crashes into him! The poor man is extremely crestfallen and lifts the injured lad onto a bench. A badly-grazed elbow is the obvious damage, but wounded pride hurts as much.

August

August 4 – Grand family day out on the *Hidden Norfolk* trail. Small villages around Fakenham are our target, and we couldn't find a more delightful starting place than little Bale, sunning itself quietly off the busy main road. A wonderful church brings to the fore the story of The Great Oak of Bale – a must for the book – and a sense of old-style serenity. We move on to Gunthorpe, the wind accentuating its lonely, lofty position, before enjoying a picnic. Shereford, Dunton and Helhoughton also call. Hard to believe we're in the same county as we leave the roar of traffic behind and find

Sign outside the church at Bale
whetting the appetite for a legend.

little communities and splendid churches nestling among fields. A rich harvest indeed.

August 18 – We prepare for the Frostenden fortnight, again exchanging houses with Shirley and David Woodward and their friend Jo. The lads have saved hard in readiness for a spending spree, but I'm sure the natural delights down the lane at Owles Hall will provide just as much pleasure. A lovely surprise awaits us – David has left a copy of Parson Woodforde, *The Life and Times of a Country Diarist* by Roy Winstanley 'as a thank you for all your help and encouragement this year'.

August 19 – The hectic carnival world of Cromer is far away as the sun beats down on rural Suffolk. A sea of stubble and growing beet surrounds us. We are willing voyagers.

August 20 – Southwold is sizzling as we pay a morning call on Mary Mussellwhite, an elderly woman who's been in touch for several months, mostly with cassette recordings of her memories. We spend nearly an hour chatting in her warden-controlled flat on Station Road.

August 21 – I listen to the rain after dark, the murmuring of the trees turning to a full-throated thanksgiving. I'm in the Owles Hall study catching up with correspondence, diary entries and various bits and pieces. Diane does her tapestry in the lounge. The boys have retired to read in bed. Was there ever a more delightful example of domestic bliss!

September

September 2 – A piece of beautiful Norfolk countryside is set to benefit from gifts left by three people who appreciated it. Sheringham Park is an area of woodland and rolling scenery owned by the National Trust, which has been left more than £2.2 million in legacies intended to preserve it. Bill and Mollie Smith took holidays in North Norfolk from their London home and were entranced by the woods which burst into blooms with rhododendron and azalea in due season. In 1983 they visited as the trust was raising funds to acquire the property and after their deaths it became clear how much they loved it. In a letter to the trust, the couple, who died last year, described Sheringham Park as being as 'near paradise as one is likely to attain this side of the divide'. They wanted their £1.18 million legacy to be used 'for the enjoyment of all'. And Mildred Cordeaux, whose cousin was the last private owner of the park, bequeathed £1.1 million. Mrs Cordeaux, who also died last year, paid for the gazebo which stands behind Sheringham Hall and was opened by the Prince of Wales in 1988.

September 15 – Fascinating day, much of it on the royal estate around Sandringham. Diane at the wheel as we go in search of more *Hidden Norfolk*. Babingley is our main target. We can't find the 'modern' church, corrugated iron and thatch, until a local points to it behind trees off the main road. It is falling down, just like its more illustrious 14th century predecessor across the fields. The unusual little church was presented to the parish in 1894 by King Edward VII when Prince of Wales. It also served as a parish room. Sad to see it overgrown and surrendering.

September 16 – Suddenly I rediscover some of the reasons for coming to live in Cromer. A walk after tea through a sun-soaked town to the front. Clouds play with a golden sunset as an evening calm falls over the sea and beach.

September 19 – Launching time for my Broads Poetry competition at the Museum of the Broads in Potter Heigham. Watercolour artist Jason Partner does the main honours after picking me up at home. He's good company and still a homely sort for all the lucrative exploits of recent

Artist, Jason Partner.

years. This sort of event is important for several reasons. It will bring the museum a higher profile and gets me involved in something else truly worthwhile.

September 27 – One of those delightful little village events destined to stay in the memory. I head for the other side of Norwich and the parish of Kirby Bedon for the Bowls Club dinner and presentations in the church hall. Hard to believe we are so close to the city and suburbs as truly local celebrations take place.

September 28 – Afternoon treat picking blackberries, first round the Beckhams and then on to Baconsthorpe and beyond. The boys are strangely reluctant to help, but are good tasters as plump fruit drop so readily. The best ones are still just out of reach amid thorns and nettles. Countryside is quiet apart from an occasional tractor coughing in the distance. Hedges are a riot of red with hips and haws galore. Clusters of blackberries revive that old childhood delight at discovering nature's bounty.

October

October 5 – Grand afternoon for trip along the coast to Paston. First, round the back of the giant gas terminal to see Bacton church and the attractive homes around it. Then it's on to Paston's delightful little Village Hall to see an impressive display of photographs of local subjects by Paul Damien. He lives in the parish and takes the official pictures each year at the Mundesley Festival. A visit to the thatched Parish Church next door to Paston's old barn is a must. The place reeks of history and there's a gateway at the back of the churchyard leading to trees and vegetation on the edge of open fields. Crows caw and soar as I snap twigs with my feet. Our first visit to a real gem on our doorstep. I pick up details of the Paston Heritage Society. I'll be learning a bit more.

October 18 – Final full-cast Press Gang outing of the year, and there's a full house at South Walsham Village Hall to greet us. Celebration time for old friend David Woodward who has just published *Larn Yarself Silly Suffolk*, a stable companion to my Norfolk volume still selling well.

October 25 – Short journey along the coast for a birthday celebration at Weybourne Village Hall. It opened 21 years ago.

November

November 1 – A treat before the start of a night of Norfolk entertainment at Whissonsett Village Hall. Doris Carter provided a refuge from the wintry weather at Brandon during the opening months of my newspaper career in the early 1960s. She comes up for a mardle about some of the characters and events from those days. I'm always bumping into little bits of my past.

November 10 – A day to savour in deepest Breckland. We take the morning road through Norwich towards Watton – and then branch off for a day of discovery on the *Hidden Norfolk* trail. Some village churches are locked, but there's plenty to enjoy as the sun beats down to accentuate glorious colours all around. Thompson, Merton, Great Hockham, Larling, East Harling, Roudham – the locations all have appeal. But we're after the jewel in the trees at West Harling. I ask for instructions but we can't find the place. Then a cheery postman points us in the right direction... only to find us flummoxed in the forest. 'I'll take you there,' says Peter, and it's a lovely sight at the end of the bumpy track. A handful of houses and a church standing back across the meadows, a wire fence separating churchyard from the sheep. I walk along the lengthy path only to discover the church is locked. We vote against finding the keyholder. 'The hall used to be here,' says our postman guide. He shows us the way out. The mainstream seems mundane after that. There's a timeless charm about these smaller villages in Breckland, the beautiful church ruins at Roudham taking top billing.

November 29 – Since it opened nearly 400 years ago, the Bluebell pub at Langham had been run by only three families. As the pub starts a new era this evening, members of each of the families are on hand to pull the first pint following a £100,000 refurbishment.

December

December 5 – Pub landlady Winnie Laws dies just weeks after celebrating her half century behind the bar at the old-fashioned Gresham Chequers. During an anniversary party customers and friends from all over the country dropped in to raise a glass to the 87-year-old, a teetotal, non-smoking

country character. 'I'm going to live here for ever,' she said.

December 13 – A Norfolk village is the pride of the county after being voted one of Britain's best. Aldborough, population 525, is given a judges' special commendation at the National Village of the Year awards in London. The unprecedented prize comes after the village figure prominently in every category but just misses out on honours.

December 25 – The boys make a festive entrance just after 7a.m, so we can't really complain about too early a start. Diane has bought me a brand new biography of James Stewart, a rich literary treat. Just a hint of sunshine in the early afternoon but it's mostly dull and very windy.

December 27 – The year was 1972. A group of local aircraft enthusiasts joined forces to form a museum in a rusty Nissen hut at Flixton, near Bungay. The sole plane on display was a Meteor from RAF Coltishall with no engines and most components missing. Now the aircraft has been lovingly restored and is one of the jewels of the Norfolk and Suffolk Aviation Museum. The museum has just celebrated its 25th anniversary. About 16,000 people a year pass through the gates.

December 29 – We may have had a wet Christmas, but East Anglia is still in the grip of the longest drought since records began. Rainfall in parts of Norfolk and Suffolk is already 50 per cent above the average for December. However, the Environment Agency says 23 of the last 32 months have seen lower than average rainfall in the region. This has left many river flows slow and ground water levels low. The drought, which started in April, 1995, is the driest period of this length since the 221-year-old national rainfall series began.

December 31 – I leave 1997 with mixed feelings. Glad to have survived another big test in the solo stakes, but still disappointed at not making the big breakthrough. Too many bits and pieces, not enough substantial slices. We were in an icy grip at the start of this year. It is a comparatively mild closing lap.

◆ ◆ ◆

1998

January

January 5 – Snow after tea, but it turns to rain as I head for Norwich and a pleasant Licensed Victuallers Association presidential dinner, full of steak and kidney pudding and squit. All diners have to tell a yarn or pay a fiver into the charity kitty. I sing for my supper and then join in the fun as the port and humour are passed round the tables.

January 7 – In one small corner of Norwich, Christmas looks set to continue for at least another six weeks thanks to a very early broody blackbird. For when it comes to feathering her nest she couldn't have picked a more festive spot. It's snug and dry, 35ft above the ground, with the warmth of bright white light bulbs for that extra bit of comfort. It's bang in the middle of Norwich City Council's giant Christmas tree. So despite the passing of Twelfth Night the conifer can't come down until nature has taken its course.

February

February 12 – Remarkable burst of weather continues. More like early summer. 'Hope we don't have to pay for this later!' is the common greeting as the sun shines out of clear blue skies. Birds full of song, snowdrops have company in the gardens and there's a real spring in the human steps.

February 13 – Norwich Playhouse is saved after months of painstaking talks lead to a financial rescue package. Cash shortages force the theatre to close in May last year just 18 months after its royal opening. Last October it was feared the Playhouse could be turned into a theme pub. Now the curtain appears set to rise again after Barclay's Bank agrees to lend them £300,000. A new board has been appointed.

February 22 – Two of Norfolk's maritime milestones are marked at a poignant quayside ceremony. Hundreds gather to remember the five Wells Coastguards who died a hundred years ago today while heading out to collect stores from gunboat *The Alarm*. Treacherous weather claimed the lives of the Coastguards, leaving 18 children fatherless, and six men from *The Alarm* also died. Plaques are unveiled to remember the disaster, and also the Dutch clipper *The Albatos*, the last regular cargo-carrying vessel to call at the town.

February 27 – The threatened touch of winter arrives after dark as Diane and I return from a happy evening at Ovington Village Hall. I'm invited to give a talk, with a chair placed up on a small stage to act as my podium. A good turn-out at the little building I have visited on my Norfolk Best-run Village Halls Competition rounds. A small community with plenty of enthusiasm and heart close to Watton. A woman from London seeks me out to stress how kind her neighbours were when her husband died. She feels moved to make the point as I mention the importance of spirit in all communities.

March

March 2 – The medieval cobbled streets of Walsingham are leaving a legacy of bumps and sprains for some of the 250,000 annual visitors. They are taking a tumble on the uneven stone, asphalt and earth pavements. The parish council is spearheading a £100,000 appeal to make them safer.

March 4 – A fierce blaze leaves the Kit Kat Club at Hunstanton a charred shell. Two women, a baby and four dogs are evacuated from an adjoining flat. Smoke fills the night sky as fire crews from across West Norfolk fight for three hours to control the flames at the seafront former dancehall and nightclub.

March 11 – Wild weather to mark my 54th birthday. Rain lashes down and there's a howling wind to keep it company. I enjoy a ploughman's lunch at the Red Lion in Cromer – but why do they insist on playing loud music? It must put older people off – and I'm almost in that category now!

March 20 – Fascinating session with the top brass of Norfolk local government as I attend South Norfolk District Council's annual dinner at Long Stratton at the behest of chairman Tim East. This is the only council to hold a sit-down function like this with chief executives and other civic dignitaries from all over the county and Suffolk on parade. They call themselves The Chain Gang and show a cheerful and relaxed side difficult to come up with at more serious events. I am there to dispense a bit of squit, but I also take the opportunity to remind this illustrious gathering of their responsibilities to dear old Norfolk. I tell them bluntly that most are unable to make telling comparisons when the big debate about development gathers pace and significance.

Taking a look round Walsingham.

South Norfolk District Council Chairman Tim East leads the Chain Gang celebrations at Long Stratton.

March 30 – It was one of the most feared and hated buildings in Norfolk. The Gressenhall workhouse provided a home for paupers from 52 parishes. Thousands passed through its gates, many of them dying there before being buried in unmarked graves in the grounds. The full story of the past is unveiled in a new exhibition at the workhouse, now the Norfolk Rural Life Museum. The striking sight of a nineteenth-century horse-drawn hearse marks the start of the exhibition. The glass-sided vehicle is followed by local children dressed as Victorian urchins to symbolise the title of the exhibition: *Life and Death in the Workhouse.*

March 31 – End of a busy month with Press Gang concerts at Mileham, Wymondham, Hempton, Tilney St Lawrence and Broadland High School taking up much of my time. I relish these evenings of homely entertainment around the halls. They continue to grow in popularity with plenty more on the programme.

April

April 6 – Short Easter break in the Cotswolds. Mid-morning departure has a sad little preamble when we hear our neighbour Frank Palmer has died in a local nursing home.

April 7 – The way homes cling to the hillsides is the real wonder of the Cotswolds. Glorious views are everywhere and it's only natural that the prospect of losing any of them is vehemently opposed. 'Why should they keep this to themselves?' is a common cry – but we know any surrender will simply cut down on the number of beauties.

April 9 – Heavy rain is falling as we leave our base at Upton St Leonards. It's still with us as we arrive back in Cromer just after 5p.m. We encounter hail, sleet, torrential downpours and flooded roads all the way home. I'll always remember virtual darkness in the early afternoon over dripping Milton Keynes, trying hard not to see it as a symbol of late-twentieth century civilisation!

April 17 – Gala presentation night at Museum of the Broads in Potter Heigham as the Broads Poetry Competition I have organised reaches its climax. Steve Snelling and Simon Proctor, my fellow judges from the *Eastern Daily Press*, are on hand with Martin Kirby, the paper's deputy editor. He announces that the winning verses will be featured as a centre spread in Monday's edition. Very cold in the museum but a warm atmosphere as prize-winners read their poems and collect their rewards.

April 23 – Filming on Cromer beach for the Channel 4 television programme *Right to Reply* after complaints about bogus Norfolk accents on the legal drama *Kavanagh QC*, starring John Thaw. Last week's episode was set in Norfolk, much of it filmed in the shadow of Norwich Cathedral, and several of the characters were supposed to be locals. We got the usual Mummerzet mixture. Protests went in and Channel 4 comes out to talk to the people affected. I say my piece under brooding skies along with Les Earl of Antingham, whose protests sparked the programme's interest in the first place. I emphasise how often the Norfolk dialect has been mocked in this way over the years.

April 24 – The agitation continues after extensive coverage in the national newspapers and on various radio stations. How ironic that every time Radio Norfolk is asked for a comment on this subject from outside, they pass the buck to me – the voice they tried to silence for being too parochial!

May

May 3 – Grand occasion at the end of Cromer Pier as I lead Press Gang deliberations to raise funds for the town twinning association. The theatre is nearly full for a concert that revives memories for me of the first Norfolk Night organised here at the behest of Dick Condon in 1984. It was the launching pad for countless sessions of local entertainment. We set up in the afternoon as the wind howls and waves lash beneath the stage, an eerie combination for the first Sunday in May.

May 4 – Villagers enjoy the ancient ritual of the Drynklings at Shipdham on this May bank holiday. Locals are invited to buy ale to raise money for the Parish Church. The practice was stopped by Elizabeth I as unseemly, but it was revived a few years ago and has proved to be a successful way of raising funds.

May 11 – On safari beyond Norwich. We search for some time before locating Hethel church down a leafy lane. My

Down-to-earth humour in a stately home – the Boy Jimma and Gal Liza entertain at Wolterton Hall.

main interest is the smallest nature reserve in the county featuring an 800-year-old thorn bush in a meadow beside the church. Cattle and horses graze contentedly in the sunshine as we hop over the stile for a close-up. The churchyard is a conservation area cared for by Wymondham members of the Norfolk Naturalists' Trust.

May 15 – A glorious evening to mark the Press Gang visit to Wolterton Hall, our first date at a stately home. Lord and Lady Walpole are there to greet us and to provide changing facilities a few floors up the grand staircase past portraits galore. Squit meets history! There's a healthy turn-out in the Grand Saloon with its splendid tapestries draped on the walls. We are here to raise funds for the Norfolk Society, county branch of the Council for the Protection of Rural England.

May 19 – Signs that our little summer could be interrupted. Diane takes Robin to Mattishall to see a specialist about his peanut allergy. As they return home the sun is blotted out near Roughton by a sea fret. The temperature drops dramatically and my chair outside is suddenly redundant.

May 21 – In search of more little bits of *Hidden Norfolk*. Our first target is Quarles on the edge of the Holkham estate.

KEITH SKIPPER'S NORFOLK DIARIES

Eight homes, one farm – and a delightful sense of community. It's hard to find and difficult to leave. The woman delivering newspapers points us in the right direction. Senior resident Norman Dack, a retired farm worker, moved here from up the road at Creake in 1945. He tells me the population is 20 with three employed on the local farm at the busiest times of the year. Another dot on the map demands attention down the lane. Waterden does have a church and a rectory but all the parish land has been worked as one farm since the enclosures. The population has always been small, reaching a peak of 44 in the middle of the nineteenth century. The Church of All Saints is in the middle of rolling fields with a neat path cut to its Norman doorways. A serene interlude before we head for Brancaster Staithe and an AA box in a lay-by, the oldest one in East Anglia, and then move on to the Magazine House in Sedgeford to complete a busy round.

June

June 1 – Warm sunshine greets the new month and it's no hardship to head into quiet backwaters for the morning. First stop is Plumstead, between Barningham and Baconsthorpe, to see if it really is as pleasant as I recall it. Old and new appear to live comfortably together. There's a Penny Black on the wall of the old Post Office, now a restored home with plants for sale in aid of church funds. We walk the street amid humming insects, cheerful birdsong and well-kept gardens. I like this spot, although it is dominated – like many of our smaller settlements in North Norfolk – by the well-heeled retired. Still, they do take a pride in their adopted homes. We enjoy the leisurely ride into Holt where we buy rolls and scones to take to Salthouse Heath for an open air lunch among the gorse bushes. Views across the marshes are breath-taking in the brightness.

June 21 – Father's Day begins with greetings and cards from the lads as I wake – and Robin's message 'my dear friend' catches the real spirit of the event!

June 28 – Return to Hardingham 13 years after my last visit – when torrential rain prevented any play in a cricket match between Caister and the home village. This time I'm here to open the Memorial Hall extension, £42,000-worth of work, and the fête outside on the playing-field. A beefy shower arrives as I praise local workers and cut the ribbon, but the weather clears to make it a busy and productive afternoon. We lunch with Henry Edwards and his family and friends at Hardingham Hall, built towards the end of the seventeenth century. I recall how Sir Bartle Edwards,

Henry's father, was on the bench at Dereham when I was a young reporter on magistrate's court reporting duty.

July

July 5 – Comeback day on the cricket trail. I agree to play for brother Malcolm's team in a friendly at Billingford where they're trying to revive the club. I have some misgivings after such a long lay-off but it goes surprisingly well. I take three wickets and pick up a few runs. We lose but I'm pleased with my contributions. The boys play with their cousins and so give the grown-ups a chance to relax with boundary banter. Old Beeston boy Chummy Hammond has the local pub, The Forge, and we congregate there before and after the match. A grand spread for tea in the Village Hall. Only blot on this traditional rural landscape is the profane language from some members of the village side. A constant barrage of foul words take away much of the pleasure in the middle. Sadly, I don't suppose those responsible consider it anything other than normal to indulge in this manner. I make a point of emphasising how verbal antics could cost the side a lot of friends and fixtures if they persist in swearing all the while.

July 11 – Small is beautiful! A grand evening at Suffield's little Village Hall. Colin Burleigh, known as the Toff of Toftwood, joins me on stage for Norfolk entertainment. A mixture of native and newcomer respond warmly to our homely overtures. Colin is easy to work with, mardling for a good half hour at a time. He has a routine but it is seamless and he is in demand at all sorts of functions.

July 13 – The countryside looks good and smells good as we wait for harvest. We visit the Duel Stone, a mile east of Cawston, next to the garage on the B1149. I need a fresh look to round off my *Eastern Daily Press* article earmarked for Thursday, August 20, the 300th anniversary of the famous duel between Sir Henry Hobart and Oliver le Neve. This is now National Trust property, but the memorial, inside iron railings, is crumbling. Perhaps the anniversary will provide much-needed attention.

July 20 – Date at Northrepps Primary School to chat to parents, governors and teachers. They've had their problems here after an OFSTED inspection and I sense I'm called in to provide a spot of light relief. A sultry evening reaches a predictable climax, thunder and lightning greeting my playground confessions from well over 40 years ago. I keep chatting as the lights go out.

July 31 – We decide to end the month with a family outing

The Duel Stone at Cawston.

despite dull skies and occasional rain. A midday stroll round Aylsham, taking in the splendid Parish Church, is followed by a visit to Blickling Hall. Over £11 for rolls and refreshments underline the cost of such expeditions. Thank goodness we are members of the National Trust! Free entry to the hall and all its splendours, particularly the library, make it a pleasing diversion. We leave for quieter pastures and the children's bookshop at Alby down a narrow, twisting lane. A cup of tea while you browse is so civilised.

August

August 15 – The call comes to appear on Radio 4's *Today* programme at the University of East Anglia. They want 'someone to defend Norfolk's traditional values' in a debate about farming and the countryside. Talk about irony! The BBC's flagship wireless programme asking me to espouse the views at national level which caused my downfall as a local broadcaster! They may not know about me and my Radio Norfolk adventures, but surely local bosses must feel a bit embarrassed that there's no one available to fight the corner at Norfolk Tower. My 'sparring partner' on the programme is Dr Ian Gibson, the cheerful Labour MP for Norwich North and we exchange a fair bit of banter on and off the airwaves. Hardly enough time to warm to the subject of Norfolk's isolation but our few minutes seem to go down well.

August 17 – Outing to Norfolk's Rural Life Museum at Gressenhall with a picnic on the field outside and a

pleasant stroll round Union Farm opposite. Children on a tight leash mock my harvest holiday memories when we had the freedom to explore field and farm, hedgerow and headland. Safety is the current watchword, but how sad youngsters cannot roam like we used to.

August 18 – Don Rudd, former chief photographer of Eastern Counties Newspapers, dies at 88. 'Chiefy' took thousands of pictures during his years with the company, 14 of them as chief photographer. He retired in 1972. During the 1953 floods he flew over the devastated coastline in an aircraft bucketing about in the gale, and captured a breech in the sea defences at Breydon while he was strapped to the wheelhouse of a boat. During his career he also lay petrified on a railway line as an express train roared towards him and was threatened with a shotgun by an irate peer.

August 22 – One of the proudest days of my life in the public eye. I open the new Village Hall on my home patch at Beeston after an eventful journey from Cromer. The rain intensifies as we get stuck behind a touring caravan from Holt to North Elmham. I suggest we continue via Brisley and Mileham. The back road is partly flooded and the downpour continues as we park in the Village Hall forecourt. A big crowd waiting for the ribbon-cutting formalities, including brother Digger and his wife Joyce. Eric and Mollie Howe represent the old guard. Meanwhile, David Wheeler of the Norfolk Rural Community Council opens a new hall at Wood Norton and John Timpson does the honours at a new £160,000 building at Toftwood.

KEITH SKIPPER'S NORFOLK DIARIES

August 28 – Interesting diversion in the shape of a visit to Anglia Television studios in Norwich to take part in the programme *Heroes and Villains*. One of the subjects is to do with regional accents and old friend producer Eddie Anderson asks me to have a few words in favour of them. I am a 'plant' in the audience to dispense a bit of squit. An American guest, extrovert in the extreme, says we still take too much notice in this country of how it is said rather than what is said.

September

September 2 – We head down the busy Yarmouth road to Thorpe where I unveil a sign awarded to locals for winning the Town and Urban Communities category in the *Eastern Daily Press* Best Kept Village competition. I then walk with Martin Shaw, from the county council transportation department, to the local hall for a speech or two and presentations. I enjoy my chat with county council chairman Graham Hemmings. I recall his role as chairman of the old time music hall when I was a young reporter at Yarmouth.

September 6 – *Thass Norfolk 'n' Good Anorl*, the third annual celebration of genuine local culture, goes down well at Norwich Theatre Royal in front of a good house. Diane's dad spends his 70th birthday laughing at the antics of Sid Kipper. I compere the show which also features Press Gang colleagues Mik Godfrey, Tony Clarke and Peter Whitbread along with singer Julie Thompson, the Ouse Washers Mollie Dancers, Sheringham Shantymen and the Norwich Schools Concert Band. David Lambert, who runs the Studio Theatre next door, again directs.

September 9 – Milestone day as Danny heads for his first lessons at Cromer High School. I offer to keep him company to the gates but he makes it clear he can cope. I did have a chat with him last evening, urging him to make full use of all opportunities and to make sure homework comes before television or other diversions after school. I wonder just how far my advice has gone.

September 30 – Farewell September! One of my favourite months has failed to produce enough cheerful weather to prepare the path to winter. With talk of another economic recession building fast, it seems the climate of uncertainty has matched the worries.

October

October 8 – Start of my six-week run of evening classes at Cromer High School as the winds blow. There are 15 for the opening night of *Mysteries and Delights of Norfolk*, and a surprisingly large number of comparative newcomers on parade. A stimulating session as my 'pupils' introduce folk they have just met and then offer opinions on all sorts of subjects. Clearly, those who live in this part of Norfolk see it in a different light to the inhabitants of places like Thetford, Bowthorpe or Brundall. I stress how life can vary in such a big county. I also draw attention to the contrast between the road from Cromer to Yarmouth and the road from Cromer to Hunstanton. The protected coastline means so much.

October 16 – It's family break-up time! We collect Robin from school and take him on to West Runton's Information Technology Centre, Kingswood, for a weekend stint – his first time away from the family. I carry on to Holt Hall for another *Heart of Norfolk* house party in this lovely Victorian mansion. Diane and Danny return to rattle around 25 St Mary's Road. The log fire blazes out its customary welcome at Holt Hall. My group is one of three on parade this weekend – walking and birdwatching are the others. Both cast anxious eyes to the skies while we look fondly on the flames.

October 29 – Family day out in Wells takes a fascinating diversion on the way home to the Iron Age fort at Warham. In fact, it's a fair way out of the village, down a straight track and across a field. The boy helter-skelter across history while Mum and Dad progress at a more sedate pace. It is dusk, best time for imagination to be at work. On the way back we look at Binham Priory and take in some of the pleasures on show at Hindringham and Thursford. It's dark and chilly by the time we reach Cromer, where they've been hanging up the Christmas lights. And Bonfire Night is yet to come!

October 31 – Rousing finale to our Press Gang year at the Victory Hall at Neatishead on a wet and windy Saturday night. Indeed, there's a standing ovation at the end of our concert after melodeon player extraordinary Tony Hall has served up delights of his 'Haddock Song'.

November

November 1 – Beeston's Audrey King, a village mother-figure who played a big part in my early years, has died. I was invited to High House Farm on Fridays for tea and to watch television. Big sister Heather worked in the house – which was so large and palatial compared to dear old Holmdene Cottages! I particularly revelled in her books lined up in the lounge, with marvellous views across the fields towards the church where her funeral service will be held next Friday morning.

November 23 – Busy day in Norwich, starting with a board-room presentation to old sporting desk colleague Peter March. He's taking early retirement from Eastern Counties Newspapers to live in Spain. I'm invited to join the official farewell party as one of the last links in his local newspaper chain. More informal session follows at the social club at teatime. Peter was a good ally in my early sports reporting days, his sub-editing professionalism and cheerful person-ality lighting up many dull hours at the desk.

November 28 – Fascinating return to Lakenham to open the St Mark's Christmas bazaar in the church hall. Good to be invited back to one of my old stomping grounds after so many years. Former landlady Pauline Preece leads the parade from the past. It's nearly 30 years since I first got close to Lakenham, taking digs near the cricket ground and walking to and from work at the press office.

December

December 5 – Snow in the air as I set out with Colin Burleigh for an evening of entertainment at Brockdish Village Hall, not far from Diss. The goose feathers are really flying by the time we leave a little after 10.30p.m. Driving with extreme care, Colin steers the squit wagon to the safety of Toftwood. I have the spare room.

December 8 – Long haul to Copdock, the other side of Ipswich in driving rain to talk to a group of Suffolk account-ants. Surprisingly low-key affair after Diane and I dress up for a full-blown dinner. We get sandwiches and cake before my chat with a small group in a hotel room. We enjoy a late fish and chip supper in Norwich on the way back. The A140 route must be one of the most boring in the country although the weather may be colouring my views.

December 12 – Pleasant evening at Fakenham with the town band in concert at the community centre. I am compere for this festive event, the first of its kind for the musicians. I accept an invitation to sample the brew after-wards at Sculthorpe Horse and Groom, a lively but amiable pub. My driver for the night is the band's musical director Danny Wakefield. Now 28, he took over the baton a decade ago to become one of the youngest in history to hold the post.

December 18 – I take the part of Santa Claus to hand out presents and a bit of squit at a party for the Tapping House Hospice at Snettisham. Patients and carers get together for a festive meal at the Rose and Crown while I wait in the wings. My chauffeur – in a car rather than a sleigh – is Myra Street, former head teacher at Beeston Primary School. I have now completed my official engagement list for the year.

December 24 – Since my switch to working from home, our Christmas Eve routine has changed to more of a low-tempo affair. We drop the customary calls on old friends in favour of a family build-up. As I tuck Robin in, he asks quite bluntly 'Do you believe in Father Christmas?' He beams at my emphatic 'Yes' and confides 'So do I.' I tell him and his brother this is the best night of the year, probably as much as a reminder to myself as an enlightened moment for them to share.

December 26 – Urgent need for fresh air and exercise take us to the new lifeboat headquarters at the end of the pier as persistent rain begins to fall. Robin invests some of his festive money in a boat at the RNLI shop and gives it a debut on the North Lodge boating lake on the way back.

December 29 – We select Holkham beach, part of the biggest nature reserve in England at 10,000 acres, for a good 'blow'. There's enough fresh air to go round. Wind is keen as we saunter through the pine trees, across the dunes and down to the mudflats. Horses and dogs share a giant stage with folk anxious for a spot of action after the seasonal excesses. Not sure our stop at Wells for a chips and sausage lunch will do much good, but the great outside does give you a healthy appetite.

December 31 – A long and difficult year in some ways, but the strength of our family ties and unyielding belief in my abilities to make a living out of Norfolk continue to mean so much.

Holkham Beach – enough fresh air to go round.

1999

January

January 6 – Back in the old routine. Residents lose a battle to prevent 41 homes being built on a four-and-a-half acre site on the edge of their village. The decision by South Norfolk planners overturns an earlier refusal taken by a seven-man sub-committee last month. Brian Hill, chairman of Tasburgh Parish Council says he's extremely disappointed but not surprised.

January 22 – After frost, the sun is out again to give the day a golden touch. On the road to Barney with colleague Stewart Orr to meet railway historian Adrian Vaughan. Stewart and I are compiling a radio programme on the old Midland & Great Northern (Muddle and Get Nowhere) railway line which closed 40 years ago. Adrian lives on the edge of this good-looking village with marvellous views over open fields. I envy him, especially on a day like this. Super-enthusiast Adrian, who used to work on the railways, is now one of our top historians on the subject – much to the chagrin of some of the academics. He speaks with rare passion and is a natural choice to lead the platform brigade in our documentary.

January 28 – The Norfolk Club was founded in 1864 by a group of Norfolk aristocrats and landed gentry in Norwich. Now this once exclusively male preserve has, in its struggle for survival, chosen a grandmother in her 80s to lead it into the next millennium. The new president-elect is Lady Enid Ralphs. Twenty years ago she became the first woman national chairman of the Magistrates' Association, the highest office a JP can achieve. As a student at Exeter University she was the first woman president of the Guild of Undergraduates. She is the widow of Sir Lincoln Ralphs, a chief education officer for Norfolk.

January 29 – Among the railway ghosts of Melton Constable as our railway documentary work continues. We meet old firemen John Wyatt and George Dack in the lay-by next door to the industrial estate which used to be home to the 'Crewe of Norfolk'. A big area with plenty of memories before the line closed in 1959. Then we moved to the edge of the village to meet two leading members of the M&GN circle who have steeped themselves in memorabilia. Phyllis Youngman and Raymond Meek chat to us in a railway carriage in the garden.

February

February 7 – High winds and snowstorms take charge of Sunday morning. I brave the elements with a walk to the seafront as waves froth and crash against the promenade. The pier looks like a strangely-shaped vegetable being tossed around in a boiling pot. Strangely uplifting for all that, although I don't take long to get back to the warmth of St Mary's Road. So surprising that the lads declined my call to join the windswept safari.

February 14 – First Press Gang outing of the year at a rejuvenated Norwich Playhouse. Our afternoon show is in aid of the Sheriff's chosen charities, Age Concern Norwich and St Gregory's Arts Centre.

February 17 – Fascinating session on the North Norfolk Railway collecting sound effects for our documentary. Stewart Orr and I are invited to travel on the steam train from Sheringham to Holt alongside the driver and his mate who keeps the fires burning. I enjoy this first-time experience immensely and so does Stewart as he points his twin microphones at all the evocative noises – steam, shunting, whistling, tooting and piling on the coal. We travel back in a good old-fashioned compartment, chatting to the guard as his enthusiasm shines through.

February 27 – As our railway documentary reaches completion, a grand old lady of steam rolls out of retirement, wearing a youthful gleam that belies her years. The George Stephenson Black Five is the star attraction of a weekend of railway nostalgia, sparking many a mardle about Norfolk's steamy heyday. She shuttles hundreds of passengers between Holt and Sheringham as a tribute to the Midland & Great Northern, axed 40 years ago. The five-mile stretch run by the North Norfolk Railway is all that remains of a network that pumped people and goods around the county and beyond.

March

March 5 – 'Time to rally to the Norfolk sound' proclaims a headline in the *Eastern Daily Press* over my article extolling the virtues of our beloved vernacular. I have floated the idea of forming a Norfolk Dialect Society and all the signs are that support is there. Happily, *Eastern Daily Press* deputy editor Martin Kirby is proving a splendid ally – and influential friend in high places. I drop a line to Professor Peter Trudgill, the internationally acclaimed linguistics expert, in the hope he will lend his academic voice to the cause.

March 21 – Rain heralds Sunday with a difference. Diane is away on a Cub Leaders course at Hellesdon. I tell the boys 'I'm taking you out for lunch!' and at about 10.30a.m. we brave the weather and walk down to the Rocket House Café. It is open despite the dodgy conditions and we say we'll be back around noon. So, how to make good use of an inglorious morning? A wander down the beach towards Overstrand is agreed. The boys take to the sands while I stick to the path beside. I bump into several people and stop for a mardle before we return eagerly to the Rocket House where a table has been reserved. Danny orders a mega-breakfast while Robin and I go for the steak pie. Danny is surprised at the size of his task but makes a good job of it. It's still blowing rain as we climb back up the Gangway and head for a quiet afternoon before Mum gets home to prepare tea.

March 22 – I'm joining forces with local press photographer Sam Robbins for a new literary venture. *Farewell, My Bewty* will feature verses and pictures to make up a last, lingering look at Norfolk in the twentieth century. It will spotlight many of the glories still on parade but also warn how many could be lost to a new millennium. We start our project in Breckland. A different world all around as we halt at Roudham church ruins. The wind is keen; pigeons wheel in and out of the tower as I walk slowly and think deeply. As we head out of the village, a tumbledown collection of farm sheds catch the eye. We stop and the lady from the chalet opposite invites us to look round. Cats, cockerels, cattle, chickens – and Enoch the 28-year-old donkey. I ask the woman how long they can live: 'Oh, donkey's years!' she smiles. I walked into that one!

March 26 – Long haul to Wortwell Community Centre, a building I opened a few years ago, for Bungay Rotary Club's 50th birthday celebrations. Getting on for midnight before the speeches are over, mine included, and we get back to Cromer past 1a.m. A pleasant event, but the meal did drag on.

April

April 1 – Fascinating day starting with morning call at Swaffham Town Council offices to open an exhibition on the history of education in the town. My reception committee includes old Hamondian stalwarts Ted Heath, Neville Crowe, Colin Burleigh and Rod Lock. In the gathering is South West Norfolk MP Gillian Shephard as I cut the ribbon and peer into ink-wells of the past. We move on to Castle Acre for lunch and an afternoon of soaking up history of the Priory. Diane decides it's time we joined English Heritage as well as the National Trust, claiming we will take full advantage in the coming months.

Ruins of Roudham church.

KEITH SKIPPER'S NORFOLK DIARIES

April 9 – Long trek to Emneth, near Wisbech, for a Press Gang concert. I travel with Peter Whitbread and we arrive at our destination well before starting time. The drive with Peter is refreshing. He hardly travels beyond 40mph and clearly treats the car with the basic respect it deserves, not elevating it to worship level.

April 10 – This will be noted as the day the big rat came into the garden. I'm writing in the study early afternoon as Diane and the boys put up a new curtain railing on the top floor. Suddenly my eye catches the nasty creature slithering towards the gate near the dustbin. I call the rest of the family – and then pest control. I have to ring a Norwich number. The man will ring me back. He does so just before the Grand National starts but says it will be Monday before anyone can turn up. They only race round at the weekend if the rat is indoors. I suggest we make it our house-guest for the weekend.

April 17 – Memorable trip home for a Press Gang concert in Beeston Village Hall, the new building I opened during a monsoon last summer. This time there are waves of laughter from a full house, including many old friends and relations. It's a day of real nostalgia as the Norwich City heroes of 1959 go on a lap of honour in the city and are fêted before and after this afternoon's 2–2 draw with Tranmere. That FA Cup run of 40 years ago remains so potent.

May

May 6 – Punch and Judy man Bryan Clarke celebrates 50 years in the traditional seaside entertainment as he lays on a show at Yarmouth Library. He picked up the skills at the age of 10 after watching a performance on Lowestoft beach. Just two years later he was billed as the youngest Punch and Judy man in the world. He performs under the stage name of Professor Jingles.

May 17 – Early rising to join photographer Sam Robbins on a mission to Aylsham market. Plenty of characters to select from for our book and there are also several excuses to stop for a mardle. We take in Sheringham allotments on the way back and also have the bonus of a ready-made picture at Salthouse as an elderly man walks uphill in a lane opposite the sun-rippled marshes.

May 21 – I take squit up-market again with an evening of entertainment at Felbrigg Hall. Joining me on Norfolk Supper night is Richard Lowe, who works for the National Trust at Brancaster Staithe. He provides warbling interludes

Characters galore at Aylsham Market.

while I tell tales, read poems and give the event a homely flavour. Perhaps we can't quite recreate the spirit of the Village Hall in a posh restaurant, but when the gathering joins in a chorus of *Hev Yew Gotta Loight, Boy?*, you know the magic is working.

Richard Lowe

May 27 – It is impossible to stay indoors on such a glorious day so I head for Cromer lighthouse with a straw hat to protect my head from the sun. A playful breeze off the sea makes it hard to keep on. I return home via Overstrand Road where traffic builds up. Plenty of fellow-strollers along the front, climbing to Happy Valley and lovely cliff-top views. It might not fall easily into the Clement Scott class, but I begin to understand how he felt on leaving a bustling Cromer for the peace and charms of his cliff-top route to Sidestrand.

May 29 – Another stimulating day on the road with Sam Robbins as the sun beats down on the Norfolk Bank Holiday scene. The lost harbour of Thornham is our main

Skipper rocks the boat!

destination, a bizarre mixture of dead and alive. Hulks of abandoned boats wallow in glistening mud as modern craft wait for water to embark on epic adventures. I chat to a man from Needham Market, who originates from Norfolk and loves this place for his bird-watching pleasures.

June

June 3 – Another night out, this time at Barnham Broom Country Club for a golf enthusiasts' dinner after a charity round or two. It's all in aid of the *Eastern Daily Press*. We Care Appeal and the event is organised by Norfolk Police to raise over £3000. I enjoy the company of Chief Constable Ken Williams, an amiable and engaging Northerner who appreciates Norfolk humour.

June 15 – A massive swarm of bees holds hundreds of Norfolk children hostage at school after a 'tornado' surrounds a mobile classroom. Around 350 pupils at Millfield Primary School in North Walsham are forced to stay indoors on one of the hottest June days so far after teachers raise the alarm. Head John Aitken says it was like a scene from a horror movie as thousands of bees swarmed round the school prompting teachers and pupils to shut windows and doors.

June 25 – A day for flowery hats and summer dresses as residents, guests and trustees of the Great Hospital in Norwich gather to mark its 750th birthday. The alms house provides housing and care for elderly people and is one of the oldest establishments of its type in Britain still carrying out the wishes of its founder, Walter de Suffield, Bishop of Norwich in 1249.

June 28 – Another day on the road in search of material for *Farewell, My Bewty*. The old red barn that never quite falls over on the road into Beeston is our first target. There are more delights to come as the sun plays hide-and-seek with memories. We pass through the village still harbouring so much for me and carry on to Fransham and Dunham. Then it's on to the quaint village shop at Guestwick, the old tailor's shop on wheels where there's just enough room to serve one customer at a time.

July

July 12 – Midday call at the Bure Valley Railway in Aylsham to meet the Norfolk and Norwich Association for the Blind Tandem Group. They are on the road for a Tandathon and this is the end of the first leg from Norwich. I enjoy a mardle with all those taking part and even allow myself the luxury

A test of balance.

of a spin on a tandem behind Mary, a charming Irish woman who nurses me though the experience perfectly. I surprise myself at getting round without falling off. After a spot of shopping in town, Diane and I head for our favourite spot on the outskirts of Itteringham to savour sandwiches and a refreshing drink. The wind rattles the trees and ripples the turning corn.

July 24 – To the Fleggburgh Village Attraction on a sultry evening for Mary Lovell-Blake's 60th birthday party. I'm asked to dispense a bit of homely squit in front of a veritable who's who of Yarmouth and the Fleggs. About 170 are here to salute a woman who's made a bold mark on local life. She was connected with the Radio Norfolk advisory council in the 1980s when we first met, just one of the countless posts she has filled over the past 40 years. Her twin brother Joe Larter (yes, they really are Mary and Joseph) bought The Village when it went into the hands of the receiver. Plenty of old friends on parade here and memories of my reporting days in Yarmouth are revived at every turn as I bump into Jack Chase, John Clymer, Harry Pascoe, Tony King, John Freeman, John Wells, Michael Cartiss, Gerry Nicholls and many more.

July 25 – Sunday trip to the tiny community of Themelthorpe for an afternoon of mardling. The invitation came from 88-year-old Edna Buckley following a plea in my newspaper column for more details about the place. Wood Farm Gardens are open and there are raspberries with cream for afternoon tea. The event is to raise money for the twelfth-century Church of St Andrew nearby. A project on the village compiled by a local lad 20 years ago is passed on to help with my research.

July 30 – A picnic in the grounds of Wolterton Hall followed by an invigorating walk past the splendid ruins of the old church tower. This is the area where the old village of Wolterton used to be. Walking with history is an uplifting experience as the old wall holds back the fields and woods. Our path leads through the trees back into the piercing sunshine glinting over the parkland lake. We stroll behind the impressive hall with all its Walpole links and progress to the farm being run on proper lines. This is a world of its own, an enchanting world that has enough reality to deflect accusations of being 'pickled in aspic'.

August

August 4 – Evening with a difference alongside entertaining colleague Colin Burleigh at the Norfolk Showground in Costessey. We are invited to dispense a bit of Norfolk culture to an international audience. NORJAM 99, an international Scouts Jamboree, is going well. It's a vast town under canvas and flags from all over the world are flying as we arrive to do our 'missionary' work in the Grand Ring. Danny, who is camping with his 1st Cromer colleagues, helps out with a spot of interpreting in the audience as we keep local yarns flowing.

August 14 – We're on the way to Dorset. We catch a glimpse of the White Horse on the side of hills at Uffington and join a long queue on the way to Stonehenge. We arrive in Tolpuddle as the heavens open and take in the museum and TUC memorial cottages, a call sadly made memorable by the po-faced reception from the warden as we call to buy postcards and a short history. We book in for bed and breakfast on a farm in Piddlehinton.

August 15 – The Dinosaur Museum in Dorchester takes up a couple of hours before a trip to Dorchester County Museum, an impressive set-up with a statue of William Barnes nearby. The dialect poet takes his place alongside Hardy in Writer's Dorset, a wonderful part of the exhibition. We hit the road towards Sturminster Newton, home town of William Barnes. Flags are flying for carnival week.

August 18 – A fresh wind accompanies our family trek around the ruins of Corfe Castle. My fear of heights keeps me on the less-than-active side while Diane and the boys climb higher.

August 20 – We agree that our Dorset expedition has done us good, not least because a change of scenery brings fresh perspective and impetus. I know places like Norfolk have similar problems when it comes to maintaining a clear sense of identity. A bit of a lottery, but the bed-and-breakfast system does mean a good deal of variety, and most of them are fine. Oh, I remind the BBC, folk in the West Country don't really talk like us – and we don't talk like them.

August 31 – When will we take these sort of forecasts seriously? Rural traffic in East Anglia could rise by more than 100 per cent during the next 30 years. Spiralling traffic levels will cause congestion across the countryside unless action is taken, according to a new report by the Council for the Protection of Rural England. Another report, more figures full of foreboding – but we know nothing will be done.

September

September 7 – Change welcome as skies cloud over and breeze springs up to make more sense of the autumn billing. I'm busy completing my verses to go with the photographs in *Farewell, My Bewty* and sorting out plans for the formation of a local dialect society before long.

September 25 – Happy return to Langley Village Hall to provide entertainment at the WI harvest supper. A full house and excellent meal. Veering away from Loddon we encounter pleasantly wooded countryside. As we pass through Claxton and peer at signposts down little lanes, I realise this is one of those 'secret' areas still thriving in parts of the county.

September 27 – Another outing on the harvest supper trail, this time by the sea at Hunstanton Methodist Church. The audience includes my Aunt Amy and Cousin Billy. I feature a tribute penned to Uncle Harry, still revered in these parts. Naturally, I was thinking about him and the family as we came through rain-spattered Thornham, where he kept the butcher's shop, but it was still a surprise to find such familiar faces in the congregation. We plough the fields and scatter the good seeds of friendship on a damp night.

October

October 3 – A big day as Friends of Norfolk Dialect are officially launched at Yaxham Village Hall – and I'm asked to fill the post of chairman. A great honour and one I accept with a deal of pride and optimism. Martin Kirby, deputy editor of the *Eastern Daily Press*, is vice-chairman and a vital ally in our fight to keep the local sound alive and well. It's a day for celebration, a day I hope future generations will salute with

John Austrin – who came up with the name Friends Of Norfolk Dialect (FOND).

gratitude. Over 40 are present and I know we have widespread support, particularly from exiles.

October 9 – Just over the border to talk to members of the Adrian Bell Society at Beccles about my favourite local writers. Then we move on to one of our favourite country haunts for a delicious meal and mardle with old friends. David and Shirley Woodward and Jo Pigot are in the gathering as I reveal some of my tastes on an occasion devoted to one of the finest writers East Anglia has produced.

October 10 – Down the lane to yesterday and the impressive Tunstead Trosh, a hymn of praise to farming's old ways. But it nearly didn't go ahead. Organisers made an 11th hour decision to plough on after 24 hours of torrential rain. They agreed to take a risk and the gamble pays off with two dry days. I enjoy a series of chats around the ground, watch the giant horses make light of ploughing jobs and hand out prizes for the best exponents driving tractors.

October 24 – Danny arrives home around breakfast time after an all-night adventure with the Sea Scouts starting at Felbrigg Village Hall. Diane collects him and then he sets out on a paper round. We allow him to sleep on while we make afternoon tracks for… Felbrigg Village Hall! I'm invited to unveil the new village sign on the green patch opposite as high winds rattle through the trees. A happy village occasion with tea and cakes to follow the ceremony.

October 31 – The first Friends of Norfolk Dialect committee meeting since our formation at Yaxham. Membership is growing rapidly and funds are coming in. We agree to launch a newsletter called *The Merry Mawkin* in January. Our first big special event will be a FOND-dew at Yaxham in the spring when we hope to have our president, Professor Peter Trudgill on parade. Lord and Lady Walpole are among those to enrol, so we can claim folk from all walks of life on our side.

November

November 5 – A hectic day of many moods. Morning call at Radio Norfolk with Sam Robbins for a live chat on air about our book, *Farewell, My Bewty*. Then it's back to Cromer as the weather turns sour for the funeral of next door neighbour Vera Palmer. Evening trek to Gorleston for our last Press Gang concert of the century. A happy return to the St Andrew's Festival at the Chapter House. A packed audience and laughter all the way to drown out the fireworks roaring and shooting overhead. It's a bit like being in the trenches!

November 10 – An entertaining evening with Aylsham and District Care Trust. After their annual meeting I present an hour of homely Norfolk fun to a full house. ACT was formed in 1985 to work alongside existing caring groups and agencies to supplement and co-operate – not to compete. The voluntary spirit is main force behind this scheme and it's clear from all comments that it works a treat.

November 20 – Cheerful occasion in the small community of Burgh near Aylsham. I'm invited to open the new Reading Room, built to replace an old Army hut that served as the local meeting place from the early 1920s. Next to the church down an old-fashioned lane, this cosy building with a bar will help revive community spirit. I write a poem to mark the opening, singling out Rosemary Topping for praise as she has led the workforce during the last four and a half years. Artist Jason Partner, often seen at work in this area, present three of his paintings to go on the walls. He's in the audience on a day pointing to the future with happy echoes from the past.

November 26 – Time to sample wartime in Withersdale! Long trip to Stewart Orr's transformed barn studios near Harleston to present book prizes to the winners of an evacuees' letter-writing competition. Stewart organised the contest after visiting local schools with his Home Front production, bringing the stark realities of wartime to life. The siren wails, gas masks and powdered milk are out and posters with Winston Churchill to the fore adorn the walls. It all adds up to the perfect climate as youngsters, with parents and teachers arrive to collect their prizes.

December

December 3 – High winds and wintry showers accompany a long trek to Wisbech for a mardle with the Fenland Wildfowlers' Association at the White Lion Hotel. My driver is the genial Tug Wilson from Thorpe, who tells me he'll be off duck shooting in the morning after an hour or two of sleep. There's a healthy turn-out for this social event despite the weather.

December 12 – Terry Davy, publisher of several of my books in recent years, dies suddenly after a heart attack at his Toftwood home. His death will leave a big hole in the local publishing scene and in many aspects of Dereham life. His work for Bishop Bonner's Cottage Museum and the local history society has taken up much of his time and enthusiasm in recent years. He had agreed to act as editor of *The Merry Mawkin*, the Friends of Norfolk Dialect newsletter. Terry's humour was on the dry side, but he was a shrewd businessman and quick to spot a good book idea.

December 24 – As darkness moves in, I wander to the seafront and see the lights of vessels just over the way beyond the pier growing bolder and bigger. I'm on my own and I tell myself these are the spirits of Christmas past, loved ones all, sending their greetings and asking to be remembered in turn. A fanciful notion, but I'm pleased with the thought. Cromer is uncannily quiet before tea. Shops slowing down at last, pubs less than frantic and people strolling rather than rushing with time to exchange greetings along the way.

December 25 – We ignore television most of the time, but tune into *David Copperfield* with its Yarmouth associations. Although the Norfolk voices are less controversial than those we had to suffer recently in *All The King's Men*, our dialect continues to evade the cream of the acting profession. Still, it seems churlish to be too critical on Christmas Day.

December 31 – Last day of the 1900s. Diane's birthday. Robin joins me for a little stroll down the seafront and pier. We decide not to go out for the traditional birthday meal – that will come later – but to celebrate quietly with a family session indoors. I write these notes in the study just before 5 o'clock. Surrounded by family and books on a dull day, I give thanks for what I have received since 1944 rather than bridle at more recent struggles. We are still better off than many. The lads are bright, questioning and good at school. They are noisy, argumentative and slow to do what they are told at times. But they are the true lights of our lives. We march into 2000 together, proud of our Norfolk connections and confident we can meet all challenges to come. My biggest bouquet for Diane. She keeps me going when life is less than easy and is a boon in all my activities. A marvellous wife and mother.

◆ ◆ ◆

January

January 1 – The year 2000 dawns bright. I take a look at Cromer after the big night before, and there are few signs of revelries. Most stores are closed but there are long queues outside fish and chip shops. A lot of people walking, some appearing to be looking for a sign that something might have changed after all that showbiz entertainment in the millennium build-up. The pier is busy as folk stroll, reflect and wonder what's on the way. The climate is slightly unreal, so I look for a thread of continuity in Bookworms.

January 9 – Here we go again! I'm asked for my views following a lifestyle survey which says people in East Anglia are the happiest and most stress-free in the country. I'll have to get busy with my 'Norfolk is the worst for…' survey in a bid to stop all this flattering nonsense.

January 20 – Death at 93 of Brian Bowle, my old chemistry master at Hamond's Grammar School. Known as Chad, peering over his desk at the world of Bunsen burners and test tubes before him, he also played a key role in the school's music ventures. Sadly, I found little enthusiasm for periods in the chemistry lab. I recall Chad pointing the finger and accusing me of cheating when I collected 14 per cent in an exam. He was fully justified in his accusations.

January 26 – Pupils expelled from Norfolk schools are to be encouraged to write poetry about their problems under a scheme funded by the Arts Council. The new reading scheme will aim to show young people how to examine difficult issues in their lives through books and writing. Perhaps if they kept a comprehensive daily diary like this they would do better.

February

February 2 – A busy and significant day. Diane drives us into the city and I head for my first meeting of the editorial advisory panel attached to the heritage visitor attraction at the new Norwich Millennium Library. Clearly I have been invited because of my local knowledge and there's determination to give the project an authentic touch.

February 6 – Long haul to Horsham in West Sussex for the christening of nephew Christopher. I'm invited to be one of his godfathers, and we hire a taxi for the 175-mile trip.

Overcast skies and constant traffic, so heavy for a Sunday, make it a memorable experience for most of the wrong reasons. The M25 is a living, snaking nightmare, and I am reminded by it and all its grisly activities that I'm so lucky not to be a driver. I remain amazed that so many people are prepared to put up with this high-speed lunacy. The christening is one of four, a block booking at St Mark's Church, a fairly new building. The font is mobile. The whole lot is done and dusted in less than half an hour.

February 15 – Norwich Playhouse has turned its fortunes around and staved off a closure threat thanks to eight out of 10 sell-out performances this year. The Playhouse reopened in January with an experimental season as a venue for touring productions.

February 21 – Family trip to Thornham Harbour. Rain goes and sun takes over as we enjoy a picnic in this enchanting spot. Plenty of other little expeditions to make it a memorable day. Waterden church in a field, surrounded by history and snowdrops. Burnham Overy Staithe, glinting in the promise of summer days to come. Wells, rubbing winter sleep from its eyes but still drowsy as half-term visitors mooch. A glorious orange sunset behind us, we savour the coastal run home.

March

March 11 – Cards and calls galore to mark my 56th birthday, and there's a healthy glow about the world. I take a stroll through Cromer towards the front to enjoy spring-like conditions. We travel to Langham Bluebell for a celebration meal in the evening – and find another table nearby has been booked by the Skippers! This is Marion, from Hindringham, daughter of the late Jack Gaskin. We enjoy a mardle, and there's more to come as Wells versifier Joyce Trett pays a call at the pub where her daughter works in the kitchen.

March 18 – Start of a new Press Gang year takes us to Rackheath Village Hall and the stage on which I appeared many times in plays, pantomimes and old tyme music hall. Old broadcasting colleague Bob Ledwidge, with me in the original Radio Norfolk team, waves the flag and shakes the bucket for the *Eastern Daily Press* We Care Appeal. I travel to and from with Peter Whitbread, who calls at the supermarket on Blue Boar Lane in Sprowston on the way to do a spot of 'loyalty card' shopping. I find it a rather bizarre prelude to an evening of Norfolk entertainment.

KEITH SKIPPER'S NORFOLK DIARIES

March 29 – Another outstanding character on the local press beat has gone. Freddie Fletcher spent 45 years with Eastern Counties Newspapers, most of them as chief reporter at Fakenham. Freddie was 85 and for 27 years lived in a caravan in Oak Street which he shared with his mother until her death. Colleagues recall how he lived on a diet of eggs and carrot juice and spent a lot of time dabbling in the stock market. John Timpson, who worked with him on the *Eastern Daily Press*, says: 'He used to twirl a little piece of hair around his finger while he was talking. It started off over his forehead and as the years went on it receded.'

April

April 1 – A full house and a lively old fashioned atmosphere make it a Press Gang winner at Longham Village Hall on April Fools' Day. It's still daylight as I travel to the heart of my old home patch and savour a few milestones and memories along the way. Auntie Margaret and Uncle Cyril, brother Malcolm and wife Muriel among supporters as we raise money for St Andrew's Parish Church.

April 15 – What a grim April day! What sunshine at Wreningham Village Hall as their latest Press Gang concert draws a crowd of over 170. This show is to raise money for the Friends of Bracon Ash church. Their Village Hall is deemed too small for the event so the larger building is put at their disposal by friendly neighbours. I opened the bar at Wreningham's hall in September, 1985, so it's time I returned for another pint.

Jim Wilson – elected chairman of Norfolk Police Authority.

April 17 – A retired journalist – and my first boss at Thetford in 1962 – is elected chairman of Norfolk Police Authority. Jim Wilson, who worked in newspapers and broadcasting across East Anglia during a 38-year career, is to chair the authority responsible for managing the Norfolk force's budget, appointing the Chief Constable and Deputy Chief Constable and ensuring the effectiveness of policing across the county. Jim was made an OBE in 1995 for services to broadcasting.

May

May 9 – A freak storm turns the streets of Diss into a raging torrent of flash floods. Force of the rain, laced with chunks of ice and hail, turns streets into rivers, sending flood water cascading through the main shopping precinct and pouring into shops and homes. Surrounding villages are enjoying bright sunshine.

May 12 – A golden evening in sunshine as I travel to Great Cressingham Village Hall to speak at Watton Inner Wheel's 19th birthday party. Cake, candles, top brass and mardling all the way as we linger on the edge of the Battle Area in a part of the county happily neglected by so many. Yes, life beyond Swaffham is different. Start of a hectic weekend with Press Gang business at Brisley Village Hall tomorrow and the Old Hamondians' annual reunion dinner on Sunday.

May 20 – Long trek to Harleston with Colin Burleigh for a slice or two of Norfolk entertainment with a fish and chip supper. We're there to mark the start of Starston Millennium Festival Week. Greeted by Keith Keeble, Arnold Wesker's nephew, who recorded *Sugar Beet*, a Norfolk cameo written by Arnold at Radio Norfolk with me a few years back.

May 21 – Lovely letter from Edward Storey, the Fenland writer who has moved to Wales to pursue his literary career. He says kind things about books I sent with a Norfolk flavour. He particularly likes *Farewell, My Bewty*, and there's a special tribute for photographer Sam Robbins – 'A poet of the camera.'

June

June 3 – Return of sunny spells on a happy evening at East Harling for *All Preachers Great and Small* in the Parish Church. David Woodward (Parson James Woodforde) and Brian Patrick (Revd Benjamin Armstrong) are in top form in front of full pews. The church extension fund will benefit to the tune of about £500. I contribute yarns, anecdotes and readings. We head home through Breckland as night falls. Chips at Watton to break the journey.

June 9 – 'I am myself a Norfolk man and glory in being so,' declared Admiral Lord Nelson when he came ashore at Gorleston to wild cheers nearly 200 years ago. Now Norfolk's most famous son is to be marketed and packaged for tourists and children in the form of an unusual teddy bear. He has a smart admiral's hat, a gold and black jacket, red sash and, of course, one arm. He is the invention of Norfolk county councillor and restaurateur Lloyd Addison. It's all part of the big build-up to the 200th anniversary of

Nelson's landing at Gorleston. A Nelson pageant will be staged there with a re-enactment of the historic occasion.

June 12 – Harold Kenneth Rose, known as HK across the county, dies at 86. A distinguished councillor with a reputation in the west for dedication to helping people, he was a keen sportsman and gifted pianist. Harold was closely involved with the Norfolk Society, Norfolk Age Concern and the Best Kept Village competition. I met him many times on duty and he always enjoyed a lively chat.

June 13 – A milestone day. It is 20 years since Diane and I met at Yarmouth. We mark the occasion with a family outing to the Dun Cow at Salthouse. A splendid meal and a couple of games of pool before our trek home along the coastline showing clear signs of gearing up for a busy holiday season.

June 16 – For the second successive evening Danny arrives home to report cricket victory and a three-wicket haul. 'I scored my first run… it came off my thumb!' he exclaims as we pass on congratulations.

June 18 – A real scorcher, so I'm glad of the breeze off the sea as I launch a sponsored line-dancing session on Cromer Pier in aid of Help the Aged. A big meal at teatime with cards and presents from the boys at my place to celebrate Fathers' Day. To be honest, I'd forgotten all about it, but I'm really touched by their thoughts. Danny went bodyboarding in the sea this morning with chum Oscar after his paper round. Yes, I was worried, but the fact he knew I would be must mean something.

June 23 – Splendid evening in the old village as a new sign is unveiled on the green. Children from Beeston School opposite do the honours and then share a potted history with a large gathering. Refreshments and mardling outside the shop afterwards has me wondering when the bus will be along to take us on the Sunday school outing. The green and pond have been tidied up. They tell me Auntie May, the formidable Miss Burrell, planted daffodils around the spot and they will recall memories of her every springtime. No doubt they'll trumpet reminders about behaviour to all Beeston backsliders!

July

July 8 – Press Gang show in a barn at Langham. This is a sort of 'taster' for the village's popular street fair later in the month and we enjoy performing on a trailer stage with straw bales at the back. The barn, provided and prepared by local farmer Patrick Allen, is a grand venue with plenty of space. The local vicar introduces me with a reminder that we stayed with two of his former parishioners in Upton St Leonards on a holiday in the Cotswolds.

July 21 – My idea to lure the 'great and the good' of Norfolk onto a country house stage comes to fruition at Wolterton Hall. *The Aristosquits*, hosted by Lord and Lady Walpole, is a success in aid of the *Eastern Daily Press* We Care Appeal. Paddy Seligman, charismatic chairman of the appeal, co-hosts the show with me in front of a full house. Home Office Minister and Norwich South MP Charles Clarke is a late call-off, but three other local MPs do play ball – John MacGregor (South Norfolk), David Prior (North Norfolk) and Keith Simpson (Mid-Norfolk) provide cheerful turns. Vice Lord Lieutenant of the County Jonathan Peel sings serious songs with his wife Jean at the piano.

Paddy Seligman

July 31 – Sad end to the month as I hear of the death of Cromer cricket stalwart Tony Lawes at 59. He was to have played a leading role preparing the wickets at Cromer's annual cricket week, which begins today. Tony, a cheerful character, joined as a first team player in the 1960s, went on to become second team captain and full-time groundsman.

August

August 2 – An eventful day split by torrential rain on the coast. We take a family trip to Sheringham where I crown the carnival queen and share the stage with four local town criers. The sun is out for the ceremony. But the skies have darkened by the time we leave and storms break as we return to the car. Torrential rain lashes down

A chime of local town criers at Sheringham.

all the way home with the road turning into a river. Holiday-makers flee for protection and the lasting image is of a child in an open buggy, crying as the rain beats on the young face and an anxious father tries to break into a run. My evening date is at Tibbenham Airfield where an international vintage glider rally is being staged. With singing colleague Ian Prettyman I am asked to provide an hour or so of Norfolk entertainment in a giant marquee. Happily, squit is international and there's a good response. As we arrive, dwile flonking is in full flight so the mood has been set.

August 12 – Annual call to do a turn at the Mundesley Festival for *Last Night of the Proms*. Phil and Joan Drackett continue to run the event, but it's clear they have to think about the end of an era after celebrating their golden wedding. Talking about the end of an era... I'll shave off my beard tomorrow morning for the first time in about 25 years. I want to see what I look like underneath all the fuzz. If I don't like the results I can start growing it again while we are on holiday in Lincolnshire.

August 13 – I leave the moustache drooping slightly, but the rest comes off at the morning sink. Not many flattering comments but I feel so different as we leave Norfolk before midday on our journey into the unknown. A stop for a picnic lunch at Gedney Broadgate brings a meeting with a colourful character on a bike. Vernon, a 73-year-old small-holder, cuts his hay with a scythe and provides a potted history of the area.

Vernon Hannah, a colourful character with his scythe.

August 14 – Our coastal safari unfolds with a trip to Mablethorpe. Holiday tripper 'attractions' abound and Diane and the boys seem delighted with all the fun of the fair. I decline all overtures to join them. A mad whirl of a machine claims Diane and Danny and it is strange to see my dear wife clinging on with eyes closed as she whizzes past. I retire to a nearby café for a mug of tea and a look at the paper. With a recently purchased Donald Peers CD in my bag, I feel really trendy.

August 15 – On to busy Cleethorpes. The boys head for the beach while I take a brief look at the town beyond. A gentle stroll along the front sees countless old folk, sitting, reflecting, remembering. You could almost hear the years falling away as they peer down on the colourful scene. Seaside towns are always brimming with nostalgia – Cromer gets its fair share – but memories must be exceptionally abundant here.

August 17 – Most of the day in Lincoln, descending into the city from the heights of the cathedral... and then climbing back again. A testing exercise made easier by the number of bookshops on the way. The cathedral is breathtakingly large, but we resent the charge of £3.50 for any adult to look round.

August 18 – Our last full day on the Lincolnshire beat centred on Woodhall Spa, described by poet Sir John Betjeman as 'an unexpected Bournemouth-like settlement in the middle of Lincolnshire'. Our bed and breakfast guest-house in the residential area is tidy enough, but a dreadful outburst of yobbery at about 3a.m. wrecks our sleep. A gang of youths yell to the background of screeching music and try to get a motorbike to start. The pandemonium goes on for well over an hour. It's remark-able that the police don't arrive.

August 19 – Heavy showers dot our way home. We make tracks for Crowland, remotest outpost of the Lincolnshire fens, to size up the remains of the big Benedictine Abbey. A wedding is taking place so we have to be content with a stroll in the grounds. This is a strange place.

September

September 2 – Intriguing date at the University of East Anglia in a huge lecture theatre to entertain University of the Third Age at their annual conference. Ian Prettyman and Tony Clarke join me on stage for a mini-Press Gang concert which is well received despite the size of the venue. I am reminded, especially after rain, just how dull and functional the UEA buildings are, a glum testament to the lack of vision and taste so prevalent in the 1960s. I couldn't imagine reading great works of literature in such a setting as this!

September 11 – I travel to Norwich for Radio Norfolk's 20th birthday celebrations at the City College. The dinner is excellent and it's good to see other founder members of the station, Julian Rush, Phil Johnson, Bob Ledwidge, Mike Souter, Leslie Dolphin and Jill Bennett among them. I have

Old colleagues meet up at the 20th birthday celebrations of Radio Norfolk.

a 'reunion' with Tim Bishop, the editor who saw me off five years ago. He shakes my hand and asks if it seems like 20 years since it all started. I am making some inconsequential reply when he is whisked off for more chats. To my surprise, I do not find any of the evening embarrassing so it is clear the recent thaw in relations has done some good. I presented a recorded tribute yesterday to Don Shepherd, the local musician who hosted the most listened-to programme in the station's history, *Dad's Favourite Tunes* on a Sunday lunchtime.

September 21 – Danny's 14th birthday and he heads for school and his first period of hockey. This is what September is all about. A gentle but bright start to the day, unfolding into a sunny saunter towards the early evening. I stroll as much as I can, reflecting on the dying embers of a seaside summer and enjoying the generous warmth. Winding-down may have a melancholy air – and old tyme music hall at the end of the pier is a sure sign of frivolities coming to an end – but it remains a favourite time for me.

September 29 – Now, this is stylish living! Lord Walpole collects me from Cromer to attend the Itteringham harvest supper in the Village Hall and returns me safely before midnight. Robin Walpole is always amiable company. A glorious sunset marks our journey to one of the most alluring parts of this area, while white owls swoop as the light fades along lonely lanes. We chat about the environment, the way Norfolk is changing and how some aspects remain strong and true. As we leave the Village Hall, Lady Walpole is busy clearing up after the feast.

October

October 2 – Predictably early start to the week as Robin rises at 7a.m. to unwrap cards and presents for his 11th birthday. After a busy day I make my way to the end of Cromer Pier to see old friend Sid Kipper excel in his new one-man show, *East Side Story*. I'm delighted Sid's talents are at last attracting wider audiences. He mixes songs with

reading and reflections, switching easily from one subject to another. It all looks so casual and off-the-cuff but he's been at it long enough to perfect this sort of impression. He must be Norfolk's most successful cultural ambassador.

October 8 – Sunday skies brighten as old friend Stewart Orr joins me for a recording round at the Tunstead Trosh. We are after Norfolk voices and farming memories to form part of an archive for Friends Of Norfolk Dialect. A few likely candidates are too shy to confront the past and a microphone but we reap a useful little crop as steam engines lead the nostalgic charge at this end-of-summer thanksgiving.

October 28 – What a busy day! First to Frettenham to unveil a splendid millennium map of the village and all its activities on the wall inside the Village Hall. Just one of Frettenham's 14 millennium projects and a stirring example of getting all ages to get involved. Then it's off into a dark and stormy night, destination Welborne Old School Room, down a narrow lane off the road into Mattishall. Welborne has a population of about 150. There are nearly 60 in the hall for my mardle as wind and rain form a mad concerto outside. Slightly better for the trip home to Cromer. We're pleased at the prospect of an extra hour in bed as the clocks go back. British Summer Time has ended in style.

October 29 – Back to Yaxham Village Hall for the first annual meeting of Friends Of Norfolk Dialect. It all passes without agitation, and Mid-Norfolk MP Keith Simpson provides an entertaining talk after the formal business. I admit to some frustrations in my chairman's report but stress the importance of getting a proper foundation before we start building. Plans for a sound archive accessible to the public on a regular basis is one of our top priorities. FOND membership is just under 200 and rising.

November

November 8 – Meeting friends after school and going to the cinema on a Friday night ought to be part of any teenager's life. But for those living in many villages across Norfolk these pastimes border on the impossible because of poor transport links. Results of the study commissioned by North Norfolk MP David Prior are stark and worrying. In a survey of 14–18-year-olds at Fakenham High School and College, 76 per cent thought their extra-curricular activities were being restricted by inadequate public transport. Also 49 students said there was no regular bus service through their village, while 75 students complained there was no bus route which went where they wanted to go at a convenient time, especially at weekends.

KEITH SKIPPER'S NORFOLK DIARIES

November 20 – This is a drab November, a drain on resources and good humour. The *Eastern Daily Press* tries to cheer me up with yet another silly survey, this time about beards. I stroke mine, a true friend for nearly 30 years (with a trial separation this summer on the eve of our family break in Lincolnshire) and there are no plans to part. I don't flaunt it as a virility symbol, I grew it out of laziness and to compensate for loss of thatch on top. There are no deeply rooted reasons to examine. I join in the squit, but feel our newspapers could spend time on more important matters.

November 27 – Author and academic Sir Malcolm Bradbury dies at his Norwich home aged 68. An acclaimed novelist, critic and television dramatist, he was also Professor of American Studies at the UEA and founded its famous Creative Writing course. I interviewed him many times and always found him charming and totally accessible. Christopher Bigsby, an old friend and colleague, says: 'I will remember his humour. He couldn't go for long without cracking everybody up. The humour in his novels was evident in his ordinary life.'

December

December 12 – Christmas lights are causing a festive headache at Holt as scores of visiting motorists clog the roads. The traffic problem has become so bad it has prompted calls for a one-way system, although many traders are pleased to see the crowds. I wonder how many drivers are spending anything but time... Meanwhile thousands of homes across East Anglia are without electricity after gale-force winds cause extensive damage.

December 15 – Real spite in the wind after a run of damp, mild days. At least the skies are clear and I prefer this brand of weather. Gloves and scarves out in force around town and on the Friday market. 'See you next week!' chorus the stall holders, sensing a seasonal bonanza. I feel much more at ease here than in the packed stores.

December 24 – Grey skies deliver the threatened rain on Christmas Eve. We enjoy tea in a cleaned-up lounge. The boys do have an occasional burst of domestic energy. There's a traditional session with *A Christmas Carol* and *It's a Wonderful Life*. The last present-wrapping and stocking filling takes us way past midnight.

December 25 – So close to a white Christmas as hail and sleet showers sweep in on a bitter wind. It's hang-on-to-hats weather along the promenade, a bit beyond bracing for comfort. A pleasant family day and a torrent of emotions

as usual as I reflect on the way years roll by, regaling the boys with yarns from their early festive seasons when they rose much earlier. Now they're reluctant to go to bed, despite obvious tiredness. Reckon that's a symptom of growing independence.

December 26 – Cheering Boxing Day news... twinned Broadland villages celebrate the withdrawal of plans to build 2000 homes and a relief road in the heart of their community. People at Wroxham and Hoveton launched loud opposition to the multi-million pound scheme floated by a London development company.

December 28 – First real snow of our winter pushes through early in the morning, and it's soon a white wonderland scene. Pretty to look at, but that's as far as it goes. Other areas have far bigger falls and the inevitable traffic chaos results. Why can't people stay still for just a few days?

December 30 – Time to start reflecting on the highs and lows of a busy year. I can report that some of the broken fences at Radio Norfolk have been mended, and my *Ghosts of Norfolk Past*, broadcast this week brings some substance to a belief that I may have a broadcasting future – although not on a full-time basis. My writing scene continues to be busy and our Press Gang fixture list suggests our popularity round the halls is as strong as ever. The boys are growing fast, taking new technology on board but not ignoring the traditional delights of reading and writing. Cromer talks of regeneration. Wealthy week-enders say Norfolk is 'cool' but still suffering from an inferiority complex for not grasping all new opportunities available. 'Poor communications' and 'a parochial outlook' are still being cited as causes for not hitting the high spots. But some people simply don't want the county to finish up like everywhere else. Norfolk will not give away its essential character easily. We await the next house-building boom with trepidation. Traffic and noise multiply. Mobile phones are everywhere, although they do have important uses. 'Poor communications' is given an ironic twist as I watch hordes of people ring each other up on either side of the streets.

December 31 – Bitterly cold end to the year and those icy winds slap our faces as we head for the Chinese restaurant near Cromer seafront to celebrate Diane's birthday. A warming family tradition to end the year 2000. We all promise to be a bit tidier in the months to come. I pledge to continue to keep my diary going on a daily basis, and to keep a beady eye on dear old Norfolk. Well, it's a habit that's mighty hard to break.